Woodrow Wilson's Heritage and Environment

ETHNIC AND CYCLIC PATTERNS IN TIME, PLACE AND CIRCUMSTANCE

by

Craighill and Elizabeth Handy

Drawings by Lorna Edwards Freeman

DORRANCE & COMPANY
Philadelphia

ACKNOWLEDGMENTS

The original publishers have kindly granted permission to reprint material from:

Athay, R. Grant, "The Sun's Flares and Earth," an article in the November, 1958 issue of *Natural History* magazine.

Blumenstock, David I., *The Ocean of Air*, courtesy of Rutgers University Press.

The Encyclopaedia Britannica.

McAdoo, Eleanor Wilson, *The Priceless Gift.* Copyright 1962 by Eleanor Wilson McAdoo. Used with permission of McGraw-Hill Book Company.

Petersen, William F., *Man, Sun, Weather*, Vol. 1, Part 1. Courtesy of Charles C Thomas, Publishers, Springfield, Ill.

Stewart, Robert Sussman, a review of Freud and Bullit's *Thomas Woodrow Wilson . . . A Psychological Study*, from the *New York Times Book Review*, January 29, 1967. © 1967 by The New York Times Company. Reprinted by permission.

Walworth, Arthur, *Woodrow Wilson*, courtesy of Houghton Mifflin Company.

Library of Congress Catalog Card Number: 68-57734
Manufactured in the United States of America

To Eleanor Wilson McAdoo
in fond remembrance

PREFACE

In the Democratic era of Franklin Delano Roosevelt and Harry Truman, it was shocking to many who had participated in the more idealistic upsurge of America under Woodrow Wilson to find how few of the younger generation's "crusaders for freedom" in the second war had any awareness of the magnitude and quality of President Wilson's service to our country and to mankind.

That service—as president of Princeton University, as reviver of the Democratic Party and political reformer while governor of New Jersey (1911), as President of the United States (1913 to 1921) and commander-in-chief of the Armed Forces, as inspired civil leader of the nation through those same years of crisis, and finally as the primary planner and creator of the League of Nations—all seemed largely forgotten.

The greatness of Wilson had been almost obliterated by his political detractors, drowned in the backwash of materialism in the 1920's, and later obscured by the gloom of the 1930's and the subsequent glamor of Franklin Roosevelt's gallant and heroic revival of the country's spirit and restoration of its economy after the Great Depression. In the British Commonwealth, in Europe and in Asia, Woodrow Wilson's stature was well remembered, but not at home.

The creation of the United Nations in 1946—recalling Wilson's ideal—somewhat revived America's interest and recollection. The centennial celebration of his birth in 1956 renewed the remembrance of Wilson throughout the country, but mainly of President Wilson the political leader, and not Woodrow Wilson the man.

In the centennial year, two of the many books published were psychological studies of the man in relation to his career. These were Alexander L. and Juliette L. George's *Woodrow Wilson and Colonel House*, a personality study, and John Morton Blum's *Woodrow Wilson and the Politics of Morality*. But for the most part, the publications of this year which marked the anniversary of his birth, dealt chiefly with aspects of his public career.

Other volumes have appeared since, most notably Herbert Hoover's *The Ordeal of Woodrow Wilson* and Arthur Walworth's *Woodrow*

Wilson—Volume I, *American Prophet*; Volume II, *World Prophet*, and Henry W. Bragdon's *Woodrow Wilson: The Academic Years*. In these works, the character and quality of Wilson as a human being emerge with great clarity, although not as intimately as in Ray Stannard Baker's comprehensive early volumes (1927 *et seq.*), *Woodrow Wilson, Life and Letters*. Silas Bent McKinley's *Woodrow Wilson: A Biography* presents a carefully calculated study of Mr. Wilson's character, stressing the effects of his upbringing. Slight but fresh and original is *An Intimate Memoir* (1960) by the President's friend and physician, Admiral Cary T. Grayson. Arthur S. Link's *Woodrow Wilson, a Brief Biography*, published in 1963 (the first in a series of biographies of outstanding Presidents of the United States), is an excellent compact review of the life and times of President Wilson, but is not an appraisal of the man or of his career and presents no fresh material. Dr. Link is editor-in-chief of *The Papers of Woodrow Wilson* currently in process of publication at Princeton, which will gradually make available much new material. Professor Link also is writing a multivolume definitive biography of Wilson.

There appeared in 1967, since the manuscript of our own volume was completed, a book which doubtless will have worldwide circulation, *Thomas Woodrow Wilson: Twenty-eighth President of the United States, A Psychological Study*, by Sigmund Freud and William C. Bullitt. Many reviews and commentaries have rejected the conclusions of this book, allegedly based on psychological analysis. Among these critics are students of the era involved: Allen Dulles and Raymond Moley, historians Arthur Link and Barbara Tuchman and an authority on Freud and Freudian psychology, Robert Sussman Stewart.

Sigmund Freud never knew Woodrow Wilson except through the voluminous notes furnished him by Mr. Bullitt. Mr. Bullitt had a deep personal antipathy toward President Wilson and Freud shared it. In fact, this shared antipathy was the reason for their collaboration, undertaken some 37 years ago. The result, as published, is what Raymond Moley (*Newsweek*, Washington, Feb. 20, 1967) characterizes as "bad history, bad psychoanalysis and even bad Freud." The wisdom of this triple characterization becomes self-evident in the careful study of Freud's relationship to the volume made by Robert Sussman Stewart and published in *The New York Times Book Review* of Jan. 29, 1967. In the course of this inquiry, Freud's daughter Anna wrote to Mr. Stewart that after reading the manuscript she concluded that "The foreword is undoubtedly my father's, but everything else is undoubtedly Bullitt's." Revisions suggested by Anna Freud before publication were rejected by Bullitt, who proceeded with the publication of this work. Dr. Freud himself had refused steadily to permit publication for six years after its completion, and agreed finally, not long before his death in 1939, when, Stewart says, he was very ill and in a state of "progressive decline."

Mr. Stewart further says of this "psychological study": "It is most noticeably a crude book, totally without Freud's customary style or play of mind: without his lucidity, his general speculative elegance or the meticulous balancing of hypothesis and verification by which he was always able to develop an argument ... it distorts and confuses even the most basic psychoanalytical concepts and materials.... From general interpretations supplied by Freud, Bullitt seems to have managed to fashion a distorted weapon of revenge."

In Chapter VI of our present volume, under *Heritage of Dissenters*, and especially in that part following the sub-title *Qualities of the Heart*, we assess Woodrow Wilson's character in terms of his breed and his nurturing, and refute the Freud-Bullitt thesis. Clear documentary refutation of that thesis, that Woodrow Wilson was crippled for life by his father's devotion, will be found in *The Papers of Woodrow Wilson* now in process of publication by the University of Princeton Press. Volume I of this series carries "virtually all the letters to him [Woodrow Wilson] from Dr. and Mrs. Wilson [his parents]. These were not found until 1963." (Quoting Arthur S. Link, editor, in a letter to *Look* Magazine, Dec. 27, 1966, where prepublication excerpts from the volume first appeared.) These critically definitive materials, of course, were unknown to Bullitt, and hence to Dr. Freud.

During the years immediately after the second World War we began to delve more deeply into our study of Woodrow Wilson, in terms of a scientific appraisal of the causative factors in his background and upbringing. It seemed to us, in the then-current revival of interest in his life, that our understanding of this man as a person could be much enriched by a closer examination of his heredity and heritage, familial, cultural and ethnic. In the ensuing years, as we have come to know his mind and heart through what he wrote and what he said and what he did, the clearer has become a profile of his character, so sharply etched in the lineaments of his Scottish and Scotch-Irish background. While altogether an American, he actually was a fairly recent American. His mother was an immigrant, daughter of a Scotch Presbyterian missionary to Canada and later to Ohio. His father's father and mother were immigrants from Ulster who settled, in the first quarter of the nineteenth century, first in Philadelphia and later in Steubenville, Ohio.

A circumstance of real significance, identifying his parents with the unique heritage of Scotch Presbyterianism, was the fact that he was born in Staunton in Augusta County, a part of Virginia originally settled primarily by Scotch-Irish from Ulster. Staunton became the pioneering frontier for Presbyterianism in Virginia; and for much of the western migration that established communities in Ohio such as Chillicothe. There, Wilson's maternal grandfather, Thomas Woodrow, came as preacher, a generation before Joseph Ruggles Wilson (who had married his daughter) was called to Staunton in 1855 as minister to the Presbyterian congregation and principal of the seminary for young ladies founded by that congregation.

Thomas Woodrow Wilson, then, was born into a family and home (the Manse) that was essentially Scotch Presbyterian, in a community whose founders prided themselves particularly on their Scotch-Irish background. The Wilsons and the Woodrows may be said, therefore, to have been in midstream of nineteenth century Scotch-Americanism. Their most notable scion, Woodrow Wilson, was in midstream of the continuation of that same heritage in the twentieth century, first as president of Presbyterian-founded Princeton University and later as political and spiritual leader of the American people. Explaining his unfailing pride in his Virginia birth, Woodrow Wilson used to say: "Sometimes a man's rootage means more than his leafage." (Ray Stannard Baker, Volume I, page 23.)

The Manse, Staunton and Augusta County, as the American scene of Thomas Woodrow Wilson's birth, first claimed our attention and welcomed our interest. From our study of that locale and of Mr. Wilson's parents, we were led to the Paisley and Glasgow areas in Scotland, whence came Thomas Woodrow and his wife Marion Williamson; and to Counties Tyrone and Down in Ulster, where were born James Wilson and Ann Adams, the parents of Joseph, Woodrow Wilson's father.

This study was not undertaken as a biography. It was conceived, and is presented, as an appraisal of one of America's most dynamic and controversial leaders, through an examination of certain essential but little-emphasized factors—family background, human relationship, historical and ethnic circumstance, geographic and climatic locale— which profoundly affected his personality and development.

The research has been confined by no means to documentary sources, but has led us into various rewarding experiences in exploring ecological factors of environment, especially in Virginia and Northern Ireland; ethnic, historical and genealogical perspectives in Ireland and Scotland; and certain climatic and astrophysical considerations rarely considered as having direct bearing on human behavior and history.

The search has been enriched by cordial interest all along the way. We count ourselves fortunate, indeed, to have enjoyed such warm and generous friendships and so much helpfulness and courtesy. Particularly, we would like to mention Mrs. Herbert McK. Smith, moving spirit of the Woodrow Wilson Birthplace Foundation at Staunton; and in nearby Charlottesville, at Thomas Jefferson's University of Virginia, the late Harry Clemons, librarian of the Alderman Library, together with other members of the Library staff, for their years of interest in and facilitation of our work. Dr. Clemons' keen appreciation of our research and vivid contribution toward our understanding stem largely from the fact that early in his career he was reference librarian at Princeton, during Woodrow Wilson's presidency there, and a frequent visitor in the Wilson home.

Since Dr. Clemons' retirement, the sustained interest in and serious concern for our work, on the part of his successor John Cook Wyllie, have done much to keep alive our determination to carry on to completion this study of Woodrow Wilson, amid the pressure of other commitments. We feel that this very intelligent scion of a literary family identified with the Glasgow area, where the Woodrows and their congeners have lived through many generations, had an intuitive comprehension of the significance of our appraisal of the factors in his heritage that made Woodrow Wilson the kind of person he was. Equally Mr. Wyllie, as a reserve officer in the U. S. Navy, has a real awareness of the significance of meteorological and astrophysical factors affecting a delicately attuned and sensitive human organism. At the same time, he has made us aware that at one point our engrossment in ethno-historical vistas was luring us too far down some enchanting but not always relevant avenues of study, especially in Ireland. (Our intoxication with these vistas was perhaps aggravated by our initiation into the charms of Gaelic culture by arriving in Dublin in May of 1957, just in time to enjoy the *An Tostal*, or modern version of the old pagan Keltic spring festival.)

The excitement and fervor that was generated in Dublin during *An Tostal* was soon tempered by a period of vigorous literary and docu-

ix

mentary research in the austere surroundings of the Library of the University of Glasgow. During the windy and rainy weeks in June, it often was so chilly that we fingered cold but interesting tomes with gloves on, while sheltering ourselves with overcoats, mufflers and berets against breezes off the north Atlantic that poured down upon us from the high open windows of the lofty reading room. It was with warm appreciation, nevertheless, that we accepted, and remember, the cordiality and interest of the University librarian, Dr. R. O. MacKenna, who made available to us literature and records relating to the forebears of Woodrow Wilson, their environment and background.

Equally, we appreciated in Edinburgh the welcome and guidance of Sir James Ferguson, director of the Scottish Records Office, whose genealogical and historical archives were opened to us.

In Washington, where much of our research centered, Miss Katharine Brand, until lately curator of the Wilson manuscript collections in the Library of Congress, has earned our grateful thanks for unfailing encouragement and inspiration over more than a decade. Miss Brand was Ray Stannard Baker's secretary when he was writing his six-volume *Life and Letters of Woodrow Wilson.* All of the voluminous files of correspondence which accumulated as a result of Mr. Baker's effort to elicit personal memorabilia from former associates of Woodrow Wilson, before and during his presidency, passed through Miss Brand's hands. When Mr. Baker died, these files came to the Library of Congress Collection of Presidential Papers, and with the files came Mr. Baker's former assistant, to add the knowledge she had acquired, through acquaintanceship with these biographical archives, to the resources of the files themselves. In sharing her understanding with many who came as we did to search for pertinent material, Miss Brand has been always generous in giving her time, and she has been kind enough to read and criticize parts of our manuscript. For all this we are most grateful.

It is with especial warmth that we acknowledge the hospitality in County Tyrone, Northern Ireland, of Mr. and Mrs. Robert Wilson. We first met Mr. Wilson in his busy grocer's shop on the Main Street in Strabane, and were invited to return another day for tea in the cozy apartment above his shop. There we met Mrs. Wilson and their daughters Elizabeth and Margaret, son Knox and younger son Thomas Woodrow Wilson. Mrs. Wilson's sisters, Kathleen and Winifred Colhoun, also were there to meet us. We soon felt ourselves completely at home with these Irish Wilsons, accorded the kind of genuine welcome that such wholesome Scotch-Irish folk know how to give in full measure.

When we returned to Belfast, Kathleen and "Winnie" welcomed us as house guests in their home in a way that made us feel genuinely akin.

One afternoon Robert Wilson closed his shop early and drove us out to the farm at Dergalt where James Wilson, Woodrow Wilson's grandfather, was born. There we met the two bachelor brothers, William and Lowther, and two maiden sisters, Susan and Mary, who lived in the very old farmhouse which, for many centuries, had sheltered the generations of North Irish countrymen from whose stock our President Wilson was descended. The house and farm at Dergalt and the open-hearted hospitality that we enjoyed as visitors that evening are described in a later chapter of this book. The old house has been taken over by the government of Northern Ireland and restored as an historic site, and the brothers and sisters are living in a new house nearby.

A source of continuing inspiration and satisfaction in this work has been a very vital relationship with President Wilson's youngest daughter, Eleanor (Mrs. William McAdoo). We became friends at the time of the celebration of the centennial of her father's birth, at the birthplace in Staunton, Va., in 1956. We have enjoyed numerous happy renewals of what has become a richly rewarding friendship with her, and with her cousin, Marjorie (Mrs. Benjamin King), whom we met at the same time and who was very much a part of the Wilson family life and of the Presidential era. For the decade since our meeting, Marjorie has given us immeasurably of her comprehension, insight and warmth of interest. Eleanor's own writings had been for us an initial source of first-hand understanding. Later, after she had given her time generously to the complete reading of our first manuscript, we spent some days with her at her home in California and were cheered and encouraged by her warm commendation of our insight into her father's personality. At the same time, her critical appraisal and constructive suggestions gave us renewed confidence that our book would measure up to the standards of accuracy and authenticity for which we were striving.

The final stage of this journey of exploration has been shared by and with our old friend, Lorna Edwards Freeman. First and foremost, her companionship in the work has been truly a blessing—it has sustained and helped us in countless ways. With unending patience and skill, she has toiled through the seemingly interminable revisions of the manuscript over the past several years. In addition, she has devoted her talent as an artist to making the drawings. All this has been freely given, out of her interest and the goodness of her heart. To her, our heartfelt thanks!

—C. and E. H.

CONTENTS

ILLUSTRATIONS

I

PHILOSOPHY AND TECHNIQUE OF APPRAISAL

The Person

"The individual is indisputably the original, the first fact of liberty. . . . There is no such thing as corporate liberty. Liberty belongs to the individual, or it does not exist."[1]

This fundamental axiom for democracy was stated by Woodrow Wilson in 1907. It was the considered judgment of an academic leader, the president of Princeton University, in an era when the individual, the human being as a person, was well nigh forgotten in the humanities and sciences, and even by Christian scholars.

The college president who preached and practiced this doctrine was a professor of political science who, within five years, would be President of the United States. The man was as unique as his doctrine. He was a devout practicing Christian in an era in which dialectic materialism prevailed among the intellectuals who were shaping and teaching all the sciences.

In 1909, he said, "You know what the distinguishing characteristic of modern society is, that it has submerged the individual as much as possible." And further: "The end and object of Christianity is the individual, and the individual is the vehicle of Christianity. There can be no other vehicle."[2]

Wilson's political science was rational and scientific in that it was based on the study of history, of governmental and political systems and procedures, and of economics. It was meticulously factual. Yet there was this that was unique in his teaching: he never lost sight of the fact that parties and governments, communities and societies are made up of *persons*. "The only responsibility to which human society has ever responded or ever will respond is the responsibility of the individual."[3] The appeal of his courses and the effectiveness of his teaching were due to his conception of the art of teaching, which was *to arouse* and stimulate his students *as individuals*. What he taught was always related in his mind to persons. And it was focused not upon "students," "a class" or "a classroom," but upon the individual persons who sat before him.

Woodrow Wilson, in his times, epitomized humanity in the throes of the first World War. Though a professor of political science, he was not, in the strict sense of the term, a scientist; and he certainly was not a romanticist. He was a great humanist of his time, and as such, he drew all men to him in the climax of international strife and victory in 1918 and 1919. It was as a humanist that he functioned in the aftermath of internal conflict and paralysis that overtook his country after victory.

What was the nature of this person, what qualities of spirit and what components of heart and mind produced such a spirit, which longed to serve as an instrument to bring the practical problems, and equally the needs and aspirations, of America and Europe into sharp focus in their time of supreme crisis?

In answering these questions, we must be entirely objective, i.e., scientific, in our appraisal of his character. We are concerned with the man, Woodrow Wilson, who was a supremely important fact in his time. Both his detractors and his admirers, to a degree, are myth-makers who, whether consciously or unconsciously, indulge in varying degrees of romanticizing, in idealization or calumniation. He had his virtues and he had his faults. At his best and at his worst, he was a romantic figure, one whose life was filled with ardor, with passion for those he loved and that which he thought good, and equally for those whom he despised and those things he thought evil in the behavior and affairs of men. His dedicated public life is as worthy as any in American history of being set up as an ideal. Yet it never occurred to him that his private life might be significant for posterity: what he *wrought* was all that concerned him.

Our concern here is not with what he wrought, nor primarily with what he thought; nor is it with the great idealist and man of affairs, of whom so much has been written. For us and for our study, he is a great humanist, so human that his own inner life and dimensions alone can give a clue to his public behavior, his hopes and failures as a man of ideas and of action. To that end, the inner life, the spirit of the man, must be divested of the aura of romance and idealization with which posterity already is clothing him. Actually we have discovered, as he has been revealed to us slowly through years of careful study, that the reality is more admirable than the idealizations, the facts more romantic than the fictions.

Voluminous are his spoken and written words, and the volumes multiply which quote them and describe his career. Yet *himself* as a person is rarely glimpsed in all this plethora of words. For this there are

2

several reasons. Although dedicating his life to public service, his sense of the sanctity of his own privacy was very intense. Although he chose to stand forth and plead the causes he believed in, he was quite shy by nature, so much so that the suggestion that he write an autobiography was repugnant to him. There already are many biographies. He is and will remain a controversial figure. What great and complex personality will not?

As a first venture in discovering the person, we have taken a close look at his background from the point of view both of his heredity and his heritage. As an organism, he was compounded of traits like those of his forebears. As a social entity, he embodied personal and cultural characteristics of their types, modified by habits of his own generation, and personal idiosyncrasies peculiar to himself.

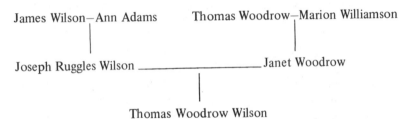

James Wilson—Ann Adams   Thomas Woodrow—Marion Williamson

Joseph Ruggles Wilson _____ Janet Woodrow

Thomas Woodrow Wilson

Through his father, Joseph, there came to him traits peculiar to Joseph's parents: from James Wilson, the robust faith in "the people," a zeal for reform, the trenchant tongue and pen, and an exuberant spirit and undaunted temperament; from Anne Adams, strong will, moral stamina, relentlessness and the capacity for righteous anger. Through Janet, his mother, he inherited characteristics which she had from her parents: from Thomas Woodrow, gentleness, meticulous reasoning, conscientious thoroughness and severity of ethical principles; and from Marion Williamson, sensitivity, aesthetic awareness, nervous fragility and the need for that privacy in which these refined traits of character can thrive.

It seems to us that the essential traits which formed the framework upon which the character of the man Woodrow Wilson developed are to be discerned in his parents and grandparents.

Philosophy of Appraisal

The first systematic explorer in the field of human heredity was Sir Francis Galton,[4] whose *Hereditary Genius*, published in 1869, is still

3

one of the most interesting treatises on this subject. This work analyzes the evidence accumulated from biographical sources favoring the hypothesis that *ability*, which is what Galton meant by *genius*, is transmitted in family lines. Whereas Galton studied a great number of notable characters in demonstrating that their genius or ability was inherited, we take a single person and study him as a whole man within his total frame of reference: his family, his home, the community and locale, their cultural and natural environment including not only the generally recognized factors, such as diet, but also the all-encompassing effects of astrophysical forces. Within this comprehensive frame we find that heredity is still the dominant factor in this story.

The habit of viewing a man of great gifts as a spontaneous phenomenon is due to failure to examine the man's background. "Gifts" implies endowment, God-given or otherwise. Actually these gifts are passed on from generation to generation. Social continuity can be understood only in these terms.

In his younger years of ardent self-development, Woodrow Wilson was very much aware of his gifts. He came to have a sense of having some part to play in great events, and of an aptitude for bringing issues to focus: "... a sort of calm confidence of great things to be accomplished ... a deep-rooted determination which it will be within my power to act up to."[5] This he wrote, while he was studying law at the University of Virginia, to an intimate of his Princeton student days. A few years later, at Johns Hopkins University, he confided in a letter to his fiancée, Ellen Axson, with reference to a triumph in the Hopkins Literary Society: "I enjoy it [speaking] because it sets my mind—all my faculties—aglow: and I suppose that this excitement gives my manner an appearance of confidence and self-command which arrest the attention. However that may be, I *feel* a sort of transformation ... [an] absolute joy in facing and conquering a hostile audience ... or thawing out a cold one."[6]

Abraham Lincoln may be taken as another illustration of Galton's point. Humble circumstances are taken to imply common or undistinguished milieu, and Lincoln often is used as the classic example of "the common man" with genius. Lincoln was of humble origin, but from a breed whose character was sharply wrought and deeply etched by the very experience of pioneering which his father's independent and self-reliant spirit had chosen as a way of life. There is no type more differentiated from "the masses," "the common herd." It is now well

4

known that Lincoln, on both his father's and his mother's sides, was descended from superior strains of Anglo-Saxon forebears. He was of humble birth, but by no means common. As Galton wrote:

> We must not permit ourselves to consider each human or other personality as something supernaturally added to the stock of nature, but rather as a segregation of what already existed, under a new shape, and as a regular consequence of previous conditions. Neither must we be misled by the word "individuality," because it appears . . . that our personalities are not so independent as our self-consciousness leads us to believe. We may look upon each individual as something not wholly detached from its parent source as a wave that has been lifted and shaped by normal conditions in an unknown, illimitable ocean. There is decidedly a solidarity as well as a separateness in all human, and probably in all lives whatsoever and this consideration goes far, as I think, to establish an opinion that the constitution of the living Universe is a pure theism, and that its form of activity is what may be described as co-operative.[7]

The implication of all this is that any man of great ability derives his qualities not only from his own forebears but in part from his fellow creatures. Another way of putting it might be that a man of superior ability is a culminating point of all the generations that lie behind him in time, and not only in his own line. This point of view makes individuality the goal and summit of the evolutionary process. The individual becomes a focal point: he makes of himself the epitome of his times, having substituted for egocentrism an awareness of The Whole. As Wilson put it in his essay *When a Man Comes to Himself*: ". . . every man hath both an absolute and a relative capacity: an absolute in that he hath been endued with such a nature and such parts and faculties, and a relative in that he is part of the universal community of men, and so stands in such a relation to the whole."[8]

One of Woodrow Wilson's greatest admirers, and one who was and ever remained his faithful colleague in the effort to establish the League of Nations, was Jan Christian Smuts of South Africa. Smuts conceived a theory and philosophy of evolution that has intimate relationship to the guiding spirit of our study of Wilson. In *Holism and Evolution*, published in 1936, he describes evolution as the progression of parts towards wholes, a progression which culminates in human personality, the goal of evolution. From the study of evolution in terms of this principle, he coins the word "holism," from the Greek *holos*, meaning whole, and defines the principle as "this synthetic tendency, this fundamental feature of 'wholes' in the universe."

> This whole-making or holistic tendency is fundamental in nature . . . Evolution is the . . . gradual development and stratification of progressive series of wholes, stretching from the inorganic beginnings to the highest levels of spiritual creation.[9]

Smuts hoped for a new science, based on the study of biographies to be appraised synthetically rather than analytically; that is, the person to be considered as a whole, and a culmination, not to be broken down into parts. The characters he thus would have studied should be those possessing a true "inner history"; that is, individuals manifesting a continuously developing life of the spirit, for it is such individuals who manifest the attributes that are essentially human.

Those possessing true "inner histories" are the creative humanists who reflect and embody humanity in their times, thereby epitomizing evolution. Woodrow Wilson certainly was one of these. Our study, then, is essentially holistic.

Taine,[10] whose *History of English Literature* was published in 1863, came, as a consequence of his philosophic interpretation of the fact that human affairs and achievements are always the consequence of the creativity of some individual, to general conclusions which foreshadowed those of Galton and Smuts. His notable and frequently quoted sentence, summarizing in a sense the history of culture, is an historian's way of saying what Smuts named *holism*, and to what Galton refers when he writes, "Nature teems with latent life, which man has large powers of evoking under forms and to the extent which he desires."[11]

In Taine's view, be it a poem, code of laws or manifesto, it is a document through which one seeks to discover the individual who created it, as one observing a fossil thinks of the creature that formed it. Behind every document is a man. "Nothing exists except through some individual man. It is the individual with whom we must become acquainted." Real history arises only when the historian uncovers "the living man, toiling, impassioned, entrenched in his customs, with his voice and features, his gestures and his dress . . . the complete thing is the man who acts, the man corporeal and visible, who eats, walks, fights, labours."[12]

The components of character of the man who acts are qualities and abilities native to him, i.e., derived from his immediate forebears;

6

qualities and abilities which experience has adapted to the exigencies of time and circumstance.

Being human entails a very complex interplay of relationships. Born into the family of a Presbyterian divine, this child whom we are studying immediately assumed particular relationships with the other members of the family and with the household: the mother who fed him, the father whose first son he was, sisters whom he came to love, yet competed with, and the servants. Beyond his immediate family, there was the circle of relatives with whom he gradually developed varying degrees of acquaintanceship. Being born in "the Manse" as the son of the Minister determined his place in the community. So, he was not just an organism dependent upon his physical environment, but a person related to, affecting and affected by, a great many other persons.

In most of these relationships, he was to assume a position of dominance. He was the gifted first son, whose place in the family was privileged from the start, and he did not take privilege passively. This remained true, at home, in the community and in his public relations, ultimately enlarged by the events of his times to include all humanity. Even in childhood, he evinced a sense of power to lead and influence others, first among his playmates, whom he "organized" into "societies" with written constitutions and "laws." A predisposition toward this kind of leadership, in fact, was a natural consequence both of his heredity and his heritage, as well as of the social milieu—that of leadership in ideas—in which his childhood was set. Ambition, the love of shining, and this despite a very real modesty, produced a love of adulation which was an inevitable by-product of a career that depended upon popularity. Such a career also developed in him as a popular leader qualities of self-assertion and regnant egotism.

His education, as guided by his parents and later chosen by himself, was calculated to enhance those intellectual gifts that fitted him for his subsequent career. He was academic in his training and interest, but the ideal of effective intelligence in *applying* his knowledge and talents was always to the fore. He was imaginative and intuitional, and aesthetic in his tastes and domestic relationships, but his art of self-expression in words written or spoken was disciplined and practiced not for pleasure but for utility, for social and political science in the service of mankind. His dynamic mind and spirit, from childhood onward, were engrossed in the planning of organizational instrumentalities—first as "make-believe," during college years as practice-grounds 'and in mature life calculated to strengthen or establish permanent means of maintaining stability in and the furthering of democratic processes. The operations of natural law and the facts of natural science, technologies, the facts of production and provision, and commerce, were phases of human relationship and activity of which he was fully aware, but they were practical matters which interested him less than the more strictly social and political phases of civilization.

Technique of Appraisal

The first consideration in our appraisal of Woodrow Wilson's character and career has been the study of heritage.

Who were his forebears, what were their characteristics, and what were the historical, ethnic, social and cultural factors that produced the unique person Woodrow Wilson, a man whose character and lineaments were so clearcut. Some of the endowment that came to him out of his heritage was definitely Irish; some was Scottish. But, withal, he was a product of the times into which he was born and in which he developed and lived. He was wholly American, a person born just before the outbreak of the Civil War, whose childhood and boyhood were spent in Georgia and the Carolinas during the war and the wretched period of the "Reconstruction." Out of this negative era of deprivation and frustration, he entered the stimulating atmosphere of Princeton College, showing there the two qualities which distinguished him later in his public life, a keen and creative mind and an innate gift for leadership. Those endowments came to maturity in both literary and academic work, which was the prelude to the creative role that he played in academic life as professor of political economy and then president of Princeton. His ability as a leader attained its full development during the years of his political career as governor of New Jersey and President of the United States.

In the appraisal of Wilson's unique character and personality we are guided by a systematic frame of reference which we have called the Genethnic Screen (fig. 1).[13]

The basic panel on this is that marked *Body*. This refers to the clinical record or physical history of the individual. Here we note two weaknesses which affected the career of this man—he was prone to bronchial inflammation and infection, which often coincided with episodes of fatigue and pressure in his career, and his was a far from robust digestion. Both of these were tied in with a nervous fragility that

8

THE FRAME OF REFERENCE FOR THE GENETNIC SCREEN

anthropological

BUILD	BREED	ROLE
BODY	INTEGRATION	EARTH
BEHAVIOR	CHARACTER	RELATIONS

Left side (vertical): temperamental

Right side (vertical): environmental

socio-psychological

Figure 1

THE GENETHNIC SCREEN

definitely was a handicap to a man who had to endure the ordeals that inevitably are numerous in the life of anyone dedicated to political leadership. These handicaps, which his stamina and vigor easily transcended, were inherited from his mother. They were no more than handicaps, which he was able to overcome until the very end of his life when an asthmatic condition, resulting from an attack of influenza during the Peace Conference in Paris, deprived him of sleep and induced a state of exhaustion that led to his collapse.

On the opposite side of the Genethnic Screen is the panel marked *Earth*. Here are the physical environmental factors that were effective in inducing the pathological symptoms and conditions recorded in the clinical record. The cycles of sun and moon both bore a direct relationship to major episodes in the life of the man studied, as did temperature, humidity and barometric pressure, whose combined effects produce weather. Woodrow Wilson was very subject to weather changes, especially when his physical energies were depleted. The panel marked *Earth* also includes variables having to do with food and nourishment, and others affecting the physique directly and indirectly.

The following summarizes the relationship of the *Body* panel to the *Earth* panel. Under *Earth* and *Body* are listed the variables on the respective panels.

Schematic Basis of Equivalence

EARTH		BODY
Sun		*Central Nervous*
Radiation	Electro-spheric	*Peripheral Nervous*
Moon		*Sense Organs*
Temperature		*Integumental*
Humidity	Atmo-spheric	*Endocrine*
Barometric		*Respiratory*
Nutritional		*Digestive*
Vegetational	Bio-spheric	*Vascular*
Animal		*Uro-genital*
Physiographical		*Muscular*
Geological	Physio-spheric	*Skeletal*
Locale		*General*

Apart from the clinical life history and the physical environment, there are two other frames of reference in which the body of an individual has to be considered. What is sometimes referred to as constitutional type is the same as *Body Build*, or form. The three extreme types of build are the rotund (endomorph), stocky (mesomorph) and lean (ectomorph). In the rotund, fatty tissue is more developed; in the stocky type there is more muscular tissue, while in the lean individual there is proportionately more nervous tissue. The three types therefore contrast in temperament—the rotund is sedentary, the stocky is athletic and the individual in whom nervous tissue predominates is more sensitive and more intellectual. It is of rare occurrence that an individual is of one form or temperament exclusively. Woodrow Wilson was a lean type, very intellectual and sensitive to both physical and cultural environment, while at the same time being compactly built and dynamic in temperament, like a good athlete. The temperament of the man expressed fully those qualities characteristic of a combination of leanness with compactness. These were exhibited in his posture and stance, in mobility and vigor of movement, in alertness and expressiveness of his face, and in the forthright energy of his speech in private conversation and public address.

What we term *Breed* refers to the ethnic traits that a man inherits. The face of an individual is a very good key to what are the dominant ethnic traits that he embodies. Woodrow Wilson's face is strikingly like that of his grandmother, Ann Adams, the wife of James Wilson. Her features are Scottish of a type that combines Keltic with Norman inheritance. It is the face of an aristocrat with clearcut uncompromising values and principles. The features express indomitable will and forcefulness. Such were traits typical of the Covenanters in Scotland and in Ulster, a very tough and uncompromising breed. Despite the gentle qualities that prevailed in his intimate personal relationships, a quality which came to him through his mother, the temperament and temper of Woodrow Wilson consistently manifested in his public life the toughness and thrust of his Covenanter forebears. His career at Princeton and as President of the United States was notable for the boldness of his attitudes and forthright action.

The four remaining panels on the Genethnic Screen are *Role, Relations, Character* and *Behavior*. What a man is—and what he does—not only reflects or expresses his personality, but modifies it. The experience of leadership and responsibility involved in a political career molds the character of the actor. It affects his relations with others in

11

evoking dominance over others, and loyalty and adulation from others, which strengthen his regnant or self-assertive inclinations. In the field of teaching and academic administration, the professor and educational leader's mind has to be adapted to the interests, aptitudes and abilities of students. His effective intelligence is adjusted to the capacity of those he teaches. In the life of Woodrow Wilson, the maturing of his mind during the years when he was a teacher and college president prepared him for the years of leadership in government and administration during his Presidency. His first constituents were the alumni of the university, and the public which he first addressed was the student body, while in his relationship with his faculty, he had a foretaste of the experience of working with the Congress which sometimes approved of his plans and not infrequently opposed him.

In the Presbyterian Manse in Staunton, Virginia, where Woodrow Wilson was born, the stage was set for the beginning of the drama of his life. A close look at the details of this scene, its physical aspects and its spiritual attributes, is essential if we are to comprehend the nature of the environmental factors instrumental in making him the kind of person he was. Hence the careful and detailed attention in the chapters that follow to the circumstances and the times in which he was conceived and born. If Woodrow Wilson had been the child of the same parents, but had lived the first years of his life in Glasgow or Carlisle or London, he would have been quite different from the person born in the Manse at Staunton, who was destined to live in the White House as President of the United States.

II

THE STAUNTON SCENE

Had Grandfather Wilson Known . . .

Sturdy James Wilson, late of Master Dunlap's printshop in Ulster, more lately of the Philadelphia printshops, then of the Ohio legislature (and finally "the late Judge Wilson") would have been proud of his youngest son in that early summer of 1885. Wife Ann had always favored young Joseph—thought him her brightest boy, and devout Presbyterian that she was, had championed his ambition to leave the family typesetting tradition and study for scholarship and the ministry. But that career had not looked too promising to James in 1851.

James, a bold aggressive countryman, was born at Dergalt farm in County Tyrone, and was as Irish as the turf he used to cut before he walked off to the county town of Strabane and apprenticed himself to a printer. To him, Joseph was a bit lacking in what seemed the elements of success. For though already a bachelor of divinity from Princeton Theological Seminary, and two years married, Joseph, in his 29 years, had but one small pastoral charge. Between his graduation in 1846 and his marriage to the daughter of that famous preacher, Dr. Thomas Woodrow of Chillicothe, he had put off his ordination, and even lately had seemed more interested in an academic career as a teacher of rhetoric.

That year of 1851 was the last year of Judge Wilson's eventful and zestful life. Struck down in the prime of health and activity by Asiatic cholera, he had not lived to watch his youngest son's developing powers. Now, four years later and some hundreds of miles south of his parental home, Joseph was making a significant advance. He was leaving a teaching post at Hampden-Sydney, a small but distinguished Presbyterian college in Tidewater, Virginia, and was accepting a call to minister to a congregation in the famed, rich Shenandoah, that broad valley in the uplands between the Blue Ridge and the Allegheny Mountains. His call was to the First Presbyterian Church at Staunton, founded in the mid-eighteenth century in this western "Valley of Virginia," as it is now best known.

Success always ranked high with Judge James Wilson, who had

known extraordinary hard-earned success in his every venture in the New World, and this move of his youngest son's represented a big step toward success. The power of the spoken word—exemplified by his own vigorous, slashing, often vituperative political oratory—appealed even more than success to James Wilson's Irish heart. Now Joseph was moving toward the fulfillment of an oratorical career of his own, and was on his way to exercizing his notably vigorous and scholarly powers as a preacher of the Word.

Indeed, father James would have felt a truly prideful stirring of the heart for this tall, robust and handsome son with a temperament so like his own; going confidently forward now to bigger things in his 33rd year. A credit to his North-of-Ireland parents and to their pioneering prowess, James would have said—though the rough and tumble of politics would have been more to *his* liking. He had liked his new daughter-in-law Janet, too—Jeanie they called her; a quiet lass, yet soundly Scottish by birth and American by upbringing. He did not underrate the Scots. Were not the stout folk of Antrim and Down, his own wife's homeland, the true Irish-Scots—returned to Ulster after subduing and civilizing the wild Pictish tribes across the water?

There was one flaw in the picture of Joseph leading his little family westward across Virginia to Staunton which might have displeased James Wilson, who in the first twelve years of marriage had sired seven sons and three daughters. Was it a weakness of some sort, that in seven years, Jeanie and Joseph had produced but two small girls?

The Reverend Doctor Wilson Comes to Staunton

As compared with the Alleghenies of eastern Ohio, where Joseph Ruggles Wilson was born and bred, Hampden-Sydney College, in the lower reaches of eastern central Virginia, was hot and uninspiring. Tall, bigboned, an Allegheny-born American of North-Irish parentage, he was a man of great vigor in this his early maturity. Robust extrovert that he was, he certainly was less sensitive to climate and weather than his physically and nervously somewhat fragile, wife. But how he felt physically was unimportant to him, compared with the upsurge of mind and spirit suddenly released from tedious teaching: teaching boys a subject—chemistry and natural science—that interested him much less than rhetoric, always dear to the hearts of preachers with scholarly inclinations.

The call to Staunton's oldest church, the prospect of serving a large congregation in this notable center of Presbyterian influence and activity in "The Valley," must have exalted his soul. For his was an exuberant spirit, and until now his sense of mastery and dedication as a preacher had been granted but meager satisfaction in the one small congregation in Pennsylvania to which he had ministered, and in two professorships in small colleges.

Of course, he had been invited to preach before the Staunton congregation before he was "called." He had seen the thriving small city in the midst of the hilly rich farmlands of Augusta County. He had met the elders of the church and some of their wives, vigorous, forthright men and women with whom he felt much at home. Here was a community that had originated as a colony of folk of his own Ulster breed, and that had become a crossroads of progress even more promising than those communities of eastern Ohio and western Pennsylvania whence he came. Here he perceived also the characteristically Virginian élan and an intellectual alertness that pleased and challenged his Scotch-Irish temperament. Augusta County, both physically and socially after the years in the low country, would, he saw, be exhilarating.

He looked ahead, in the delightful privacy of the new home, to the moments of expansive elation characteristic of his nature, but not suitable to public expression. The intimate and tender affection that prevailed in their household naturally engendered such a mood in his spirited soul. Jeanie, his wife (whose letters show her to have been capable of serene delight), had always enjoyed his exuberances and risen to meet them. Her quiet bright joyousness was for him just the right foil. She likewise had been bred in an invigorating trans-Allegheny community of southern Ohio and rejoiced with him in the change of environment. And the glee of the two little girls would surely make the austere Manse and its secluded garden ring with gay play: always seemly and not too noisy glee, as befitted their mother's sense of propriety.

Having been a professor of natural science, Dr. Wilson knew that the Valley of Virginia promised to be more interesting than Prince Edward County had been. Hampden-Sydney College at Kingsville was a little college founded in 1776 as Prince Edward Academy. It lay in the rolling sandhills of the outer fringe of the Piedmont, low in altitude, hot, and in an area of mediocre small farms and much "scrub" pine. Yes, undeniably it had had a dampening effect upon them all. Like most folk in that area they had, in that day, endured occasional bouts of ague, locally known as "chills and fever," with frequent resorts to quinine and calomel to cure or fend it off. Joseph himself, of robust physique to start with, had enjoyed a relative immunity, devoted pipe-smoker that he was, and not averse to an occasional drink of good whisky with faculty colleagues. But beyond the physical benefits of Staunton's thousand-foot elevation and its well defined changes of season, he reckoned the stimulus of a new and vigorous community and the challenge of new opportunity, and on these he reflected as the little family journeyed to their new home.

The train journey to Staunton was slow but not tedious. Coming up into the Piedmont they had "changed cars" in Lynchburg, the great Virginia tobacco market of the day—the town "built on seven hills" whose streets went straight up at precipitous angles from the shore of the broad James River where the railway station stood. North of Lynchburg, the train wound through interminable foothills of the Blue Ridge, passing small tobacco farms in every bit of flat land, stopping here and there at unkempt towns, dusty from good old Virginia red clay. The hilly farms were sadly gashed by gullies, but there were pretty streams in the narrow valleys, and along the railway the fences, bushes and trees were festooned with honeysuckle, filling the air with sweet pure fragrance. The jumble of hills and little mountains were thickly wooded with pine and cedar and oak, locust and black walnut; and in "bottoms" along streams stood majestic tulip-poplar and sycamore.

As they slowed for Charlottesville, they again "changed cars." From the station there was little to be seen but dingy small houses, a few warehouses and little factories. But as their train turned westward toward the Blue Ridge, hazy in the distance, they could see above and beyond the tracks the buildings of Thomas Jefferson's University of Virginia. They passed just below the beautiful Rotunda of the University and could even see part of the line of handsome faculty homes east of the Lawn, and the cloistered West Range of student rooms. Even this glimpse was uplifting to a man who had read and reread with warm interest Mr. Jefferson's "Notes on Virginia," the first general exposition of the natural history of the New World and still one of the best. How his father had revered the noble and practical idealism of the great Jefferson as philosopher, experienced politician and man of affairs! As newspaper publisher and legislator, James Wilson had battled vigorously in print and in the political arena for the Jeffersonian principles. Indeed, it was Thomas Jefferson's pen that had lured the young printer's apprentice to take passage for America from Londonderry;

16

and it was to Jefferson College at Cannonville, Pennsylvania, that he had sent his son Joseph to be educated.

No sooner had the train left Charlottesville than the nature of the country changed. It opened into the generous rolling hill-and-meadow pastures typical of Albemarle County, perhaps the noblest of Virginia's counties east of the mountains. Now, running along a recently completed rail line connecting Charlottesville with the Shenandoah Valley, they were heading straight for the Blue Ridge. From a distance, one wondered how a train might pass through or over that Ridge; but there was much near at hand to claim attention. Among the increasingly hilly farmlands on either side nestled many neat homes surrounded by apple and peach orchards. Here, in these sunwarmed uplands, apple growers were developing the Albemarle pippin that was beginning to make the county famous. Joseph recalled the story of an Albemarle farmer who had sent a barrel of his finest pippins to Queen Victoria as a complimentary gift; and it was said that these apples became so famous at the court of England that several English gentlemen came to settle here!

Now the train swung out past wooded hillocks, and suddenly, no longer obscured by the rolling foothills, the hazy forested wall of the Blue Ridge was spread before them close at hand. This was not Joseph's first view, to be sure, but this time it thrilled him to the depths of his heart to realize that just beyond, in a cool bustling midland town, with mountains all about, lay a home and a great work for him—and for Jeanie, whose quiet eagerness equalled his. For her, as for him, it meant moving back into a country and among a people more like those she loved best in southern and eastern Ohio, and in Tennessee where she had gone to school. Then too it was a move that brought her much closer, as miles are reckoned, to her beloved father and elder brother, who still lived in Chillicothe, her own old home.

The grade steepened and the puffing engine suddenly was enveloped in its own smoke as they entered the tunnel under Rockfish Gap, and they were all coughing and laughing and, with the other passengers, trying to get the windows down, half blinded by the smoke. After emerging from the tunnel and passing the village of Waynesboro, the Blue Ridge now behind them, they must have felt themselves a grimy looking family to be presenting themselves to the elders of the Church who would be greeting them soon in Staunton! But as they stepped off the train they were welcomed with warm cordiality by a little group of gentlemen and ladies delegated by the First Presbyterian Church and

—Lorna E. Freeman

The Manse at Staunton, Virginia, from the Garden

the Female Seminary to greet them and conduct them to the Manse.

How good these people are, thought Joseph. There in the ample pantry was all they could need for days to come. Even several mannerly colored servants awaited them with friendly warmth. And a horse and buggy in the stable! Supper already was prepared and ready to be eaten after their hosts had made them feel welcome and then considerately bade them "Good evening," knowing they must be tired from their journey and in need of privacy to "clean up" and rest a bit. Yes, a good town, good folk!

Later, in the sunset, as Joseph stepped out upon the second floor verandah overlooking the secluded back garden, he thought with satisfaction of what a good place to think and write this would be on summer days when he had some leisure. He gazed out past the town to the wide rolling farms beyond, to east and west, the Blue Ridge and Alleghenies flanking all—truly, a Land of Promise! That evening the family prayers were more than usually devout, for thankfulness and a strong presentiment of imminent blessings were in the hearts of husband and wife. Joseph was moved to read Psalm 84, for this was his first true pastorate; and this dignified Manse, in the mellow June twilight, seemed already to be enfolding them with a sense of substantial and spiritual wellbeing.

O how amiable are thy dwellings, thou Lord of hosts!

My soul hath a desire and longing to enter into the courts of the Lord, my heart and my flesh rejoice in the living God . . . .

Blessed are they that dwell in Thy house; they will rejoice in praising Thee.

Blessed is the man whose strength is in Thee, in whose heart are Thy ways . . . .

They will go from strength to strength . . . .

For the Lord God is a light and defense; the Lord will give grace and worship, and no good thing shall be withheld from them that live a godly life . . . .

A Retrospective View

There was scarcely a day, in those which followed upon the family's settling, that did not find the minister at some hour refreshing his mind

19

and his eyes with the view that stretched away south and west from the upper verandah which at first glimpse so invited him. In between the pastoral calls which were acquainting him with his new congregation, the session meetings and the preparation of sermons, he found what time he could for quiet contemplation there, overlooking the garden.

This summery late afternoon, as he sat there while Jeanie was bathing the little girls in readiness for supper, he was reflecting, with a fascination born of his own background as the son of a pioneering family, upon what he had been reading and what he had been told here and there of late about the human story of this pioneer community. From his vantage point, he could look over the lower part of the town to southward, and northwest toward the succession of hilltops beyond "Gospel Hill" which marked the favored residential area. Gazing to the left toward Beverley Street next beyond the Manse, and then down into the lowland, he mused upon the beginnings of Staunton town, there around its mill, more than a hundred years ago when all the region hereabout had been known as Beverley Manor. William Beverley of Essex County, Virginia, having been granted these thousands of acres of forested upland and virgin valley bluegrass, had chosen this confluence of the forks of Lewis Creek as the site for his mill. The Colonial Government in Williamsburg had made the grant of lands in 1736, with the express stipulation that they promptly be settled and cultivated—a development regarded as imperative, both in order to assure the extension of Virginia's claims to the west and as a bulwark against the probable threat of Indian wars along the so-far peaceful frontier.

With an even livelier interest, Joseph Wilson reflected upon the circumstances which had antedated the arrival of William Beverley, for here was something akin to his own background. The old fort on Lewis Creek, over to the northeast of the mill that Beverley installed, had been built in 1732 by John Lewis, the first independent settler, and John Lewis had been an emigrant to America from Ulster, as had Joseph's own father in 1807. John Lewis—The Founder, as members of Dr. Wilson's congregation liked to call him—and his family of stalwart sons had become legendary in Valley history, throughout the pioneering era and the Revolutionary War which followed. His family, and the other Scots and North Irish settlers who accompanied or followed him, had already carved out large settlements for themselves by "right of the plough," several years before William Beverley had arrived from Williamsburg with his grant from the King's Governor.

20

John Lewis, Ulster-born of French Huguenot emigré parentage, had fled from Ulster during a period of Church-of-England persecution and Irish rebellion, entering the Colonies by the hospitable gateway of William Penn's "City of Brotherly Love." From there, pioneering up the Shenandoah River from the German settlements at the Valley's northern or Pennsylvania border, he, "Dissenter" that he was, had not bothered even to ask for the improbable grant of the lands he settled on, but had made his own peaceable arrangements with the nomadic Indians of the Valley.

Joseph's own parents, he was remembering, had emigrated seventy-five years later from the midst, not of rebellion, but of the hard times following rebellion, and entering also through the City of Brotherly Love, had pioneered more directly westward, across the Ohio River's southflowing stream, at Steubenville. The courage of a young Scotch-Irish lad and lass to leave home and family for a new land overseas must have been greatly strengthened, Joseph thought, by the tradition, strong in Ulster, of all those who had gone before them in more dangerous times to swell the strength of colonists seeking religious freedom and ready to die for a new concept of independence.

Thinking of this—his gaze straying over to the white portico of his church across the ravine—Dr. Wilson reflected with satisfaction upon the surprisingly peaceful conjunction of the Beverley and Lewis "plantations" in those years immediately following 1736. There was gratitude to God as well as satisfaction in his reflection, for he realized that upon that fact hung the establishment of the Presbyterian faith in these Southern colonies—first its toleration, and then its peaceful spread from this Valley of Virginia to the south and west. This Staunton church to which he had been called was at one of the mainsprings of his Faith in America.

Dr. Wilson's training in church history had given him ample acquaintance with both the persecution and interdiction which the Presbyterian church had endured in the New World, for that was a policy carried out as determinedly in the English Colonies of North America (except perhaps William Penn's) as in the Old Country. He therefore had been astonished to learn, in the course of his study of the Augusta County community, that as early as 1739 a Presbyterian minister had been supplied to that newly begun settlement at the settlers' solicitation. The Reverend John Craig had come from the Donegal Presbytery of Philadelphia, named after the Ulster county next to that in which his father had been born, and by 1740 two rude meeting houses had been built for this ministry, with others soon following. Even more astonishing, the presence of this first "settled" Presbyterian divine in all the Colony of Virginia had been looked on with equanimity in the Valley by the newly-come King's grantee, William Beverley, and by the Colonial governor himself.

Perhaps, thought Joseph Wilson with a chuckle, the fact that the then-Governor Gooch was himself a Scot, though in the King's service, might have had something to do with it. Quite likely, too, the presence by then of hardbitten Scotch-Irish clansmen in large numbers in the settlements—seasoned "rebels," ready to fight Indians for their lives if need be, or King's soldiers for their religion's sake—had had even more to do with it. But, be these surmises guess or gospel, the undeniable fact was there, that William Beverley himself, though he had brought in the Established Church of England along with his English settlers, also had aided the Dissenting congregations. It was he who arranged for the arrival on his lands of the two families of gentry from Scotland and Ulster, the Pattons and the Prestons, whose settlement in 1738 near Tinkling Spring gave impetus to the building of that famous early church, some 15 miles from Joseph's church on Gospel Hill.

Indeed, he understood, Beverley had taken every measure to assure the wellbeing of the Scotch-Irish already in the area and to encourage the continued immigration of their fellow countrymen by way of Pennsylvania. This was a consistently calculated plan, as Dr. Wilson could well understand. On the side of the settlers, the appeal of these rich grass-and-plough lands would have been irresistible (once their religious liberty was assured) for displaced and land-starved emigrants from chaotic North Ireland with its succession of wars and famines. On the government's side, dependable settlement at the earliest was what was essential in Virginia.

It was a matter of church history, told with pride to the new minister, that following the settling of the Reverend John Craig of Scotland and the regular establishment of his congregation here "on the Triple Forks of the Sherando," the taking up of the new lands in Beverley Manor, which had lagged seriously for the first year, went forward now with startling speed.

The Lewises and other pre-grant settlers, Joseph understood, not only had been given the opportunity to clarify their titles but took a natural and prominent place of leadership in town and county councils when community organization became effective some years later. Friendly cooperation seemed to have been the rule in those early days. It was so between Scotch-Irish and English, and between whites and Indians. The most singular instance of this, in Joseph Wilson's mind, had come to his attention only recently in his perusal of the history of his new charge.

For some time before the building of the First Presbyterian Church in Staunton town, around 1805, the town-dwelling section of the congregation, dissatisfied with driving the several miles to the old Augusta Stone Church which stood northward along the Valley Road, or to the still more distant church at Tinkling Spring, had accepted an invitation to worship in old Trinity, first erected as Church of England, now, since Independence, known as the Protestant Episcopal Church of America in Staunton.

What a reflection upon the sinfulness of man, thought Joseph, that these good and amicable relations could not have endured, in all directions. For twenty years there had been a general peace between those earliest settlers and the Indian hunters who for generations before them had roamed the Valley as their most abundant source of game. Fort Lewis, built as a natural adjunct to pioneer life, had remained practically unused. Then, as settlement became more indiscriminate, and as wild frontier characters became part of the floating population (in that flux of movement further westward of which Staunton was a center), frictions and provocations accumulated.

"Spirits" had provided the final tinder, according to the story told him by a descendant of one of those early settlers. The picture of that incident was very vivid in his imagination—a small party of Shawnee braves returning northward to their homes beyond the Ohio, flushed with victory over the Chickasaws of Carolina, with whom they carried on a perpetual feud; a pause, according to custom, at one of the plantation establishments, where they were bidden to spend the evening; a beef roasted over a campfire and hosts and guests gathered around it; the warriors then plied with whisky until their natural bravado flamed into raucous boasting and wilder gestures as they performed their heathen victory dance about the fire,—then finally sank into drunken stupor.

"That white man's plot touched off ten years of warfare and widowed many a Valley woman," Joseph's friend had told him. For it *was* a plot. A few of the host's neighbors, who had endured occasional thievery and other minor depredations at Indian hands, hit upon a plan to gain revenge safely (they thought). Their plot was to stupefy this band of warriors whom chance had brought into their hands, and murder them all in their sleep. Murder them they did, but not with impunity.

Joseph Wilson, growing up on the Ohio frontier in the 1820's and 30's, had heard in his boyhood enough stories of early Indian raids and massacres to know that no one can best the savage in ingenious plans for revenge, and he could gauge something of the terror to which isolated settlers in the Shenandoah region were subjected in the years that followed as a result of this outrage. To be sure, from the very first, the whites had had to learn to endure high-handed demands for rations, occasional pilfering, and frequent loss of grazing cattle to marauding Indian bands on the hunt or the warpath, but with patience they had been spared more than the rarest incident of personal violence. Now by one stroke of folly, all was changed, and every Indian became a potential or active foe, treacherous or declared.

Taken to visit "The Founder's" grave some days before, Dr. Wilson knew from the inscription that John Lewis had been a captain of Militia. That, he mused, probably would have been at about this time when concerted defense became necessary. It was a time, moreover, when France had declared her claim to lands not only along the Mississippi but along the Great River's tributaries as far east as Pennsylvania. This aggravation led to bold British resistance in the border colonies and to more widespread Indian wars, especially against those tribes whom the French had secured as allies.

What changes could be wrought by man in a hundred years! Looking out over the thriving town and off toward the peaceful rolling countryside it was difficult to envision roving herds of buffalo or catch the clamor of Indian hunting parties. More difficult still to see this land through the eyes of the first seventeenth century white explorers or those of the early eighteenth century—transient visits all, but leaving their written record of a natural and uninhabited wonderland to lure the imagination of later pioneers. And at this point his mind turned away from the terror and bloodshed of two wars—first the prolonged war with the aroused Indians of Ohio, Delaware and the Carolinas, whose "Great Trail" traversed the Valley from north to south, and then that later war against the soldiery of an English king, whose advisors lacked the good sense to leave well enough alone in his thriving New World colonies.

24

Joseph's parents had come to the new America only thirty-one years after its founding as a nation—the United States. But he well knew the temper of the thousands of Highland Scots and Ulster Irish who had preceded them and had been a mainstay of General Washington's patriot army of volunteers, gathering in Pennsylvania and the colonies to the south. Scarcely a family name in his congregation—or for that matter, in the whole Dissenting Congregation of the Shenandoah—was not enrolled in the annals of the Revolutionary Army. And now, during the half century of peace that had come to the Valley, prosperity had blessed it with a lavish hand.

Throughout the countryside, there were rolling green pastures and cultivated fields encircling the eminences on which stood the sub-stantial homes of estate owners. Staunton town had become not only, as in earlier years, a crossroads for the pioneers moving westward into his own native state of Ohio. Since his recent familiarity with Virginia, he had recognized with quickened interest the source of the many town and county names in the southern part of his home state—particularly in the area of his wife's family home at Chillicothe, which might well be a transplanted section of the Old Dominion. Staunton had become a thriving market center for the whole Valley and transmontane region of Virginia. The old pre-Revolutionary family names were attached now to solid, often handsome brick homes on hilly tree-lined streets or winding lanes; the Courthouse square had taken on a look of well-established authority; and in addition to the churches, the community had built schools.

The first—in accordance (he thought rather pridefully) with the tradition of his faith—had been built by his own Presbytery here: The Augusta Male and Female Seminaries. The Episcopal Diocese had built Stuart Hall Female Seminary and the Augusta Military Academy for boys. These notable schools drew their pupils from far afield, especially the male academies, which trained the sons of the entire Valley's more substantial families for entrance into Thomas Jefferson's University, over the Blue Ridge at Charlottesville.

One thing in this culture Joseph Wilson found difficult to accept— the slave basis of the prosperity which its chief families enjoyed. He had understood previously that the slaveholding institution prevailed chiefly in the large plantation areas of Tidewater and Piedmont Virginia, east of the mountains, and that the Scotch and German-settled region of the great Valley was relatively free of it. But he was surprised, on arrival, to recognize the prevalence of Negroes in the population, and more surprised still to learn that from earliest settlement in Augusta County, the sturdy Scots and Ulster Irish, even ministers of the Gospel, had not been averse to owning Negro servitors. Of late years, he knew, there was growing discussion of the issue in church circles and increased aversion to the practice; indeed a considerable number—proportionately small but still considerable—of the slaves had been freed. But then this, he knew, was a growing tendency among all but the largest slaveholders, throughout the state.

Dr. Wilson entertained no illusions about the practical and economic difficulties involved in a large-scale change of status for slaves and owners. Indeed, since his term of residence in the South, he had grown in appreciation of its people and its problems, and he deplored the ill-considered racialism of the New England Abolitionists who sought to press the Southern States into a premature and impossible situation relative to slavery. This attitude of understanding was to deepen through the coming years; to become indeed a forthright championship of the Southern cause, not on the issue of slavery but upon that of the right of secession, a right strongly attractive to a man of his breed and heritage, and an attitude that was to lead to a serious break with his own brothers, several of whom served in the Union Army.

It was in such a climate of sympathy and conviction that the boy Tommy was to be nurtured in his most formative years. This, strengthened by vivid childhood memories of war close at hand, of privation, heroism and soldiers marching ragged and wounded in defeat, was to put an indelible impress upon the youth, together with a passionate love of his homeland and an equally passionate bitterness against the folly of war. All of it put together, on the purely personal side, was to lead the mature man to say; "The only place in the country, the only place in the world, where nothing has to be explained to me is the South."[1]

There was an occasion during his first year at Princeton when, with some fellow students (Northerners presumably) he was discussing the War Between the States and the excesses of "Reconstruction," when "Wilson's face went white with feeling, and he cried out, 'You know nothing whatever about it,' and turned and left the company."[2] After four years at Princeton, it seems he was still so much of a Southerner that he wrote to his fiancée in Georgia from Baltimore that, as a member of the Johns Hopkins Glee Club, he and three others "had no little difficulty" in learning "The Star-Spangled Banner," because "four members of the Club [including himself] had never heard it before."[3]

But all this lay in the years ahead. Now, with his characteristic independence of mind and strength of conviction on matters of right and wrong, Joseph was feeling the unquenchable hope that a workable solution for this critical problem was soon to be found. And as dusk fell and the sounds and smells of supper preparations invited him indoors, he felt a rising thankfulness that at least the cheerful servants in the Manse household were no longer in human bondage.

The Teacher at Staunton

There was one aspect of Joseph Wilson's part in the Staunton scene in which he took great pride, even while he was inclined to find its duties somewhat irksome. That was his relationship to the Augusta Female Seminary, on whose grounds his church stood. He felt pride in the institution itself, as a tribute to the acknowledged leadership of Presbyterians in establishing seats of learning wherever they settled. But he felt also a certain impatience with what seemed the trivialities connected with the education of females, when there was such a big task to be wrought in the doing of the Lord's work in a man's world.

His son, years later, would have the same qualms about his own professorship in a "female college"—Bryn Mawr.

But to return to Joseph Ruggles Wilson—he was not at all averse to educational activities. Indeed, teaching ran as a recurring strand throughout all his most vigorous years, ever since his brilliant record as a student at Jefferson College, where he was valedictorian of his graduating class in 1844 and much esteemed for both his personality and his scholarship. Upon graduation he chose first to teach, and only later had he decided upon theological training. Even after completion of his studies at Western Theological Seminary and at Princeton, he had taught for two years at the Male Academy in Steubenville. Not until after his marriage did he enter upon his first pastorate. Soon, however, came an irresistible opportunity to teach rhetoric in his own Jefferson College; then came the offer from Hampden-Sydney College in Virginia, to teach "the natural sciences." It had seemed during these years that he was destined to teach rather than preach. Actually one of the most notable episodes in his later life was to be connected with a professorship at the Theological Seminary in Columbia, South Carolina.

Yet what he wanted with his whole heart was to be a great preacher of the Word. So when the call to Staunton came, he was glad. That the new post involved direction of the school was due to the resignation of the principal.

The Seminary was not very old. It had been founded in 1842, exactly one hundred years after its masculine counterpart, the Old Fort Academy, later known as the Augusta Male Academy. The first Presbyterian minister in that area, Dominie Craig, had founded the Old Fort Academy in 1742 close by the Stone Church, built near John Lewis' fort, before Staunton was a village. This was years after Presbyterian pioneers began homesteading farms in what became known as the Beverley Grant. Even historic Hampden-Sydney, proud of its establishment in the year of Independence, 1776, was an upstart, Joseph reflected, compared with this academy for Presbyterian boys founded by his Scotch-Irish countrymen in a wilderness where Red Indians hunted, roamed and stealthily stalked and killed men, women and children.

He approved of the Church's recent zeal for female education—provided it be sound and practical and encouraged no social vanities and no scholastic nonsense. Jeanie's mind had been well-nourished indeed by her schooling in Tennessee. Certainly in her it had encouraged no vanities, either social or scholarly. Her gentle mind and ready wit would have remained unspoiled under any circumstances. Already this new school's high reputation seemed to attest to its own soundness in this respect.

Miss Mary Baldwin, a graduate of the Seminary and an able woman, became Jeanie's good friend. Dr. Wilson knew her as a good Sunday school teacher. (In 1863 she was to become the first woman principal of that fine school for girls, whose trustees, after her death, renamed it Mary Baldwin College.) Yes, it was a good school, and if females were to be taught they should have good female teachers. Yet he would feel a certain amount of relief when his own directional responsibilities toward the Seminary were ended. Joseph Ruggles Wilson was essentially a scholar, preacher and pastor of souls.

From upper windows looking southeast in the main building of the school, one can see a symmetrical small wooded hill, one of a pair that stand picturesquely just outside the town, where together they form the first notable feature that comes to view as one approaches Staunton along the highroad from the Blue Ridge. These two are famous in the annals of this Virginia county settled by Scots and Ulstermen. As "Bessy Bell and Mary Gray" they survive here as if in homage to a

28

very ancient Scottish legend, long celebrated in balladry. Only fragments of the ballad were still remembered and quoted to us by graduates of the College, where once in earlier days it was memorized complete and sung by all the students:

> O Bessy Bell and Mary Gray!
> They were twa bonnie lasses—
> They biggit a bower on yon burn-brae,
> An' theekit it ower wi' rashes.
> They theekit it over wi' rashes green,
> They happit it round wi' heather;
> But the pest cam' frae the burrows-toun,
> An slew them baith thegither.

And the concluding stanza:

> They thought to lie in Methven Kirk,
> Beside their gentle kin;
> But they maun lie in Dronach haugh,
> and beak fornent the sin.
> O Bessy Bell and Mary Gray!
> They were twa bonnie lasses—
> They biggit a bower on yon burn-brae,
> An' theekit it ower wi' rashes.

What surprise a few years later in County Tyrone, Northern Ireland, when two similar hills were pointed out—and the gay lilting voice of a "wee Irish lass" suddenly piped into an Ulster version of that same first verse, there near the River Mourne! Might Joseph Wilson have heard this ballad in his childhood? For the small singer was Miss Margaret Wilson, youngest daughter of our host on that occasion, Mr. Robert Wilson of Strabane and Dergalt. And the hills were in the countryside near the farmhouse in which the emigrant James Wilson was born more than a century and a half before, and where quite likely he had hunted rabbits round about them as a boy.

Joseph A. Waddell,[4] historian of faraway Augusta County in Virginia, wrote in 1902 that "seventy or eighty years ago," boys and girls used to climb the twin hills to gather nuts and berries. Quite likely Dr. Wilson of Staunton had followed those winding paths with his two little girls, taking them chestnutting in the colorful autumn, perhaps reciting to them the ballad, heard certainly at the Seminary, if not in his Ohio home. And may not Tommy Wilson, two decades later when he was courting cousin Harriet Woodrow, have taken her walking there? She was attending Mary Baldwin College, he was a law student at the

"Bessy Bell" and "Mary Gray," near Staunton

—Lorna E. Freeman

University of Virginia, and many were his visits to her in those days. But he did not know of "Bessy" and "Mary" in Ireland. He "liked to think" that he had Irish blood in his veins, but he had no assurance of his Irish background and never visited Ireland in search of it.

Certain it is that he did not know of the Scottish source of the legend, carried to Ulster by the Scotch-Irish settlers there, nor that the source lay deep in pre-Christian Keltic naturalistic lore and symbolism which saw the two "lassie" hills as the breasts of Mother Earth. Neither he nor his father would have approved of such an interpretation!

In Staunton, Waddell recorded the accepted version of the Scottish legend around which the ballad was composed. These two hapless lassies, close friends, and daughters respectively of the lairds of Kincaid and Lednoch, built their woodland bower as refuge from the pestilence which swept the country in 1645, and there they lived in seclusion for some time. The missing verses of the ballad carry the romantic and tragic irony of their fate; a lad who, it is said, loved them both, brought food to them and it was through his tender solicitude that the plague sought them out in their woodland retreat. Waddell is explicit as to final detail: they died in their bower, and were buried by the river Almond not far from Lednoch House, "which is seven miles northwest of Perth."

So was their memory immortalized,—in Scotland, in Ulster, and in the Valley of Virginia. The Augusta County countryside of rolling pasture and wooded hills is beautiful at all times. Especially charming to the eyes of folk in Staunton who loved the beauties of their county was the view of Bessy Bell (some here call her Betsy) on a summer evening after a shower of rain, with the setting sun glinting on her wooded summit. And at other times, wrote Waddell, "when the clouds gather around her head, and 'Bessy Bell puts her nightcap on,' we see her in another phase scarcely less attractive."[5]

Professor of Natural Science

Jeanie will enjoy what I have to tell her of today's explorations, thought Dr. Wilson as he urged his horse homeward one afternoon. But the horse was well travelled and preferred to amble comfortably, and the driver, his mind full of many things, was content to muse and allow the beast his own gait.

This day, as he was returning from a call on members of his church family whose farms lay north of the town, he had stopped in to have a talk with "Jed" Hotchkiss, the professor of natural science and engineering at Mount Solon school (later to become Major J.E.D. Hotchkiss, General "Stonewall" Jackson's civil engineer).

A full day indeed, yet more full of natural history than of theology or pastoral duty! A minister's mind is refreshed and vitalized by such communing with Nature and with men who know her as a book. Would that more of us who preach the Word of God were versed also in the book of Nature—as is brother James, mused Joseph.

Dr. James Woodrow was Jeanie's brother, the younger son of the family, and one of whom each of them was deeply, even passionately proud. Moving south out of the Ohio home, he had become an eminent preacher and a notable teacher of natural history. It was not until the mid "eighties" that the General Assembly of the Southern Presbyterian Church—profoundly shocked by the expression of his belief that the new theory of Evolution was amply proved by the known facts of geology—called him to account. In 1884 he was tried for heresy—a famous trial which lasted through another year and drew to him many zealous partisans. (Among these was his nephew Thomas Woodrow Wilson, then a graduate student at Johns Hopkins University and already author of his major work, "Constitutional Government." In defense of his position and his teaching, Dr. Woodrow wrote one of the most penetrating analyses of the apparent but irrelevant conflict between scientific and theological doctrines ever written, and one still worth reading by scientists and churchmen of today. It inspired in his nephew the most ardent approval and admiration, and led him to express his own religious faith in no uncertain terms.[6])

Mr. Jefferson had known this Valley like his own "Monticello," Joseph reflected, and had described it in 1782 when Augusta County was bounded on the east by the Blue Ridge, on the south by France's Louisiana, on the southwest by Spanish Mexico, on the west by the Pacific Ocean, and on the northwest by the Great Lakes and Canada! As for the Valley formation itself, Mr. Hotchkiss confirmed Mr. Jefferson's opinion, stated long ago in his "Notes on the State of Virginia:"[7]

> . . . that this earth has been created in time, that the mountains were formed first, that the rivers began to flow afterwards, that in this place particularly they have been dammed up by the Blue Ridge of mountains, and have formed an ocean which filled the whole valley; that continuing to rise they have at length broken over. . . and have torn the mountain down from its summit to its base.

33

That "Blue Ridge" is a backbone of hardest green and black basalt thrust up from the core of the earth, formed in gneiss and schists where the original crust was metamorphosed by pressure in the era of up-thrust and during the more recent slipping and faulting of the crust.

Joseph's thoughts turned to recollections of his father's and mother's descriptions of the parts of Ulster whence they came—of Dergalt in the rolling hills near Strabane in Tyrone County, where James Wilson was a farm lad; and of Donaghadee in County Down, where the farmers were also fishermen. He knew that geologically Northern Ireland was, like the Blue Ridge, formed of basalt, and that there were even prismatic outcroppings in these mountains of Virginia resembling the "Giants Causeway" that lies along the coast of Antrim facing Scotland, where there are vestiges of the same outpouring of basalt off the coast. The soil of Tyrone County, in which Dergalt is located, lies upon gneiss and schists as do the farms on the slopes of the Blue Ridge. The hardy settlers of these Virginia "hollows" and slopes, some living right up on the Ridge itself, as poor and as hardy as those Scotch-Irish who cling to their land in northern Ulster, are of the same breed, thrust back like their forebears, to struggle for a living in a harsh environment by low-landers with sharper wits but no whit more brave.

This great valley of rolling farmlands that the minister's eyes swept over appreciatively made up three-fifths of the county, six hundred square miles of fine terrain. Actually an undulating plateau of limestone, once ocean-bottom, now from 1,000 to 2,000 feet above sea level, it lay slightly eroded by rivers, encompassed by the Blue Ridge and the Appalachian ranges. Hotchkiss was later to describe it in a paper on "The Physiography of Augusta County" as "a natural blue-grass country, the larger portion of which is the best plow-land or pasture-land; and good for wheat or corn, or for other grains, favorable to the raising of fruit, and that naturally clothes itself with park-like forests, chiefly of hard-woods."[8]

Here in this valley lie the headwaters of two of the great rivers that empty into the Chesapeake Bay—the Shenandoah, which flows north-ward into the Potomac, and the James, with its tributaries to the south. It is a land of living waters, such as the "Big" Spring near Waynesboro and "Bold Spring" near Paterson, which gush forth in volume like small rivers out of channels comparable no doubt to some of the great caverns which have been discovered beneath nearby farmlands.

This county was not only the focal point for the peopling of the

West, but a cradle for its young science. It was right here that Professor William B. Rogers had begun to study the rock formations of Virginia in 1835, and here determined for the first time the American order of succession of geological epochs. His brother, Professor H.D. Rogers, adopted and applied the same order in studying the Pennsylvania terrain. "And all this," thought Dr. Wilson, "in my time! A great country in which to work, and a wonderful time in which to live!"

Yes, Jeanie would enjoy his account of the day's interest as they supped this night. She was just asking a few nights past about the county's therapeutic springs that bring so many visitors from the less salubrious lowlands the year round but especially in summer months. The Hot Springs, Warm Springs, White Sulphur, Woodell, Yellow, Stribling, Lebanon, Variety, Crawford—oh, there are too many to remember! All arise from Lower Devonian slates and sandstones, out of which the minerals are dissolved into waters oozing through soft decomposing rocks, rich in minerals, which were washed down from the highlands in ages past and deposited in lowlands and along river shores; long buried, now exposed in places. But the great deposits of the minerals thus laid down by the Creator for man's uses—coal and iron— these lie in incalculable quantity in the Appalachian ranges to westward.

That evening, it is probable that Joseph took down from his shelf his copy of Mr. Jefferson's *Notes* and turned to Query VI, *"A notice of the mines and other subterraneous riches,"* to read again of the exact locations of gold, lead, copper, iron, and of the areas "replete with mineral coal"; of marble of fine quality, and of precious stones such as amethyst and emerald.[9]

Life in a Lush Valley

Time passed swiftly in that early summer as the family settled into the life of Manse and Church, and the doctor into his studies and an exploration of the wide area of which the town of Staunton was the center.

In addition to the townfolk, Dr. Wilson's congregation included many of the large landed families as well as small farmers, descendants of early settlers or of more recent immigrants from Ulster and Scotland. Many were the gifts of provender that he brought home in his buggy on the days when he visited the homes of his rural parishioners—luxuries mostly, such as fresh poultry, venison, cottage cheese (the Scotch "lopper" that Jeanie remembered from her childhood), and apples, grapes or peaches to please the little ones. But to know a town, he thought, to know its people and the countryfolk who feed the town, the market is the place to go.

Saturday mornings it was a common sight to see the tall minister strolling down the market street, to greet the menfolk of town and country, many who knew and had come to revere him as the weeks and months passed. He liked the bustle of the day—the press of people about the farm wagons drawn up along the sidewalks, laden with fruit and garden produce, "Irish" potatoes and even southern "yams." He enjoyed the lively talk, the calling of wares, the squawking and bleating from the pens of live poultry, lambs, pigs, hogs and calves. The stands piled with pork and mutton and beef, slaughtered yesterday and butchered this early morning; with cured "side meat," hams, bacon and corned beef piled to one side along with crocks of butter in plenty and great round cheeses, all this filled him with a thankful sense of the abundance of this land. This was the day, too, to buy flour, oatmeal and cornmeal fresh ground from the mill.

A minister's "pittance" did not allow of luxuries unless given in free will, but Jeanie had the Scotswoman's shrewdness and sense of what was most substantial for her family, and she selected and bargained wisely. They were living well. Especially the wee girls were growing soundly, and blossoming in this bracing climate.

On market days, the bustling crowds seemed more teeming week by week, despite the constant flow of emigrants to the west and southwest. Completion of the railroad had made access to Augusta County and beyond more easy from the Tidewater and Piedmont sections. The mines of the region, to which Mr. Jefferson had pointed a generation before, now were also far more accessible for development.

The very opening of the railhead and the mines had brought its evils, however. Unhappily it had increased the slave population in this land as yet relatively untarnished by the wretched system. But what other crude labor was there? Here was an issue the local Presbytery was meeting honestly, but it was not one to be solved by fine resolutions, nor by the spectacular writings or plots of hotheads in New England and New York and the West.[10]

But it seemed to Dr. Wilson that not only the northern abolitionists or Deep South hotheads made this western part of Virginia turbulent at times. He remembered with serious disapprobation (but with an irrepressible chuckle) the story told him by members of Tinkling Spring

36

Church near Fishersville, regarding the "Irish Rebellion" in February of 1850—only five years before. "Shanty Irish" they were who started the trouble. Too bad they were bringing those ignorant South-Irish immigrants into Virginia, he thought. Poor folk, Roman Catholic and unlettered as they were, one had to pity them, coming by shiploads to this country to escape famine and the English tyranny!

When the tunnel through the Blue Ridge near Rockfish Gap was under construction, the Central Railroad had brought in train loads of the "Corkians" for the job. A party of "Fardowners" (the North Irish) were hired to work on the rail section near Fishersville. The Corkians warned them off. When the warning was ignored, they marched through Waynesboro 235 strong and attacked the Fardowners in their quarters, beat the men, tore up their boxes of belongings and burnt down the house. Then they returned to the mountain in high spirits, no doubt elevated by whisky. The militia was called out, and fifty of the ruffians were arrested. But the trials were turned into a farce by the ready wit of the Irish defendants. Only two were convicted, and judge, court and community had ended the proceedings in a mood of amused leniency.[11]

This early autumn day, bright with sun and rich with harvest, was surely no time for forebodings. The future was full of promise, thought Joseph, so long as the core of the town's citizenry was this body of God-fearing Presbyterians; so long as the bulk of the land lay in the hands of the original settling stock—these law-abiding, hard-working Scotch-Irish and German plowmen—the skilled farmers who, with God's help, had brought about such a bountiful yield.

And with these comfortable thoughts uppermost, the minister again climbed the steep hill of Frederick Street toward the pleasant Manse.

Mistress of the Manse

The first Staunton autumn and winter had passed beneficently in the minister's household. Now as spring came again, a new life was in the making in the Manse.

The mother who conceived and was carrying the unborn infant during the genial spring, summer and autumn of 1856 at Staunton was now in her third pregnancy since her marriage in June of 1849. More than two and a half years had elapsed since the birth of the last little daughter when this latest conception occurred. Now an early winter had set in and the time of her labor was drawing near.

Janet Woodrow Wilson—Jeanie to family and close friends—had just passed her 30th birthday on this 20th of December, 1856—eight days before her son, Thomas Woodrow Wilson, was to be born. Her health was considered somewhat delicate in the period just before and immediately after this birth, and there was not to be another completed pregnancy for almost ten years. From all accounts, however, she had been a young woman normally vigorous physically and of exceptionally vital spirit, hampered only by a certain nervous frailty—outcome of the childhood experience of terror and hardship at sea which soon after had culminated in the death of her mother.

That disaster had occurred just after Jeanie's ninth birthday, in the bitter winter of 1835-36, when the Atlantic seaboard of the North American continent was lashed by ocean tempests, and its northern latitudes by a notable succession of Arctic blizzards. What memories of mountainous waves, roar of lashing wind, bitter cold and near ship-wreck long obsessed the mind of the sensitive young girl, and still brought tremors of recollection!

Now, twenty-one years later, the young woman approached her ordeal in another winter of exceptional cold—the historic winter of "the Big Snow" in Augusta County, when the Blue Ridge close at hand and the Alleghenies to the west were stark and frozen, sending their icy blasts down into the snow-drowned foothills of Staunton and across the Shenandoah River and the entire Valley of Virginia with unprecedented severity.

Her childhood in a temperate English climate had not prepared Jeanie to endure easily those first violent winter months of 1836 in New York, during the family's first American sojourn, nor had subsequent years of residence in Southern Ohio—with school interludes in Tennessee—increased her stamina or accustomed her to climatic rigors. Probably the never-forgotten dread of that earlier winter with its sad accompaniment of loss now touched her waiting spirit, as the time of her labor drew near and an iron cold penetrated even the stout brick walls of the snowbound Manse. "Dead of winter," and a low point for the human spirit and the body's energies—even for a body quickening with new life and a spirit quickened by expectancy. At such a time, waiting can become interminable through short cold hours of daylight and the long and colder nights—tinged with something of dread even for the stout-hearted.

Janet Woodrow was stout-hearted, as became a Scottish lass of firm faith and character and stern Presbyterian upbringing; but she was not the proverbial stout-bodied Highland Scot, conditioned by environment, stock and training to bring both an intrepid spirit and durable nerves and muscle to every hard circumstance. Everything in her background had tended toward the opposite. She had been gently nurtured, in a family whose traditions were those of generations of town dwellers in the Lowland area of Glasgow and Paisley. Her own childhood environment had been set in the household of a scholarly and respected minister and teacher in an urban community. She was treasured by parents and elder brothers alike as the first daughter in a line of sons, her gentle spirit encompassed by an exceptional warmth of family affection. Later, in the New World, her quick mind had been enlivened by educational advantages to a degree unusual for females of her generation and one therefore calculated to set her somewhat apart.

Reserved, too ("proud," her husband's parishioners sometimes called her), Jeanie Wilson did not always welcome the well-intentioned solicitude and proffered ministrations of the ladies of the congregation. So it may be that save for her husband and the two little girls, and the Negro servants of the household, she found herself meeting this winter's ordeal in an outward loneliness even greater than the depth of winter itself would account for.

But outwardly only. Inwardly, for a woman of Jeanie's temperament, the family warmth, the intimate happiness of snug evenings together around the big fireplace in her bedroom, would have been enough. Always, privacy and the precious sense of individual family attachment had been and was to be her greatest treasure—attachment to father, to brothers and the one younger sister, to husband and to each child as it came into the world. It was in the close-knit family circle rather than the wider social group that all her predilections centered and her loving nature flowered—a flowering that her children basked in and, in maturity, came to understand and value as the truest and loveliest expression of her character.

That Janet Wilson was to be a potent influence in shaping this first son's destiny—as potent as was that of her dynamic and scholarly husband—is clear, not only in the after-view, but in terms of what she was, in this year of his conception and birth. To his shaping, in physical stamina and in temperament, she contributed her nervous energy and delicacy, her spiritual force and intensity, the clarity of her mental gifts, the depth and need of loving attachments, her capacity for wrathful indignation "in a righteous cause"—qualities which were to mark the man conspicuously throughout his lifetime. And in the earliest formative years, she was to arouse and direct his imagination, to help fix in him her own idealism and uncompromising sense of principle, her own unalterable religious faith, and perhaps without effort or intention, to mould in him that conception of womanly gentleness, staunchness, lovingness and dignity which was to serve him as his measure of womankind in all his later relationships.

These gifts of Janet Wilson to her son were out of her own Woodrow heritage, but strengthened, we may be sure, by the fortitude which her own mother, Marion Williamson, must have possessed, along with the gentler womanly traits for which she too had been beloved.

The fortitude we assume for Marion Woodrow seems implicit in the readiness of a gently bred woman of 46 (in that day accounted old) to accede to the "call" her husband felt drawing him to the mission field in wilderness America—the Canadian wilds being his original goal. To uproot herself and her family from what had come to be an accustomed and comfortable home in Carlisle and to undertake a hazardous winter voyage across the Atlantic by sailing vessel with her brood of seven (the youngest, little Marion, being but three) demanded fortitude indeed. Of the quality of her courage during that violently stormy two-month passage, we have the testimony of her husband, writing in desolation to his father-in-law the grievous news of his wife's death at the end of it. We know of her constant ministry to the sick on that voyage, even though ill herself from exposure and privation, and of her steadiness and faith during the several episodes when all on board gave themselves up for lost and "commended their souls to Almighty God" and to eternal life.

But here a distinction must be made between fortitude of spirit and bodily constitution. That she alone of the family succumbed to the exposures of that violent winter, soon after weathering the voyage itself and before reaching her 47th birthday, is an indication that Marion Woodrow's fortitude of spirit was not equalled by physical stamina. Here is the strain of bodily fragility which passed to her daughter Janet, and in some measure, to Janet's son.

We know from the bereaved husband's letters something of the "sweetness," "gentleness" and "loyalty" of the lost companion—terms often used descriptively of her daughter Jeanie, too, in later years. And may we suppose for Marion Williamson a measure of subdued and very private gaiety, such as Jeanie had? Gaiety would seem to have been her legacy, for it is said by those who knew all the men of the family, father and sons, that the Woodrows had none! Certainly this passed too, to a marked degree, into the temperament of Thomas Woodrow Wilson. Perhaps from her mother came also Jeanie's fondness for music, her love of singing songs to her children—a tradition of family singing which her children carried into their own families later on, and which was to show itself notably in the fine tenor of her first son's singing and in the vibrant timbre of his voice in public address.

If the Reverend Thomas Woodrow had no humor in his makeup, he at least had a great fund of affection and quiet charm, as attested by such family letters of his as remain, and by the loving recollections of his descendants. If his religion taught of a stern and wrathful God, he nevertheless believed in the gentle fatherhood of man and his Maker, and himself practiced it. He could be stern and even unforgiving in theological matters, but love was the essence of his personal relationships, as was true in the lives of those of his sons and daughters, about whom we know anything at all, and equally of Jeanie's son, Thomas, whom she named for his Woodrow grandfather.

For the sake of his motherless family, Dr. Woodrow had forsaken his intended mission field in Canada, because of the rigors of its climate, and accepted the pastorate of the Presbyterian Church of Chillicothe, in southern Ohio. Here the young folks grew up under the care and firm guidance of their maternal aunt, Isabel Williamson, who had accompanied them from England, and Chillicothe remained "home" for them always, the haven for summer visits, even after all except brother Thomas had moved away.

Here too, Dr. Woodrow himself grew in reputation in the New World, where the Dissenters' faith had spread widely and rooted deep in the soil of freedom. Bred in the notable tradition and faith of Glasgow University, and with the solid experience of his fifteen-year ministry at Carlisle behind him, he soon became known as one of the foremost preachers of the state, noted throughout the Presbyterian East, indeed, for his scholarly discourses and his impeccable theology. That his two daughters should marry rising young ministers was a source of great happiness to him. He was later to watch with keen satisfaction the career of his youngest son, James, who during his own lifetime brought to flower the family's chief claim to scholarly and ecclesiastical fame in America. But though Grandfather Thomas Woodrow had a long life, dying at 84, he did not live long enough to know that Jeanie's first son,

Thomas Woodrow Wilson, whose childhood and young manhood he had watched with affection and pride, would be his most distinguished descendant.

The Manse Becomes A Home

It was anything but an austere home into which this boy was to be born in the pre-war year of 1856. The father, called to the vocation he adored in a prominent church community where his oratorical gifts and natural wit made him very popular, was exuberantly happy and content. The mother, for all her gentleness and dignity, was a young woman of unusually lively spirit, and in her little family she was famous as a teller of dramatic and fascinating tales. Perhaps more unusual for a minister's household of those days were the occasions on which we hear her singing to the accompaniment of her beloved guitar, a gift of her brother Thomas a year or two before, and remaining among her cherished possessions always.

There already were two lively youngsters in the home, the girls, aged five and three. The elder, Marion, was assuredly a potential worshipper of the longed-for baby-brother-to-be; the younger, Annie, probably relatively unaware, possibly even a bit jealous at resigning her own privileges as "Baby." It is a measure of the youthful relationship which developed, that much later, after his sister Marion had married and moved West, brother Tommy was to say that no sort of young companionship could be so close and contenting as that between congenial sister and brother.

From either the upper or the lower balconied porch which looked out above the terraced garden that ran downhill from the rear of the house toward the town, one could see, upon the next hilltop, Dr. Wilson's two-storied white brick church with its columned Greek portico, less than two city blocks to the westward. This was on Frederick Street, one of the earliest east-west thoroughfares of the community, and it was the first Presbyterian church built within the town precincts. Ten years before, in 1846, the church had bought a half-acre lot on which to build the Manse as a residence for its minister's family. This lot was at the corner of Frederick and Coalter Streets, quite on the eastern edge of town. Solid and handsome without being pretentious, gracious and comfortable within, "the Manse" is still a pleasant landmark of a sturdy and gracious era of living that was not long to last unmodified or unmarred by war in either Virginia or the Deep South.

First Presbyterian Church and Augusta Female Academy, Staunton, in 1856

—*Lorna E. Freeman*

From an exterior view at least, this new home must have seemed familiar to Jeanie, for it strikingly resembled the Manse in England which her family left when she was nine. The framed picture of the Carlisle house, gift from the Carlisle City Council to President Wilson, hangs on the wall of the Staunton Manse today. It shows that the main difference was that the Carlisle house was smaller and of red brick, while the bricks of the larger Staunton house were painted white. Inside, one suspects that the Staunton house was considerably more commodious, and not only because of its three stories, for the rooms opening off the wide central halls, on the street floor and the one above, are spacious and high-ceilinged, the windows broad and rather deeply embrasured. The lowest floor, being half-basement at the front because the house is built upon the hill slope, contains the dining room and kitchen with the servants' rooms at the back, and its hall opens directly onto the brick-paved garden porch and the garden itself.

During the summer, as the new child grew within her, Jeanie would have spent much of her leisure time in that pleasant garden, a shady secluded place, its upper levels planted to fruit trees and flower beds, with flowering shrubs sheltering the little summer pavilion against the fence, and a great wisteria vine clambering up the grillwork of the balconies. For formal visitors, the garden was reached by a path that came around the house from the Coalter Street gate, but the familiar way was in through the Frederick Street gate, or out from the house through the dining room hall, and it was here that the family loved to gather in the early evenings.

This was a family for whom the natural cycles of daylight and darkness were the arbiters of household routine. Neither parent was given to burning the midnight oil; and all the precious hours of daylight were made the most of.

In April, after Jeanie had conceived, daytime already seemed more lasting than night. By April the sun rises earlier and sets later, until the summer solstice of June 21-22. From then through the hot weather of July and August, the slightly later rising is hardly to be noticed, for all nature is astir long before dawn. In fact, except on threatening or stormy nights when tree frogs and locusts are silenced, the wooded hillsides and gardens seem more teeming with life at night than by day.

The busy life of the Manse began with daylight. Because Staunton was both a market town and a point of passage to and from the frontier, its bustle of riders and wagons began with the rising of the sun.

44

Neither the minister nor his busy wife wasted the early hours of the lovely summer mornings. In that well regulated household the rule had always been, by preference as well as a matter of duty, "early to rise and early to bed," and the hours between were busy ones until evening tea, always followed by family prayers, Bible reading and a hymn. Then came a leisurely time in the peace of the cooling evening, the children playing happily in the garden below the house while the mother and father sat quietly in the cozy nook at the garden entry to the lower hall, or on the porch above.

It was especially pleasant above, for from there they could look out over the garden plot and the stable, and across the lower town to the rolling farms where sheep and cattle and horses were grazing. Beyond that the green fields widened to the gentle curves of the mountains that seemed to sleep in a transparent haze. Then, after a little reading, some quiet talk of the day's doings or plans for tomorrow, the little girls were put to bed before nightfall. Come dusk, it would not be long after candles were lit that the parents too were sleeping. Bright lights had not yet established man's habit of lengthening the day into the hours of the night and then, at least in Joseph's opinion, losing the best hours of the next day by sleeping long after dawn.

So it had been through that long summer. As summer slowly changed to autumn, dawn came later and dusk earlier, with lamps lighted right after tea—then during tea; and as November gave place to December, they must be lit even before tea. Now days are shorter, but something is in the air that makes the busy household move with more alacrity. And in the cooling house, as nights became colder, with only a grate fire for warmth, there was but a little reading, less talk, then lights out—and to bed!

By November, Jeanie had become heavy with child—plainly a big child. With earlier and earlier dusk, she was glad to be able to excuse herself and rest in bed until Joseph had finished his reading and knocked out the ashes from his last pipeful on the fender before coming down from his study. Then, lighting the candle by the bedside, she must have included in her murmured prayers one of thankfulness that she was one day nearer her time, for the duties of housekeeping, and especially the stair-climbing, demanded daily greater exertion, and her energies seemed very much consumed by the growing child.

Does the timing of a household's routines during the infancy of a child establish habits that last through life? Is it possible that the time

45

of rising and going to bed, habits of work and movement by day and quality of sleep by night affect the growing foetus? Certainly here in the Manse, with its substantial, careful round of living and regularity and assurance in worship and faith (and works), we see the very antithesis to the agitation and desire for distraction typical of many a modern young mother today.[1][2]

We find here in the Manse the setting of the pattern of living that was to be typical of Woodrow Wilson through all his mature life, until the vicissitudes of the World War years and those following forced a change, much to his detriment. His normal diurnal routine was to rise early, to apply himself completely to the tasks of the day, be punctual and expect punctuality from others; then over the evening meal and in the hours that followed before an early bedtime, to relax, enjoy conversing with his family, sometimes reading, but not working after supper. Like his parents, he was never in youth, in the years of his academic career, nor during his early terms in public office (until outside pressures obliged him to change his habits) one who "burned the midnight oil."

In that unusually cold winter of 1856, most of the family life centered in the first-floor rooms—perhaps mainly in the big front bedroom where the baby was to be born, and later in the adjoining nursery which looked out upon the snowy garden in the rear. The Manse was a big substantial house, with four large chimneys and an open fireplace in every room, but still it would not have been too easy to keep it warm, and above stairs probably only the doctor's study was regularly kept heated in the coldest weather.

What fun winter was for the little girls! In their warm coats, boots and leggings, they would leave their play and run down the hill to meet their father at the foot of the garden slope, where Dr. Wilson stabled his horse and buggy. He was always a gay playmate with his children, and there doubtless would be many a boisterous romp with him in the snow on the way back. Then would come a clamorous invasion of the warm fragrant kitchen as they entered from the garden level, where fresh hot pones or molasses cookies would be doled out—or maybe not, according to whether old "Aunty's" mood at the moment happened to be indulgent or "pesky," her attention concentrated upon the all-important ceremonial of the family meal in preparation.

The family meals, in these years before the war of secession, would have been ample at this season. There would be the dried and preserved provender of a fruitful summer, gathered from the vegetable garden down near the stable or bought in the well-stocked markets of this foremost market town of the luxuriant Valley. The most nutritious foods were relatively inexpensive in those days, and in a new minister's family they were amplified often by delicacies proffered by parishioners during the season of abundance. There might be, for instance, a gift of calves' liver or newly ground sausage after a farm slaughtering. In the summer, there was fat fish from the mountain streams. In the hunting season, some huntsman would bring them in a wild turkey or a brace of wild ducks from the game-rich environs of Staunton. And during the preserving season, a crock of Mrs. Preston's famous "yellow pickle," a jar of Mrs. Paris' delicious watermelon-rind preserve, or brandied peaches, or Mrs. Lewis' tomato marmalade found their way to the pantry shelves of the Manse.

During the four preceding years, while Dr. Wilson was on the faculty of Hampden-Sydney College in the Tidewater, the family had had time to become accustomed to, even perhaps enamoured of, the then justly famous Virginia style of cuisine. And now Mrs. Wilson, dependent as she was upon the "dyed in the wool" and practically unalterable methods of their amiable but dictatorial Negro cook, probably made little attempt at modification of the prevailing diet of the region. And why try? Joseph loved the rich and substantial dishes served up to him, and he and the little girls were thriving on this excellent fare, gaining a new soundness of physique after the somewhat debilitating climate of sea-level. She herself recognized the fact that during the summers of 1855 and '56, this high-plateau climate and the enriched food it produced were building fresh strength in her own body, and in the new life she was now nurturing.

Particularly as the heavier late months of her pregnancy passed, Jeanie probably had been content to leave matters almost wholly in Aunty's capable hands below stairs. And out from the snug kitchen and onto the family table across the hall would come a saddle of mutton for dinner, roasted on the spit in the big kitchen fireplace, its savory odors filling the lower house. With it there would be plump butterbeans, best of the autumn garden vegetables, served drenched in cream; boiled parsnips or beets, and tempting "batter bread," its corn-meal base made rich with eggs and milk and spooned out hot from the sizzling baking dish. For dessert, Joseph favored one of Aunty's steamed puddings, or her toothsome sweet-potato roll, or maybe an

47

apple dumpling, while Jeanie herself enjoyed more a dish of smooth and delicately flavored *blanc mange*, the French dish recently become so popular in Virginia.

All the family had come to love Aunty's luncheon specialty—a Brunswick stew that varied in content, according to the season, in its squirrel, veal or chicken base; thick with white potatoes, fresh grated corn, tomatoes, butterbeans and savory herbs. For hours before meal-time, it would be simmering richly in its big iron kettle hanging from the fireplace crane, tantalizing the nostrils of young and old alike. Sometimes it would come on table together with a light loaf of Sally Lunn which Aunty had removed at the last minute with loving care from the capacious Dutch oven beside the fireplace; sometimes it was companioned by her firm and flaky beaten biscuit. But in garden season there was more apt to be a light chicken gumbo, the fresh-fried chicken joints steeped long in broth with tomato and tender okra, and served up with rice and spicy cole slaw, and walnut pickle.

In her early years of southern housewifery, Jeanie had been inclined to look askance upon the prevalence of hot breads in the Virginia dietary. "Bread," the only proper bread, she soon learned, meant hot soda biscuits, cornbread or hot rolls. Loaf bread, or "light bread" as it was called, was eaten cold, but infrequently and never highly esteemed, even on the day when it was freshly made (beyond that day it was used only for toast under game or ham slices or for stuffing fowl, or perhaps for a rich bread pudding). But she was soon accustomed to those dawn sounds from the kitchen, which meant that light rolls were being set from the ever-ready yeast sponge (which a provident cook never allowed to become diminished), in readiness for breakfast baking. And she acknowledged that, together with a thin-gravied hash and brown pan-fried tomatoes—or sausage and fried apple rings in winter—there was no more tasty breakfast, unless it be the buckwheat cakes and maple syrup so plentiful here in the Valley, and which Joseph doted on, eaten along with a thin piece of steak, well pounded and slow-fried in its own juices.

Now the spring dishes were past—the turnip salad and pork jowl (boiled together), the tender lamb and new green peas ("gathered in your garden while the dew is on them," so the cookery book ordered), the young frying chickens and green onions. The summer luxuriance was over, too—the tender young cymling squash fried with bacon, Aunty's sweet-corn pudding of which her family could never get enough; beans, the green "snaps" cooked with pork middlings; and fresh corn fritters for breakfast. All these were past, along with the wealth of peaches from the many orchards round-about.

Now had come the season of roots—sweet potatoes and turnips, parsnips and salsify; of winter cabbage and dried corn ground into "grits;" and "blackeye" peas, from all of which Aunty could concoct delectable and substantial accompaniments to the beef and mutton, ham and fresh pork always available in the market place. There was an abundance of eggs and milk, and Aunty had been making her delicate boiled custards quite frequently of late—"good suption for the baby, ma'am," she would say; and certainly tempting to a less avid appetite.

Now preserved berries and spiced peaches and jellies took the place of summer fresh fruits and sauces, and the abundant apples of the region were a main item in the family diet. Little Marion, out with her father to search for wild chestnuts, even loved to gather the wild persimmons as they fell in the nearby wood lots after the frost had touched and shrivelled them to sweetness; but small Annie, once outraged by the mouth-puckering misery of an unripe fruit, would have none of them!

What bounty, thought Jeanie with thankfulness, as autumn had deepened into winter. With what bounty the good Lord had blessed this Valley together with themselves, her precious family, so soon to be augmented by another so richly nourished little life. And she blessed God devoutly for this comfortable and happy home into which the new life—the ardently hoped-for son—was to be born.

III
A PRENATAL BIOGRAPHY

Thou hast light in darke, and shutst in little roome,
Immensity cloystered in thy deare wombe.

—John Donne

The story of the first stage of this life begins with the spring equinox and ends with the winter solstice. The child who was born on the 28th of December was conceived and began life very nearly at the time when the sun's return northward brings the springtime resurgence of life in nature.

Usually a biography will give a rather brief account of the subject's parents, and their forebears perhaps, and then proceed to the date and place of birth, assuming that the life story begins then, and omitting the nine months of embryonic life in the mother's womb, a period of supreme importance in the whole span of life.

The conditions surrounding coitus and conception, in particular the health and spirits of the prospective mother, her diet and habits, are of great significance in the life of the child then conceived. The circumstances affecting the mother while the embryo and foetus are growing within her, as well as the circumstances, time and conditions at delivery—all these taken together are perhaps as significant as is the nature of the child's heredity. Therefore, in assessing the child and the man, we must remember that the baby who was to be named Thomas Woodrow Wilson was nine months old when he was born.

There is a Maori creation chant whose opening lines have a peculiar cogency in relation to the inception of a human being. Creation for the Polynesian peoples was conceived to have been accomplished pro-creatively, that is, by propagation.

> Seeking, earnestly seeking
>   in the gloom,
>   on the bounds of the light of day.
> Looking into night,
>   night had conceived
>   the seed of night . . .
> The life pulsating and the cup of Life.[1]

50

In the darkness of the womb, "the seed" (sperm) seeks its fulfilment in the ovum.

Spring and its Concomitants

On or near the spring equinox in the year 1856, one minute spermatazoon plunged into a human ovum, also microscopically minute, yet as much larger than the sperm as a small pond would be larger than a pebble. And instantly there commenced series upon series of responses: multiplication of cells, differentiation, an embryo, a foetus, a male child born, destined to become a man whose mind and heart, whose good works and creative efforts—and equally whose myopias—like wavelets on a pool's surface, would change the lives of millions then living on our planet, with effects lasting until now, and beyond.

Hippocrates, whose practice as a physician gave him abundant opportunity to observe variations in human tone and type as affected by differences in environmental conditions, recorded his conclusions in the following generalizations. Referring to what he termed "The Coagulation of the Seed," he wrote:

> With regard to the states of the weather . . .
> that which is northerly braces the body
>   giving it tone, agility, and color . . .
> But the southerly relaxes the body
>   and renders it humid, brings on dullness . . .
>
> For where the changes of the seasons are most frequent
>   and most sharply contrasted
> there you will find the greatest diversity
>   in physique, in character and constitution . . .
>
> Generation, too, varies in the coagulation of the seed,
>   and is not the same for the same seed
>   in the summer as in winter,
>   nor in rain as in drought.[2]

Staunton, with an elevation of about one thousand feet, with high mountain ranges on two sides and seated on its limestone plateau in the Shenandoah valley down which chill winds from the north flow during half the year, was a locality in which northerly weather "braces the body, giving tone, agility and color," and in which "physique, character and constitution" are stimulated by frequent and sharply contrasted changes in weather. The "seed" that was to become Woodrow Wilson coagulated during the lively growing time between spring seeding and fall and early-winter harvest.

Born at normal "full term" on December 28, 1856, Woodrow Wilson would have been conceived in the womb of his mother approximately 280 days previously, i.e., about March 23 of that same year, during the weather episode of the spring equinox, which is generally turbulent. The vitalizing influences of the changes of seasons were very active then. The near coincidence of conception with the spring equinox, of birth with the winter solstice, gestation during the spring, summer and autumn of the year—these were circumstances favorable to sound growth.

Dr. William F. Peterson, author of *Lincoln–Douglas: The Weather as Destiny; Weather and the Patient; Man, Weather and Sun*, more than once in personal conversations has expressed the conviction that the human embryo whose original substance, which later produces the cells of the whole body, is entirely derived from the ovum of the mother, is profoundly and permanently conditioned by two primary environmental factors affecting her during the early phase of gestation. Especially important are the diet and tonus of the mother's body, and the weather at this time.

With respect to diet, recent research has shown that the child of a mother who during pregnancy and nursing is eating a diet ample in vitamins and minerals (specifically ascorbic acid, thiamine, riboflavin, niacinamide and iron) is capable of manifesting his maximum intelligence; while children of mothers deficient in these essentials show less intelligence. Investigators further indicate that a rural diet, if it is well-rounded and abundant, is more likely to contain all the needed elements than an urban diet.

Jeanie Wilson's son, then, was to have a very favorable entry into his life span on this count. It is quite certain that the diet of this Scotch-American family, husbanded by the robust Joseph Ruggles Wilson, was solid, sound and ample in all important ingredients. Both the place and the times produced sturdy and vigorous men and women in this Valley, the finest farming section of the Old Dominion and one of the richest agricultural counties in America. So, with sound, strong stuff to build on, the minute one-celled, then two-celled, then eight-celled, then multicelled living creature that was to become Woodrow Wilson set about the physiological business of splitting and multiplying cytoplasm, the work that occupies the time of an embryo. Here was superior human cytoplasm enjoying the best of nourishment from a well-conditioned mother in an ideal environment.

Weather also played its part. This biological building process was begun just at the turn of the spring, when the genial warm air mass from the south Atlantic and Gulf of Mexico, weighted with moisture, begins to push inland in such quantity that the cold Arctic airs still dominant over the northern half of the continent rush in furiously, and there results that episode of turbulence in wind and weather associated always with the spring equinox. After a stressful period of harsh winds when all nature is ill at ease, a slackening of wind and warming of moisture-laden air will result in a period of low barometer and high humidity. Following an episode of rain, the barometer will rise, temperature fall and again there is wind—out of the chill northwest. This is a time, and the kind of weather, in which domesticated animals (including man) are stirred in every cell and tissue and organ, even as the forests are stirred, by the swift-changing fortunes of the elemental war. It is the season *par excellence*, when a vigorous masculine temperament turns dominantly to thoughts of love.

The Book of Days, an old Scottish compendium of lore, depicts March as a man of tawny color and fierce aspect, wearing a helmet. He leans upon a spade and holds in his left hand a blossoming branch, and carries on his arm a basket of seed. In his right hand is the sign of the Ram, which the sun enters on the 20th. The horns of the Ram symbolize the rays of the sun, which, at this time of the spring equinox, begins its return north with augmented power.

Perhaps it was no coincidence that this child, whose life spanned the era including our Civil War and the first World War, and who was to become America's commander-in-chief, was conceived in March, the month in the Julian calendar dedicated to Mars, the god of war. This Roman name is said to be cognate with the Greek *marnamai* "I fight," and with the Sanskrit *mrnati* "to smite."[3] Coincidence or not, it was in the midst of this period of turbulence and stimulation that Jeanie Wilson conceived her first son, whose life would be one of turbulence, whose supreme crises were to be related to and much affected by season and weather, and not infrequently to coincide with the equinoxes.

Elsworth Huntington, in *Season of Birth*, has shown the relation of season of conception and birth to genius, demonstrating that the conception of highly intellectual and strong-willed types is peculiarly influenced by the weather prevailing at the time.[4] Huntington has found that especially in the southern states, gifted intellectual people are born in the colder part of the year, about midwinter.[5] It is not that weather controls or directly affects the mind, but that the central nervous system is sensitive and responds favorably to the freshening cold weather; that the glands, nerves and organs of the body which influence vitality are stimulated by cool air and high barometer.

Tonus of the mother's body, then, and "weather" (a complex set of astrophysical influences) are conditioning factors. It was early spring, after their first strengthening winter that followed the years of low altitude and high temperatures and humidity at Kingsville, a locale that had been suited to the physical well-being of neither parent. Undoubtedly after the move to Staunton there was a great renewal of vitality and vigor in the bodies of Joseph Wilson and his wife.

And the genetic elements whose coincidence with good tonus and right season produced the gifted man Woodrow Wilson? Good genes from forebears on both sides were available to produce cytoplasm of superior quality and sensitivity in this child of Jeanie Woodrow, sired by Allegheny-born Joseph Ruggles Wilson, whose restless, strong masculinity roused to meet the stimulus of the spring equinox in this his first year in Staunton. Temperature probably was a primary influence, but unquestionably a complex of factors is involved, such as increasing solar radiation, the rising tide of life in all organic things, freshening diet, systemic changes in the human organism caused by these, and the upsurge of psychological and spiritual delight in the joys of spring. The spring equinox in Staunton is the time when pastures are "greening up," maples and other early deciduous trees are beginning to burst their leaf buds and clothe themselves in filmy pinks and greens, the fruit trees are in blossom—apple, pear, plum and cherry. Some lambs are a month or six weeks old and gamboling and frolicking and bleating; later comers are being "dropped." All livestock, including man, is glorying in life.

Dr. Wilson's was a town church, but his congregation included many prosperous farmers. When he went buggy riding these fine spring days, visiting these country folk, he listened to the talk of the women about nursing orphan lambs, about calves and colts aborning. With him, or as related by him, Jeanie shared these visits, the talk, the delightful sights and smells and sounds of springtime in Valley Virginia. Back to the Manse from country and market came the "first fruits" of the season, laden with minerals and vitamins. From the windows of the manse Jeanie Wilson looked down upon a garden in which iris, lilies and other bulbs were abloom, violets were blue, roses budding, lilac and althea leafing with promise of loveliness to come. The last week in March in Staunton is like early May in New York and New England.

When she knew that she was to be a mother again, there was surely the hope in her heart and in Dr. Wilson's, and probably there were prayers, that this would be a boy, for she already had borne two girls. Whatever her hopes and her prayers, they were definite, gentle and strong, for such was her character, and there was joy within her heart to match the delights of her surroundings.

For the next seven months, the nutrients and vital energies flowing to this embryo through the mother's body would be out of the abundance of the season of plenty in a land whose soil, climate and weather were as ideal as could be found in the world.

Predestination

When we study the development of the embryo and of the man, from the germ plasm transmitted through his parents, it is evident that the lineaments of character are laid down in a pattern of heredity at conception. This one might term a predestination of internal controls.

But also at work is a complex of external controls within which the pattern of internal development which determines character has to operate. There is predestination of another sort here.

Predestination, the concept that human destiny is foreordained, is a curious doctrine for the Scotch and Scotch-Irish to have adhered to, for never was a people less prone to accept existence fatalistically or more capable individually and collectively of taking their lives into their hands and working out their own destiny. No trait in his character was more typical of Woodrow Wilson than his certainty that his own faculties and choice determined his destiny. But did they?

The record of Woodrow Wilson's life is one in which, in every major transition, circumstance rather than preference was the real determining factor in his decisions. He surrendered his desire for a literary career to the necessity of teaching as a means of livelihood. On becoming president of Princeton, he gave up teaching, not by choice but because he recognized the step up as a greater opportunity for the kind of service that had been the theme of his teaching. Then he stepped out of the academic world into politics, and once he had entered that field by becoming governor of New Jersey, it was momentum rather than deliberate choice which carried him into national politics and on to the

White House. As President, his heart was set on internal national reform and progress, but the outbreak and progress of World War I compelled him to abandon his effort to stand apart and maintain neutrality. Once America had joined forces with the Allies, and the war was won, the maintenance of a united front automatically evoked the plan for a League of Nations. Once this had been formulated, all his hopes for creating an era of responsible internationalism were concentrated in the League, but his effort to bring the United States into the League met an insurmountable barrier in the obstructionism of conservative isolationists of the Midwest and the Far West.

Hence, we say that Woodrow Wilson's belief that he himself wrought his destiny was not true of the course of his private and public life. His career necessitated repeatedly the surrender of his personal choice and intentions as circumstances and world events required.

It is true that his genius wrought his destiny, but within clearly drawn limits. Predetermining factors affected his well being, which may be appraised in the light of predestination of a sort that he himself was little if at all aware of. Man's life, said Sophocles (*Antigone* 622-624) is woven "with a shuttle of adamant." In the warp and weft of Wilson's life, certain phases of his physical environment swept back and forth with the precision of a shuttle which unswervingly wrought the design, regardless of the will of the man who believed his was the weaver's hand.

Aside from and beyond the shaping of his destiny by national and world events, another and larger frame of reference must be borne in mind as we appraise this man's life. History, the course of human events and every individual's activities are subject to the complex astrophysical forces of the universe which control climate and weather. Woodrow Wilson was extremely weather-sensitive. Later in this volume, we will demonstrate how accurately his personal career reflected the rise and fall of solar energy through the current sunspot cycles of the years in which he lived and worked.

That Woodrow Wilson was an individual directly responsive to the impact of energy released by the sun becomes evident when the record of his days and years is studied against the background of the seasons and years through which he lived. It would be interesting therefore to know what Wilson's response would be to the following statements of a physician whose study of astrophysics has convinced him that, as Heraclitus stated, "there are things foreordained wholly."

56

In our region of the world, weather—and the longer environmental rhythms therewith connected (season and climate cycles)—govern the well being, the moods, illnesses and death.

The government of the air mass is, in final analysis, solar. Some individuals may be directly responsive to the impact of energy so released. For a larger group, a tide that may be lunar or solar (or both) is apparently of some importance.

Certain is one thing. We as individuals and as a group either conform to the demands of the environmental forces or we perish. To this extent destiny is determined by the "music of the spheres"—the silent symphony of the vast forces of the universe.[6]

Heredity

Another kind of predestination is revealed by the study of genetics. The body contains a unique substance called the germ plasm. From a single cell of this—the ovum of the mother, combined with another single cell from the father's germ plasm—a new body grows by multiplication of cells. The new body does not produce germ plasm, but merely transmits it. It seems that there is a quality of physical immortality in this germ plasm so long as reproduction continues from generation to generation. But when "reproduction of its kind" ceases, it is finished. And as long as reproduction continues, there is predestination in it, for the germ plasm contains all the genetic determinants of the breed whose combined effects, manifest in dominant (expressed) and recessive (repressed) traits, will make up the substantial form that is the man. The body is the substance of traits foreordained. The germ plasm may be likened to a reservoir of potentialities peculiar to the breed.

There is no fusion of traits. The individual is not a blend of the parents, but rather a new mosaic whose pieces are derived not from the somatoplasm or body substance of the parents, but from the germ plasm received by them from their forebears.

The germ plasm appears to be immune to modification as a result of growth processes or environmental influences affecting the body of the individual who carries it, except that it can be crippled by certain diseases and certain poisons.

None of these were present affecting the germ plasm from the Woodrow and Wilson heritage. The soundness and normality of the organism that came from it proves this.

However, inherent in the organic heritage of any lineage are qualities that predispose the organism to particular functional disturbances. Two such conditions affected Woodrow Wilson from youth to old age, and these, it would seem, were inherited in the sense that they were inherent in the somatoplasm or body substance that originated in the germ plasm transmitted by his two parents. One of these conditions affected his digestion, the other the respiratory system. The malaise of both was so definitely associated with hypersensitivity of the sympathetic nervous system that there is good reason to suppose that herein lay the cause of both digestive and respiratory troubles. His mother was delicate and, we know, was invalided by typhoid fever late in life. And her mother, Marion Williamson, died from "lung fever." It is reasonable to conclude, therefore, that these "predispositions" came to him through his mother and his mother's mother.

The Seed

> 'Tis only from the sturdy and the good that sturdy young are born; in steers and steeds, appear the merits of their sires; nor do fierce eagles beget timid doves.
>
> Yet training increases unborn worth, and righteous ways make strong the heart; whenever righteousness has failed, faults mar even what nature had made noble.
>
> —Horace

As a single grain of pollen penetrates and fertilizes the open blossom, matured and ready for this miracle of nature, so a male *sperm* enters the ripe *ovum* of the mother and sets in motion the sequence of complex processes which produce the embryo, the foetus and the child.

We adopt the simile of the pollen grain fertilizing the flower, because the process is universal, and this gives us a precise simile that places this incident, minute in time and space, within its total frame of reference. Actually the human process is more akin to mating and reproduction in the lower orders of life in the sea, for it all transpires in the medium of fluids that have physical and chemical composition closely akin to seawater. The human process is a perpetuation of the most primal life process. The sperm actually swims by means of the lashing of a thread-like tail up the channel (or tube of the ovary) where the ripe ovum lies waiting, even as many fish make their way upstream or upriver to breed.

The word *sperm* is derived from the Greek word meaning *to sow*. Pollen and seed are not sown in nature as single grains. They are lavishly dispersed. So it is with the human sperm which are numbered in hundreds of millions. Of these millions from the male at the moment of mating, one and only one comes to fruition in the good soil of the ripe waiting ovum. The race is to the swift. The person who was to come from the union of the nuclei of the sperm and ovum here united would ever be one who so ran in each contest as to be first, and who won every race except the last, in which the goal was beyond his power of endurance, because he entered that race with vital reserves already exhausted. Woodrow Wilson's last and greatest effort to achieve his goal ended in physical collapse, due to exhaustion following illness in Paris during the final weeks of the Peace Conference.

But in this race of the spermatozoa toward their goal, the mother-egg, every contestant is fresh. Each is a microscopic entity, its head encompassing the vital nucleus of inheritable germ plasm evolved through countless eons of human and prehuman evolution, the vital substance whose organic particles, in combination with those of the nucleus of the ovum, determine precisely the characteristics of the individual that will result.

At the moment of emission, the race is on. There is an exact analogy in the behavior of fish, such as the salmon or the carp, which fiercely swim upstream, driven on by the most urgent motive that prevails throughout nature, the urge to propagate. Only one out of many thousands will satisfy that urge. That one sperm, entering the waiting ovum, will cease to exist as a separate entity the instant it joins its minute nucleus with that in the mother cell. In that merging, the individuality of the two, respectively male and female, will cease to exist, and by a little-understood process of splitting of molecules, the joining of certain ones and elimination of others all in precise mathematical arrangement, there will emerge the tiny entity that will grow into a new creature endowed with specific traits, some derived from the father's side, some from the mother's, not blended, but rather selected in terms of which ones are dominant.

Herein is the clue to the meaning of the union of two nuclei from male and female. In every union there arise possibilities of a very wide range of variation through recombination. Herein lies also an important fact explaining evolution by survival of the fittest—it is not "by tooth and claw," but through endowment, energy, and drive. So it is in social competition in a democracy. The man destined to grow out of the single sperm that won its race at the spring equinox of 1856 would be a winner. He would be first man in the race of his times, not only in his own country but in the race of humanity toward its destiny; his ideals would become a goal for all men.

As conception is a natural process that finds its parallels throughout

59

nature, so the mechanics of the combination of nuclei is based, like all mechanical operations, on mathematics. The germ cells of all organic life forms contain a precise number of carriers of heredity, and that number is constant. Each human nucleus contains 46 threadlike particles called chromosomes, and each of these contains a series of still more minute particles, the genes that control heredity.[7]

The Wilson and Woodrow traits embedded in the genes transmitted to their son were not at all affected by the fact that Joseph and Jeanie were or were not born and bred in America, for germ plasm is unaffected by physical or other influences which modify the physique. But that *behavior* is largely an attribute transmitted through the genes is proven by the study of identical twins.[8] Here we are dealing with the foundation of somatopsychic behavior, affecting temperament, emotion, sensitivity, mentality.

It follows that at the instant of the fusion of the nuclei from which was to grow the embryo that would become Woodrow Wilson, the basic design of the character of the man was laid down. The mature man grows out of the child, the child out of the foetus, the foetus out of the embryo, the embryo out of the union of the nuclei of sperm and ovum. The faculties, attributes and temperament of the man who became the 28th President of the United States were implicit in the germ plasm of his father and mother, and this germ plasm was out of the Scotch and Scotch-Irish breed, one of the most definite human strains that came to America from the British Isles.

Those traits were to be etched as sharply in the man as if he himself had been born in the land of his ancestors. Much of this would be due to the way he was reared, but his mind and his temperament were determined basically by somatic factors. The type of person he became was foreordained, in the union of a particular sperm and ovum. Oats do not grow from wheat germ, nor oak from pine, nor Hindu from Scotch-Irish. The germ plasm there joined had a definite immortality of its own. It was and is timeless in the sense that, existing in the present, it contained the plan, limits and destiny for the person it became, and the record of its own past. That past was the foundation of the future growth.

The complex of traits inherited from the Wilson and Woodrow lines in this process of selection and joining of chromosomes was not to be altogether good, as has been indicated in Chapter I, for many were incompatible, and hence would become a source of conflict and frustration in Woodrow Wilson's life and career. A bold forthrightness, the combativeness characteristic of James and Joseph Wilson were there, but always lurking within was a shyness, a delicacy that prevented him from being bold, and made him aware that fighting was an unhappy business. The intellectual ambition, the will to power of the masculine Wilsons were chained to an almost feminine dependence and sensitivity. A vigor and stamina which should have been housed in a robust physique like his father's (a physique inherited from farming forebears) was housed in a body that inherited the fragilities of a delicate mother descended from sedentary townsfolk, gentle, artistic and intellectual. His was a mind and heart full of conflicts—heroic faith and self-doubt, pride and humility, exuberance and despair, gaiety and grief, pugnacity and charity, independence and the desire to be possessed. These conflicts arose out of the very persistence, the indelibility, of Wilson and Woodrow traits which were antipathetic to each other.

But whatever there was of conflict was to be resolved and transcended largely by the mind and spirit of a man to whom stamina, strength of character, singlemindedness and integrity, nobility of purpose and a lofty sense of human values came as endowments from both parents. The conflicts were a source of struggle within himself, but in every supreme crisis and decision, the choice always was dictated by values that transcended any consideration of personal or selfish issues. To what extent was this a matter of heredity? There is no way of knowing. What one inherits is a combination of dominant and recessive traits. Those that are dominant are the basis of what we call character. Certainly a very favorable assortment or constellation of hereditary factors of a high order derived from, or through, both parents were the fortunate heritage of Woodrow Wilson.

Is "the way the chips fall" a matter of chance? By chips, we mean the genes that determine the somatopsychic makeup of the individual through central and peripheral nervous systems, the sense organs, respiratory, vascular and digestive organs. The character of the man that will grow as a result of this union will be affected by his having a poor digestion, by developing arteriosclerosis, and by suffering frequently from bronchial inflammation and infection. Gifted with keen senses and high sensitivity, he inevitably will suffer acutely in the course of a life that subjected him to great ordeals, due to the keen and powerful intellect that masterminded his career. The physical and nervous conditions mentioned all greatly affect both his character and his career. The psychic effects result from somatic traits inherited during the re-shuffling of genes when the nuclei of sperm and ovum become one. Was it mere chance that threw together the particular combination of traits which were characteristic of Woodrow Wilson?

We cannot say positively yes or no. Certainly the hypothesis that it is pure chance is tenable, but equally tenable is the thesis that intelligence and purpose are at work. This is not to say that they prevail in *every* human conception, but here in the Manse at Staunton, at the spring equinox of 1856, we can reasonably believe that unusual intelligence and purpose were involved. To have a son was the heart's desire of this man and wife—a gifted son.

The time and the place were right for it. Other children there were. The two girls, neither particularly gifted, and born before Joseph's work had come to focus, were, so to speak, just the natural consequence of a congenial marriage. A second son would be born ten years later, as a good but average human being. By then Joseph had fully recognized the quality of the child born in Staunton. His heart and mind were already dedicated to fostering and feeding the mind of the gifted ten-year-old "Tommy." And this final pregnancy came at a time when Jeanie's stamina was scarcely equal to the task, and when the ardor of her devotion was concentrated upon sustaining her existing little brood in the immediate post-Civil War period of deprivation, rather than upon the desire for a fourth child.

Most human affairs perhaps are a matter of "happenstance." This may be true, in the case of most children born, of "how the chips fall" in the assortment of their genes. But we see all around us *human* achievement accomplished with acute calculation into which no element of chance is permitted to enter: creations such as intricate machines, engineering, industrial or military operations, a musical composition or work of art. We cannot believe that in a *natural* order, where every detail operates strictly according to law, the same degree of intelligence that men bring to bear in such human calculation is inoperative as affecting the nature of an embryo at the moment of conception.

Growth in the Womb

"The Intelligent"

> You thought Nature intelligent . . . How can she have reason or purpose being pure mechanism? Yet at length she made you, you with your reason. . . .

Bethink you too that perhaps in knowing me [Nature] you do but know the instrument of a Purpose, the tool of a Hand too large for your sight as now to compass. . . .[9]

The individual life in virtue of its mind uses strategy to promote its life and that of its seed. . . . To the unconscious "urge-to-live" is added conscious "zest-to-live."[10]

Conscious zest to live a life of calculated purpose was the particular endowment of Woodrow Wilson. Calculated purpose is intelligence. Intelligence, in him, comes to sharp focus.

A verse comes to us out of the philosophical teachings of ancient Hindu literature which shows that thousands of years ago, sages were aware of the nature of spiritual intelligence of the sort that was manifested in the career of Woodrow Wilson.

Now man is a creature of will. According to what his will is in this world, so will he be when he has departed this life. Let him therefore have this will and belief:

The intelligent, whose body is spirit, whose form is light, whose thoughts are true, whose nature is like ether (omnipresent and invisible), from whom all works, all desires, all sweet odors and tastes proceed; he who embraces all this, who never speaks, and is never surprised,

He is myself within the heart. . . .[11]

In this, his biography while yet unborn, it is worth pointing out that, like all his species, the first and fastest growing thing to manifest itself in this child's development is the nervous system surmounted by the brain. Unlike many, perhaps most of his species, this man will choose, from earliest youth onward, to give first place to the continuing development of this highly specialized instrument of perception and intelligence, and to train and apply it with ceaseless one-pointed effort for the good of his fellow men.

By the third week after conception, the surface of the tiny elongated disc that is the incipient embryo develops a depression down its center, gradually enclosing a core of nerve tissue like a tube. Little by little during the first month, this core of nerve tissue becomes differentiated, and at the head end, the beginnings of a brain are already visible. By the end of the second month of pregnancy, the cerebral hemispheres are prominent features of the developing brain, and the cerebro-spinal nerves and ganglia of the sympathetic nervous system are well formed. The basic endowment for the acute mind and highly sensitive nerves that will distinguish the person this embryo is destined to become has been laid.

"The Light Divine"

It is not our purpose in this "biography of the unborn" to review the entire progress of embryonic development, but merely to point up, in some of the successive stages, the incidence of certain traits or features peculiar to Woodrow Wilson, the boy and man. We have noted briefly the earliest of all embryonic changes—that leading toward formation of the spinal cord, brain, and nervous system. Development of the sensory organs, those most vital links of brain and nerves with the outer world, is another case in point. This has been proceeding during the first two months already considered.

The fact that the fully evolved organism lies enfolded or dormant within the germ plasm is nowhere better evidenced than in the emergent process by which the sensory organs develop. These are not sensitized appendages imposed or developed from outside *inward* by the impinging of external stimuli such as light, sound or other vibrations. Consider first the eyes, which in the man we are studying were to be not only one of the most important tools of his training and of his academic career, but also a compelling feature of his will, of his power to win faithful followers and to sway crowds the world over, even to chill unmercifully those whom he regarded as ingrates or imposters.

The organ that will register the light vibrations of a particular range takes form as a result of the pushing *outward* of appendages originating *in* the brain.[12] As development proceeds and optic stalks, lens cups and even pigment appear, the true marvel becomes apparent, that eight months before the eyes of this small body will be exposed to light, the eyes already are there, literally projected by the mind; and even the pigmentation, that typically Keltic-Anglo-Norman blue that chills to gray, has become evident. The physical type of the breed is here asserting itself significantly very early in the growth process. And who could say that the pigmentation and structure of those eyes is not related to the temperamental and mental set of the psyche?

> There is a Power Divine within the Heart of things . . .
>   bodied forth in him whose soul
> Reflecting Good itself, doth comprehend the whole
>   . . . wherein the Light Divine
> Though hid by darker veil, hath never ceased to shine.

—Laotze[13]

It is worth considering what has transpired in the rest of this minute body by the time brain and nerves have come to this degree of development. A rudimentary face is there, an appendage to the brain, with eyes, nose, mouth, ears, and a beginning of the nerves that will sensitize these organs. Very short folded extremities are there, with fingers and toes, and the rudiments of the internal organs, even the final plan is all in order. But, interestingly, not until this eighth week is there the beginning of that internal framework upon which the organism will depend for its mobility and its strength. Here is a recognizably human body, though the head is larger than trunk and limbs together, but it has no skeleton whatever. Here is head but no skull, spine but no backbone, lungs and heart but no housing of ribs, abdominal organs but no pelvis, arms and legs, hands and feet—all without the bony processes which are to make them do the will of the brain. There is no need as yet for a rigid frame of bone for this soft growing thing that floats at ease within the warm womb of the mother.

Now two months of growth have passed, and most of it has been devoted to the making of this already demonstrably human brain in its well-formed head, which at this point is truly monumental by comparison with the rest of the body—fully half the length and more than half its volume and weight (at birth it is one quarter, in maturity one sixteenth).[14]

This head, which by the time it is born will be encased in bone, will be a critical hazard for it will barely, and at great risk to mother and to infant, pass through the pelvic orifice as the new human creature plunges head first into the outer world. Head first it must be, because this, the most precious and the most vulnerable part, must lie throughout its waiting time safely encased in the mother's strong almost unbreakable bowl of pelvic bone, which this scion of the most royal of all the kingdoms of the world's creatures wears like a crown—yet wears with an humble grace as it sleeps in peace, awaiting its great day when it shall lay aside its crown and enter the lists of worldly strife and human brotherhood.

"The Giver of Life"

> Gods, men, beasts, live by
> breath.
> Breath is life and is called
> the giver of Life.

> —Mandukya Upanishad[15]

Although the full term of life within the mother's womb must elapse before "the breath of life" is given, the intricate preparations for its reception already have begun during the very early weeks of gestation. During this process of growth leading toward the finished artistry of the upper respiratory tract, arches, grooves and paired buds have appeared in the primitive cellular material of the trachea and pharynx. By the time the arches and grooves have been transformed into apparatus for inhalation and exhalation, for speaking, hearing, smelling and tasting, these buds have developed into two lobes, supplied with bronchial tubes for breathing. These lobes remain compact until their sudden inflation at the moment of the first cry of the infant after it emerges at birth, when the compact cells suddenly become elastic and pneumatic.

So grew the organic apparatus whose sensitivity would be one of Woodrow Wilson's greatest problems until the end of his life and yet whose matured and cultivated quality would be one of his greatest assets. The carrying quality of his voice, which enabled him to be heard distinctly by great crowds (before the era of microphones and loud-speakers) was partly a matter of the precise articulation for which his preacher father meticulously trained him, and for which likewise his grandfather Judge James Wilson, coming from a breed notable for such precision and vigor of speech, had been famous in the "spellbinding" style of his era as a member of the Ohio State Legislature in the first quarter of the nineteenth century. Equally the fine clear timbre, which gave Woodrow Wilson's voice great charm, and which he cultivated, and consciously and so effectively used in private, in teaching, and in public speaking, that was inherited. This is a quality, a timbre, a kind of voice with which one becomes familiar in Scotland, and even more so in Ireland.

"Intestinal Fortitude"

There is one thing that even his most violent opponents and detractors, as well as his ardent admirers, were, are and always will be agreed on, and that is that "W.W. had plenty of guts." That expression is good old English. In the more polite but less forceful and less specific professional terminology of World War II, he exhibited "intestinal fortitude." Whichever way you say it, he had it, and he inherited it from his Irish and Scottish forbears. Ann Adams and James Wilson were Irish Scots who survived as young folk in areas (County Down where slaughter was commonplace, and County Tyrone where Strabane faced hostile Donegal across the River Mourne) through an era ("the bloody '98") when anyone who survived had plenty of both guts and horse-sense, self-control and ingenuity. The hotheads, the troublemakers and the stupid amongst the "teenagers" of those times were presumably, as now, congregating where there was a rumpus—and they often suffered the consequences. The sensible, purposeful youths and maids—and such were young Jimmy Wilson and Annie Adams—kept out of it. And many emigrated. As for the gentle but forceful young minister, Thomas Woodrow, and his refined artistic wife Marion Williamson, they certainly showed plenty of intestinal fortitude (if not too much sense!) when they set sail from Liverpool in 1835 to cross the North Atlantic in November in a small sailing ship. (Probably the young missionary was able to buy a passage cheaper for himself and family at that time of the year.)

In brief, we are justified in assuming that the embryo now firmly rooted and growing vigorously in the mother's womb has inherited from all four lines, represented by its grandparents, an abundance of dominant genes calculated to produce that mosaic which results in a physique and temperament characterized by intestinal fortitude—highly sensitive guts, but firm and hard. It is almost axiomatic now, since World War II, that the truly brave, those who are dependable in crises, are not those "who know no fear" (i.e., the stolid, indifferent) but those who are acutely aware of danger and fear and whose adrenal cortices are thereby stimulated to pour into the bloodstream the hormones which accelerate the heart and alert the sympathetic nervous and muscular systems for action to meet crisis. Such was the temperament of the man this embryo was to become. As Dr. W. B. Cannon[16] first demonstrated, this syndrome centers in the celiac cortex of the peripheral nervous system (the "solar plexus") and in the chain responses involving the adrenal cortex, the heart, the stomach and the intestinal tract.

In the embryo, the alimentary tract appears first as a cavity surrounded by the inner surface of the infolded plaque of now rapidly multiplying cells into which the ovum has been transformed. This connects with the yolk sac of the ovum, the source of nourishment for the embryo at this stage of development. The cavity lengthens into a passage with a smooth lining (which becomes the foregut) by the time the yolk sac disappears, and this forward end contacts the ectoderm or outer skin of the embryo, penetrates it, and becomes the mouth. A similar process produces an opening for excretion of wastes at the posterior end of the gut.[17] By the time the child is born, the entire complex of the organs of digestion will be complete and ready to function the instant milk from the mother's breast is drawn into the infant's stomach by the sucking movement of lips, tongue and throat.

In Woodrow Wilson, this digestive apparatus, like the respiratory, will be hypersensitive. It is intimately related to the sympathetic nervous system, and will act at times so acutely as to be a great burden and problem to him. He once quoted as an axiom in education a remark of his father's, to the effect that human intelligence is not to be compared to "a prolix gut" which expands by being stuffed with facts. It seemed likely that the man Wilson's complete dedication to his own intellectual development and the exercise of his mind, which resulted in a lack of interest in eating and the neglect of his digestion was, rather than any hereditary weakness, the cause of his gastrogenic difficulties.

Prepotent Geniture

Prepotency in breeding is the power to impress on offspring traits characteristic of the sire or dam. Breeders of sheep and cattle utilize this principle in maintaining and improving their flocks and herds.

Prepotency is a matter of heredity. It rests entirely with the germ plasm, which is unaffected by environment. This germ plasm resides in the gonads or reproductive cells of the man and woman, and is there produced and subject to control of, but not to modification by, the medulla of the adrenal gland and the pituitary.

In a person predominantly masculine in physique and temperament, or in a complex, highly sensitive person such as Woodrow Wilson—very masculine physically but in feeling and temperament quite feminine in interpersonal awareness, in no sense a "man's man" or a "he-man" —prepotency is a manifestation of a complicated interplay of factors of body and mind that are of hereditary origin. The predisposition in this case was strengthened by physical and cultural factors of his environment in childhood. The "precious son" of a dominant and notable Presbyterian scholar and preacher like Joseph Ruggles Wilson—the son who, as Joseph recognized very early, possessed especial gifts to be fostered, tutored and evoked; the boy and youth who soon would sense that he was more learned and able than his playmates, who would dream of leadership and fame, even as a small child growing up in "the Manse" in a succession of important Southern Presbyterian communities of Virginia and the Carolinas and Georgia—this person provides a clear example of the complex interplay of the hereditary and conditioning factors of which we speak. In a home such as his, in the era of Reconstruction when Southern white morale and leadership were being put to the ultimate test, he was to have, strengthened and deeply wrought into his heart and mind, those traits of purposefulness, one-pointedness, responsibility, devotion and idealism which were "natural" to him in the sense that they were characteristic of the breed from which he sprang; for they are traits highly developed in responsible Scottish and Scotch-Irish Presbyterian families of the intellectual sort. They are not simply a part of heritage, strengthened by conditioning. They exist only in a person who, as an organism, has the necessary physiological constitution, which is a matter of heredity, not heritage. What was the nature of this combination of heredity and heritage in the case of Thomas Woodrow Wilson, about to be born in Staunton, Virginia? At this point let us glimpse a Wilson album, and speculate upon what lay behind the likenesses it portrays.

The Face of a Warrior

Ann Adams, Joseph Wilson's mother, was a Scotch-Irish Presbyterian of the flinty type. She was born near Donaghadee, an old County Down town in Ulster that sprawls around a wee bay opening on the Irish Channel. Here for nine months of the year, harsh winds and rains sweep out of the northwest, passing over and through the Western Isles, right off the polar icecap. Or else the sharp easterlies from the continental sub-Arctic blow over the Baltic and North Seas and the Highland ranges of Scotland, the hills of the Lowlands and bleak ridges of the English Lake Country. These winds, bringing chill waves and spray, rains and fogs, whip the worn granite forelands of Antrim and Down, indented by many coves and bays.

These shores and small harbors have been the beachheads for brutal invasion and fierce defense through all the ages of human habitation. Prehistoric shore-dwellers descended from Ice Age men fought here with stones and clubs against the seafaring pioneers and herdsmen armed and armored with bronze, who were the first true "Irish." In turn, these had to battle against later invaders who came armed with iron—Keltic horsemen and herdsmen whose waterborne migrations swept out of the Danube Basin, across Switzerland, down the Rhine Valley, around the Cornish Coast past Wales and fanned out along the shores of the Irish Sea.

Here at Donaghadee, near the deep lough on which the city of Belfast now stands, the Gaelic descendants of those Iron Age Kelts later fought fiercely for the precarious foothold which was their home, against oncoming waves of Danes and Norwegians—merciless pagans whose aim was to loot the treasures of the monasteries and castles of Irish Christendom. These receded, and on the flow of the tide of migration that followed their ebbing came invading Scots from the Western Isles to slaughter their distant kinsmen, offspring of the same ancient forebears, to fight for a place on the paternal shores, to intermarry and produce that formidable breed, the Scotch-Irish of Ulster.

The strife of clan against clan and family against family continued even after the next invasion, that of the English in the seventeenth century, bringing their Anglo-Norman culture and Anglican Catholicism, their skill in warfare and their genius for organization—gifts little appreciated and steadfastly resisted during long periods of smouldering hatred and sudden outbursts of violent rebellion. Nor was there any oil for troubled waters during the generations that followed, when from the lowlands of Scotland and Northern England came dedicated Calvinists in search of respite from persecution at home and with the determination to make Presbyterians out of the "wild red-shanks" of the Highlands and long-suffering native Irish-Scots of Northern Ireland.

These newcomers, these "Covenanters," were men and women of iron will and the kind of stamina it took to survive in a new environment in those wild and troubled times. Their own new faith—and the persecutions they had suffered for it—made for an utterly irreconcilable spirit. They were adamant of will, unshakably "for or forninst"—"for" none but those of their own faith, "forninst" especially the tyrannical English bishops and their repressive laws and beyond them "Popery." For them, "Popery" included its "pawns, the paddy Irish" with their priests and prelates—all "instruments of the Devil" and enemies of free worship and "the true faith."

The folk that comprise the population from which Ann Adams came were, then, the survivors of five millenia of selective toughening of the severest kind. The face of Ann Adams, framed severely in the style proper for an elderly woman of quality of her time, is as hard as the granite of Donaghadee's foreland, and could be as aggressively resistant. That bleak penetrating eye has behind it a mind as keen and sharp as a Nor'west or Easterly gale. The chin is like the prow of an icebreaker, and the jaw behind it is massive; the mouth is wide, thinlipped, powerful and dour; the prominent aquiline nose, those heavy-lidded, hard, calculating eyes with epicanthic overfold (inherited from Norse or Norman ancestry) which could gaze with cold condemnation upon a wrongdoer or an enemy—this notable physiognomy might better be framed in the shining metal of a helmet instead of the stern straight hair of an old lady, drawn tightly over the temples under a knitted cap tied coquettishly under the chin with a velvet ribbon. (Teutonic warriors, we may add, *were* coquettish, even as is a male or female lion!) Yes, this is a face that looks like that of a Viking or a Norman knight disguised as a Presbyterian old lady of pride and distinction.

Her son Joseph's features show the same powerful lineaments. And these very same will be notable in "the fighting face" of Woodrow Wilson, the leader, the President, the crusader, the commander-in-chief, the Covenanter. From Woodrow Wilson these same features were to pass to Jessie, his second daughter, but more gently chiselled, softened into classic beauty through her mother Ellen Axson. And through Jessie they have passed to her son Francis, in whose expression gentleness is blended with massive strength and masculinity. Through five generations this prepotent strain traces its lineaments, pictured before our eyes.

Mechanism of Prepotent Geniture

Prepotency in one parent—that is, having greater power than the other to transmit inheritable characteristics to offspring—implies the existence of uniqueness in the central and sympathetic nervous systems, and in their agents—the glands of internal secretion which dispense those hormones that mobilize the organism by way of the nourishing bloodstream. The kind of temperament that a man had to have in order to behave as Woodrow Wilson did—both as a family man and a leader of men—requires a sound mind and sound body. Even more essential is a vital pituitary gland, well balanced and functioning efficiently, with its dependent centers that make up the endocrine system: particularly the thyroid, adrenal and sex glands (or gonads). From the physique of the normal individual grown to maturity, and from his behavior, may be inferred the previous normal development of that individual from embryo through infancy and childhood. And this may be inferred not merely for the whole organism but for particular parts as well. In this case it is from the after-look that we may surmise what was laid down in the embryo.

71

Peculiar gifts, strongly marked characteristics such as Woodrow Wilson possessed, denote unique nervous and endocrine development. Typical of his career were long-sustained periods of tremendous outpouring of energy, episodes of over-exertion and relentless effort, which would be followed by a temporary nervous and physical exhaustion. These periods of exertion were the response of a mobile and powerful nervous mechanism to the challenges of exigencies of his academic and political career. He was by no means chronically driven by an urge to ceaseless activity, regardless of circumstances. Consequently, we see no reason to believe that his behavior evidenced hyperthyroidism. One observes in some photographs the prominence of the eyes. But this is a condition that is anatomical. The nose, lips, ears, chin and jaws are all prominent in his rough-hewn face. The prominence of eye is not disproportionate. Nor is the fact that the eyeballs bulged somewhat in anger or excitement anything out of the ordinary, considering the mobility of his features in times of stress. He was a man of intense but controlled passion. In a letter to his beloved, Ellen Axson, in 1884, he wrote: "It isn't pleasant or convenient to have strong passions. I have the uncomfortable feeling that I am carrying a volcano about with me."[18]

What caused and what governed the "volcano" of which this man, both in youth and maturity, was so keenly aware? Here we verge upon the immensely complex physiological subject of endocrinology—the study of the glandular secretion of hormones which not only control body growth (size) in postnatal life, the contraction of muscles, and the proper functioning of all the organs of the body, but which account for potency (or its lack) in all bodily action, for sloth, rage or passivity, swift response or dullness in crisis, be it physical, mental or emotional. This is not the place for detailed elaboration. Let us be as simple as we can in the case in point—the person, Woodrow Wilson.

Integration of the Growing Organism

Just as the central nervous system surmounted by the brain is the controlling organ in the subsequent growth and functioning of the entire organism, so a tiny gland enfolded in the base of the brain is the controlling agency whose hormones govern the development and operation of the rest of the complex of endocrine glands. This is the master gland—the pituitary. By the second month of embryonic growth it is already prominent; a very small organ called the thalamus (meaning

72

chamber), its lobes impinging upon the upper end of the spinal cord.[19]

The Inner Springs of Personality

This hidden chamber of the mind is the control room through which pass impulses between the brain and nerves of the skin and of the eyes, ears, nose, palate, throat; in fact of the whole peripheral nervous system, which is the communications network that keeps the inner man (the brain and beneath it the central nervous system) in contact with the external work of persons and things. Of the minuteness, complexity and extensive activity of this network, the most highly evolved of all forms of living substance known on this earth, Dr. George W. Crile[20] has written:

> The most delicate structures known . . . a network so vast and so intricate that, were all the tissues of the body removed except these nerve mechanisms, there would remain an effigy of the body as a whole. . . . Like a battery, the brain is wired to every muscle and gland of the body. The spinal cord is a cable that carries thousands of connecting wires, and the nerve trunks are lesser cables. . . . The brain, heart, thyroid, adrenal-sympathetic system, these control muscular action, glandular secretion and emotional expression, thereby generating and controlling intelligence, power, and personality. . . .

If this is true for the generality of animals and men, how much more so for any man of Wilson's delicacy of feeling and acuteness of mind.

The person who is a potent factor, as Woodrow Wilson was, in shaping the events of his time, is obviously one with acute intelligence. Intelligence depends upon the physiology of the brain, and this, as shown above, is controlled by the genes in the germ plasm of the two parents. The nature and combination of these genes in the embryo determine the size and number of convolutions in the developing brain—and it is upon the intricacy of convolution rather than upon size that intelligence depends. As W. H. Mottram[21] states: ". . . As intelligence largely determines personality, one main basis of personality must be determined largely by inheritance. We are what we are largely because we inherit a definite type of nervous system."

In how far may the vigor, growth, sensitivity and agility of this master mechanism which controls intelligence, power and personality be stimulated by exercise and practice? Woodrow Wilson consciously cultivated his mind and regarded it as an instrument to be used, an organ to be developed by use. Though keenly aware of physical and nervous fatiguability, it was his firm conviction that the *brain itself* never tires. Apparently he had trained his mind to respond and act, regardless of bodily fatigue or illness.

The hormones of the master gland also are believed to control the growth of the sex glands, whose maturing marks puberty; likewise the development of the reproductive cells, the sperm in the male and the ovum in the female.[22] The sensitivity and responsiveness evident in Woodrow Wilson's family life, his deep affection for kith and kin, his devotion within the magic circle of family to mother, sisters, wife and daughters, and equally to father and brother, reveal a normal and balanced organism, yet one resilient and sensitive. Such resilience in the sexual phase of the endocrine complex is an essential part of the well balanced and sufficiently powered physique of a dynamic individual, such as this one which was in the making in Staunton in 1856. His deeply affectionate nature flowed outwards. It was not buried in the unconscious.[23]

The Adrenal Mobilizer

As with the affections, so with the emotions of anger and fear and the tendency toward or later habituation to such emotions in the developing personality. They too are dependent upon the prenatal growth of brain, glands and nervous systems. Here again the pituitary is indeed the master, in that it directly controls those portions of the adrenal glands known as the cortices, which pour adrenalin into the bloodstream at times of crisis, rousing the whole organism to action for offense, defense or flight. It is this regulatory fraction of "gray matter" which prevents man from being a physical automaton.[24]

The resiliency, the capacity of the organism that was Woodrow Wilson for extreme tension and the outpouring of energy and power when aroused, and for total relaxation (deep sleep, sociability, humor), also typical of him and of the breed from which he came, indicate high development of the adrenal cortex, which is intimately related to the sex glands and to the celiac or "solar" plexus, servant of the master gland.

Here enters one of those questions which science does not answer, as yet, but which is worth pondering. Given this inherited capacity, was the activity of this component in his physique increased (and if so was the cortex enlarged) by his habit of feeling and expressing passion? This was a habit which was most certainly strengthened in early life by the

74

like behavior of his father, whom he admired so ardently. "Righteous anger" was for Woodrow Wilson a virtue, and one to be cultivated. Expressing "righteous anger" was a part of his careful, conscious, histrionic self-training for political leadership. Exerting his will over individuals, companions, crowds and audiences for the ends which were his ideals was the form of power he exerted. Physiologically, it may be said perhaps that Woodrow Wilson unconsciously cultivated and exercised his adrenal cortex, as a professional "strong man" consciously develops his muscles. The quality and capacity of the organ was determined genetically, a matter of breed, but specific reactions and actions—behavior, judgment, values—are very much a matter of habituation. Woodrow Wilson was Scotch and Scotch-Irish racially, but culturally he was Presbyterian, and an American Southerner.

Probably these same cultural factors (and others) were, at least in part, to be determinants of the famous Wilson "drive" in later life, as contributors to the prenatal conditioning of the thyroid gland (another important collaborator of the pituitary).[25] His then typically American zeal for a "cause," his fierce loyalty to the "Lost Cause" of the Southern secession, his crusading spirit and stubborn will, bequeathed by generations of "Dissenters" in Ireland and Scotland—all were a part of his cultural heritage, and all influenced his postnatal development.

"Hyperthyroid" and "Hypothyroid" are the well-known medical diagnostic terms which indicate an excess or a deficiency of energizing hormones, an overactivity or a sluggishness of the thyroid gland in its task of converting bodily nutrients into energy for every part of the organism. Whether during the nine months of growth before birth a tendency to overdevelopment of the thyroid occurred, to be augmented in later years, we cannot know. Whether his driving ambition, the quality and force that enabled him to dominate or sway people and events to the extent that he did, could be interpreted as indicating a degree of hyperthyroidism is not certain in the absence of clinical records. But the "temper of the man," his zeal, may not have been due to any clearcut situation involving the thyroid, but rather, and in a more primary way, to an overactive pituitary. This may be a case in which the master gland, as the servant of the brain, became a tyrant, acting as the accomplice of the conscience, will and ambition of "The Crusader," mobilizing the thyroid and the adrenal cortex to the point of "overdoing." In popular phrasing, The Crusader "outran himself," got "ahead of his times."

But manifestations such as these were to be mere recurring episodes (though no doubt cumulative and all pointing to the final episode of physical collapse) in the life of the individual now building so snugly and soundly in his mother's womb. By far, the preponderance of experience in that life-to-be was (again from the after-look) of another quality altogether, but equally based upon the activity of these glands we have been discussing. Elation, joy, enthusiasm, the sense of great things ahead—from youth onward (and often explicitly expressed by him) those would be "feelings" characteristic of Tommy Wilson the ardent student, and of Woodrow Wilson the teacher and leader. They were expressed not only in his own personal confidences to intimates, but in action, in the dynamic, enthusiastic quality of his teaching which made his courses the most popular at Princeton in the time of his professorship; in the exuberant gaiety of his social activity during the periods of his rising success and recognition as an academic administrator; in the sweeping optimism and spirited appeal of his nationwide lectures and later of his campaign speeches.

This mood and behavior involve a smooth interplay of the pituitary with the adrenal cortex to stimulate deep breathing. This deep breathing surcharges the blood with fresh oxygen that in turn stimulates the mind and nerves toward that sense of well-being and elation which induces a relaxation of tension in the whole body. This is the mood of happiness and laughter, of courage and achievement. This mood was to be notably in the ascendant throughout Woodrow Wilson's zestful middle years, despite periods of discouragement when particular ideals and goals of achievement met with rejection.

In contradistinction to the physical impulsion of elation, the adrenal cortex is also stimulated by shock, distress, fear, pain or anger to pour into the bloodstream quantities of cortisone. This too causes the heart to beat faster, pumping blood rapidly and in quantity through the whole body, and into the lungs to cause fast breathing. A continuing aspect of this syndrome is the withdrawal of blood from the digestive organs, a "blanching" or contracting of their tissues and the temporary cessation of their operation—all this in consequence of the diversion of blood to the motor or muscular mechanism of the body now poised for the action involved in fight or flight. The mature Woodrow Wilson's behavior, in every crisis of his public life, was to give outward evidence of this complex syndrome of inner activity—the blanching of his countenance, reflecting that of the digestive tract suddenly thrown into paralysis by the body's need for a sudden effort of will; the tensing of the figure into taut immobility while within there was a gathering of forces for the plunge into—fight, but for Wilson never flight!

There are many reports of this. At the fateful faculty meeting at Princeton when the president's carefully wrought plan for "the Quads" was voted down, a colleague saw "a tightening of the muscles in the President's long jaw and a curious pallor spread over his face. . . ."[26] In another instance: "His face was ashen gray," reported his Secret Service guard, Colonel Starling, standing beside him in the ordeal of asking Congress for a declaration of war against Germany after he, dedicated to peace, had "wrestled with his conscience and . . . done what he thought was right."[27] His daughter Eleanor describes his face as "gaunt and gray"[28] in the weeks that followed the shock of her mother's death; and the rigidity of his face and form in times of suppressed irritation or "cold anger." He was "white to the lips," with "burning eyes," when Edith Galt first saw him after the whispering campaign concerning their probable engagement had come to his ears.[29]

May we not read, in the deadly episode of frustration, shock and exhaustion that was to come at the end of his active career, a comparable stagnation and corrosion of temperament? This, on the level of mind, feeling and will, could be a counterpart of the physiological frustration just described. Might not this stagnation of spirit be the natural consequence of the denial of that success toward which all the passionate hopes and efforts of a lifetime had been directed, when the powers of a dynamic soul are at last effectively suppressed and paralyzed?

The Architectonics of Bone

So far in this "biography" of the unborn child that was to be Thomas Woodrow Wilson, we have been concerned chiefly with the brain and its servants—the sensory, the glandular and the nervous systems which would largely determine what he was to be in nature and temperament, ability and strength. What of that which, in the most literal sense, was to be the physical support of this body?

That beautifully wrought mechanism which, with its leverages and tensions, upholds the tendons, muscles, tissues, integuments and organs of the mobile body, is not merely a frame upon and about which these parts of the organism are laid. It is a system of supports that grows from within.

Here again the earliest development is in the area of brain and head. At three weeks, just as the spinal tube of primitive nerve tissue is making its appearance, the first evidence of growth that is to become skeletal is the notocordal plate which manifests as the central beginning of a skull. Yet not before the sixth week is there even an observable beginning of the centers of future bone formation, and it will be two weeks more before the first indications of potential ossification appear at and from these centers.

By the tenth week, the centers are more pronounced, and by the twelfth, the bony structure is really taking form. By selecting and absorbing from among the nutrients of the mother's body the phosphorus and lime essential for strength, and then by exuding this, much as a coral polyp exudes the beautifully modelled walls within which it lives, these centers of human bone formation slowly create the body's inner frame—first as semi-firm cartilage, later as solid bone.

It was in the substantiality of this inner frame, its essential soundness, that the child Jeanie Wilson was carrying would enjoy an incalculable blessing throughout a life of crowding tasks and all but crushing events—a "sturdy frame" that gave him his notable endurance as a fighter. This was an endowment of his Keltic breed. But again the beneficent gifts of the Valley of Virginia helped.

The broad rolling fields of this valley plateau, so richly carpeted with blue grass, had for millennia been the grazing grounds of wild game of all kinds. For millennia it had been the seasonal hunting ground of innumerable Indian tribes, trekking along the length of the Atlantic seaboard and from the Great Lakes and the mid-region west of the Alleghenies to hunt the herds of bison and deer—and each other, as the animals did. The white men followed the red men. To wild game they added domesticated livestock—swine, sheep, cattle and horses. Had all the skeletons of all the animals and humans hunted and slaughtered through the ages been preserved on the surface, both open plain and marginal woodland together would have been strewn quite literally with bones. But all this phosphorus-bearing refuse of myriads of creatures had decayed and gone into the ground, to be reabsorbed into the vegetable and animal bodies growing in and on that soil. Thus to new generation after new generation of every plant and creature nurtured thereon was given a special richness not found in average types of terrain. So it was that the Valley, with its phosphorus-laden earth and its wealth of limestone springs, contributed richly in both preconception and prenatal periods to the sturdy bone and cartilage framework of this growing child.

Through the first three generations of Wilsons in America a phenomenon not unusual in this country is observable—a progressive lightening and refinement of the physique together with increased sensitivity and intellectuality. This change was marked as between James Wilson the pioneer—rugged of frame and magnificently impervious to the political darts which his own vitriolic tongue invited—and Joseph Wilson, his youngest son, strongly but not massively built, endowed with unflagging energy and a barbed wit but with a gentler, deeply affectionate cast to his more scholarly mind and nature. And now in ,this first son of Joseph's begetting there was laid down the toughly knit bone and fibre (typical in the strongly developed mesomorphy of the Wilson constitution) which, though not too rugged, was to sustain, over longer years than those of his grandfather's life, the relentless drive of a more powerful brain and the "shocks of battle" to be endured by a far more sensitive nervous system.

Actually, the skeleton, seemingly the most fixed part of the body, is the least stable. From the moment it begins to grow, it is in a state of change, from its embryonic first budding to the progressive ossification of old age. For, from maturity onward to senescence, a process of fusion will reduce the number of separate bones, and fusion will mean less pliability—the familiar "stiffness" of age. Are physical and mental stiffness correlated? The man this embryo was to become was of the bodily type that reaches maturity early. May this be related to a noteworthy rigidity of mind and purpose from early middle life on, until, at sixty-four, illness withdrew him from the arena of battle to the contemplative life and mellowing reflections of a recluse?

"The Heart Stands Forth"

This unborn child had inherited no Wilson or Woodrow *blood*. In the yolk sac of the ovum which begins to grow at conception there appear the "blood islands," which in reality are specialized cells which multiply and remultiply to produce the life-sustaining fluid that nourishes the body. During the fourth week, genuine primitive blood cells and their rudimentary vessels are present. In the fifth that human chalice, the "cup of life," already has become dilated into the small beginnings of what will be the great chambered muscle called the heart.

The heart . . . stood forth . . .
Self-existing . . . in the gloom.
It grows in gloom—
The sap and succulent parts,
The life pulsating and the Cup of Life.
—from a Maori Creation Chant[30]

By the sixth week, the primitive blood vessels have made the connection between heart and head and bodily extremities. During the eighth week, the complete circulatory system is delineated. Some blood had been forming in the liver in the preceding week, but not until the twelfth does the true blood chemistry begin in the marrow of the bones, those innermost laboratories which have only just reached a stage of development adequate to the essential chemical processes that must go on in them for all the years of a hot-blooded human life. Here proteins and carbohydrates, phosphorus and other mineral elements, hydrogen and oxygen, will be combined and transmuted into the white and red blood corpuscles, floating in serum, on which the health and functioning of that life will depend.

The mother's body is well supplied with all the essential ingredients for the alchemy going on in this organic laboratory. In the flesh of herds and flocks and wild game on which her body has been nourished, in the richly stored mineral elements of the vegetables and fruits which this Valley soil produces, in the calcium, iron and manganese which the famous springs of the region bring up in their waters from the depths of what once was an ocean floor, in the salts and fats and proteins of the milk she drinks, and in the eggs she eats, golden with sulphur, she has stored within her during a winter and a summer all that this complex scheme of organic chemical synthesis will need.

In the fourth month, the enlarging muscle which is the heart takes on a quality of compactness which continues steadily to increase, until at birth it gathers its forces to begin, at the first gasp and rush of air into the baby's lungs, that rhythmic pumping of the life fluid, that ceaseless automatic pulsation which is perhaps the supreme marvel of nature in the physiology of man. During all these nine months of gestation, this growing heart rests "in bliss of calm and quiet," drawing its sustenance through the placenta rooted in the wall of the mother's womb. The tiny body is still like the curled-up plant encased within the kernel of a seed planted in warm soil.

This small heart now growing silently in the embryo will pulsate

80

about seventy beats to the minute, quietly, faithfully, at times more, at times less, but skipping never a beat for sixty-eight years, one month and one week. In cold, in illness, it will beat with faster, more urgent strokes; in times of spiritual and emotional exhilaration with quickened élan; in fatigue and sorrow or in sapping heat, with a slowing rhythm; in episodes of calm and contentment, with an even, peaceful flow.

At the last, weary from a long ordeal at the close of a life of relentless effort, this heart will relax slowly until it lies still again, as before birth, while the spirit of the body it has animated to carry the torch of humanity for a brief span of arduous years, reenters the womb of night.

On that day, February 3, 1924, when the heart stops, mankind, remembering the seeking spirit and the valiant effort, will pause for a moment and mourn; and through press and radio (then in its beginnings), a tide of prayer and gratitude was to rise from multitudes over the world.

> Thus the progeny of the Great Extending
> Filled the heaven's expanse;
> The chorus of life rose and swelled into ecstasy,
> Then rested
> In bliss of calm and quiet.
>
> —Maori Creation Chant[31]

The Face of a Covenanter

In this chapter titled "prenatal biography," we have stressed certain phases of embryonic development because they focus an especially significant light upon the character of the person in after-life; and as a corollary we have in most instances brought an "after-look" to bear upon the embryonic picture, in order to give relevance to the appraisal in hand.

No part of the body embodies more definitely and more completely hereditary traits affecting qualities of character and temperament than the face, while at the same time its lineaments record the effects of environment and experience.

The facial features which perpetuate the traits of forbears may become softened and neutralized where there is an expression of docility or complacence. There was nothing of docility or complacency in the nature of Woodrow Wilson. When he discovered what he wanted to be and to do, he did it with all his might. He vigorously exercised and trained his intellect, his ability to write and speak. He was vital and purposeful in personal relationships, his tastes were acutely discriminating, his attitudes were always positive. His was a face that told a long story, of background and breeding, of nurturing, of experience: the face of dominant self, generally conquering, occasionally defeated, but always pressing on.

The Embryonic Face

Reposing in the night of womb-life, the face of the foetus, which has taken form rapidly from the fifth to eighth week, after the eyes and mouth have been well formed, has every appearance of profound sleep. The eyelids are closed, the mouth is shut, lips tight together. Actually the body *is* asleep; its life is literally vegetative. The foetus is a parasite, rooted in the wall of the mother's womb, drawing its sustenance through the placenta. Not until the sixteenth week does the face have a really human look. And then it is the face of a sleeping creature, which will not wake until after it is born.

After birth, the awakening of the brain and nervous system is very gradual. The creature still sleeps most of the day and all of the night, its waking times mere episodes of very short duration. Actually the animation of the face is a process extending through all the years of the central nervous system's slow maturing. The features of the face which frame the orifices of the external sensory apparatus—eyes, ears, nose, mouth—are organs that are extensions of the central nervous system. These antennae will become modified by environment and use; but basically in this baby, their form is determined by genes inherited from Woodrow and Wilson forbears.

As the features themselves are true to form, so are their movements and behavior. The expressions of calm or agitation, concentration and mobility, pleasure and pain, while individual and unique to a degree, would all be registered in ways characteristic of the breed. The forehead, the brows, eyes, ears, nose, mouth, jaws—they are altogether Woodrow Wilson, a descendant of Anglo-Norman-Keltic lowland Scots and North-of-Ireland Irish-Scots.

Symmetry

Symmetry is to be one of the most notable characteristics of this face from youth to old age. Cover one half of the portrait and look at the other in any photograph, and the features are the same—the broad, rather square intellectual forehead; evenly arched full eyebrows; large, outward, searching eyes with heavy lids like Joseph's and Ann Adams':

large even nose and even nostrils; full lips, large chin flanked by a long jaw; large fleshy ears, and high even skull. Ears, eyes, nose and mouth are those of a man too well-bred and self-controlled to be sensuous in any vulgar sense or way, but vulnerable and emotional as only a sensitive refined soul can be. It is a face like his mother's. This vulnerability would be one of his greatest handicaps for the career he chose.

Normally, even when the mouth and eyes are tense, there is a quality of firm repose. Unposed views reveal weariness, ill health, sorrow. But in these the symmetry is still there. It is a symmetry of wholeness. The inner man is spiritually whole, and the face expresses this wholeness. It is only when anger has thrown him off-center that the symmetry is destroyed—as in the Princeton campus photo in which his striding pace evidently matches a strident temper in a distressed heart and distraught mind thrust in upon itself by distortion of his hopes and plans. (This snapshot probably shows him returning from the faculty meeting in which his beloved friend Hibben had disappointed and seemingly deserted him.)

Winthrop Daniels, a colleague at Princeton and later in Washington, once described Woodrow Wilson in terms of a photograph of the historian Mommsen in Wilson's study:[32]

> The eye of Mommsen was the eye of Wilson, searching, significant, penetrating, unforgettable, with an unquestionable gravity, and at times almost protuberant as if by an internal and intellectual impulse. His play of facial expression was always dominated by his eye. His features were sensitive and mobile; his lips fine and full, and at times the tip of his nose, especially when he was amused, would tip slightly downwards, out of alignment with the nasal bridge. His countenance was at once arresting, sometimes grimly arresting, but always distinguished.

Poise

The wholeness of heart and mind revealed in this face is that of a man whose nurturing through childhood and youth had established substantial values and wholehearted faith in self and surroundings. It is a masterful face because it expresses confident poise, combined with alert outgoing intelligence. It is perhaps a less handsome face but more attractive than that of his father, for instead of the forthright arrogance (which is a form of obtuseness) so notable in Joseph's portraits there is in his son's a searching sensitive awareness. He was sure of his gifts and his capabilities, because they were hard-earned, after having been discovered gradually and developed by application and practice. The mastery that the features express, is, then, not merely a matter of innate character, but more a mark of achievement. That mastery increases with the years, until, during the episode of trial and suffering towards the end, when the physique was crippled, the unconquerable will reaches out through the eyes with a thrust, perhaps sharpened rather than diminished by physical weakness and the reversal of his hoped-for achievement.

Mobility

In many instances, a physiognomy that is markedly symmetrical, with an expression of profound repose, is one that is rather immobile. Woodrow Wilson's face, for all its symmetry and repose, was extraordinarily mobile. This mobility of expression was an important component in the magnetic power of his personality. Acute thought sharpened his features and concentrated his gaze. In expressed anger, which was rare, his jaw set and his eyes blazed. More often anger or deep indignation was repressed, and then his jaw worked and his eyes had a steely look. In moods of love, sympathy and appreciation, there is said to have been incomparable charm and tenderness in his eyes and general expression. His daughter Eleanor remembers that his gray eyes became blue at such times, while in moments of anger, the gray darkened to gray-black.

When gay and facetious he was a gifted mimic, in voice, gesture, posture and facial expression. Photographs taken in the course of his career at Princeton and in politics, show an infinite variety of moods expressed—austere seriousness, exhortation, persuasiveness, attentiveness, pugnaciousness, calculation, elation, laughter, sportiveness, but never vague geniality, insouciance or nonchalance.

A study of photographs showing his whole body, taken through the sequences of his later life, gives the impression that the symmetry characteristic of his face, from youth onward, was equally true of his entire physique. The shoulders are set evenly, his left and right arms and hands are alike. Seated, his torso is erect, alertly poised, never slack or twisted. Standing, his stance is firm, on both feet, and his step in walking or marching is vigorous and even. There is never any evidence of drooping, leaning or slackness in these photographs, even in those taken at times of great fatigue, or as he aged—before the onset of invalidism.

While as a child and youth, his own preference for day-dreaming, and later for intellectual exercise, and his father's dominant interest in developing his mind, may have deprived him of the sort of physical development that would have made his mature years more comfortable and heightened his endurance in times of strain, he was by no means a sedentary youngster or young man. His college intimates remark upon his passion for baseball (although he coached more often than he played) and his love of long walks, alone or in company. His daughters and other members of his household also record this. His young sister-in-law, who grew up in his family at Princeton, remarks on his delight in long walks, and says that "his usual brisk constitutional at the end of the day" was from two to three miles.[33] Edwin Alderman (later president of the University of Virginia) knew Tommy Wilson in the Wilmington days, and remembered him there as "a tall slender youth of curious homeliness, detachment and distinction . . . proud-spirited, . . . ambitious" but "never sturdy in body;" and elsewhere in the memorial address, delivered before Congress in 1924, he speaks of the mature Wilson's "quiet grace of dignity" in form and action.[34] Joseph P. Tumulty, his private secretary from the New Jersey governorship through the two Presidential terms of office, writes of "the fine poise of his head" in all public addresses.[35] William Allen White, a Republican and by no means an undiscriminating admirer of the President, writes of his second Inaugural in 1916:[36]

Woodrow Wilson that day loomed the largest figure in the civilized world. Four years in office had not broken him, but they had changed him greatly. His face was lean, his body straight and strong. A commanding resonance had come into his fine tenor voice.

Edith Bolling Wilson, his second wife, remembers his lightness and agility and fondness for dancing, and how in the evenings in their private apartments in the White House (before the growing pressures of the war deprived them of all leisure), "he would put a record on the Victrola and say, 'Now, I'll show you how to do a jig step;' " and how he often said "he envied Primrose, the minstrel dancer, and wished he could exchange jobs."[37] Colonel Starling, his Secret Service guard, also remembers the President's "natural lightness of foot," and how in his daily walks in Rock Creek Park with Mrs. Edith Wilson "along the woodland paths, he leaped over the smallest obstacles, or skipped around them."[38]

Of later days, in France after the war's end, Mrs. Edith Wilson recalls the President's Memorial Day address at the military service at Suresnes and how he stood, "head bared—and how white the hair had grown those last few months—his tall, slight form tense with emotion";[39] and at the signing of the Treaty of Peace in Versailles Palace, "his figure, grown more slender in these months [of "unremitting labor,"] but alert and alive."[40]

This vigor and elasticity of physique, carrying him through the most stringent ordeals of a political career and world war leadership, and in spite of a not too robust frame, could have come only through sound and superior genes and a body well-proportioned and well-knit during its embryonic development. Although in childhood, he did not build an athletic body and became subject to dyspeptic disorders, actually there were to be only a few episodes in his career when illness or disability interfered seriously with his intellectual work or his statesmanly leadership.

CHILD OF THE MANSE

The Waiting Time

The winter solstice, three to four days before Christmas—those gray brooding days when snow often falls silently in the night, is when nature is in a state of profound repose. It was on the day of the shortest hours of daylight that the pagan Keltic and Saxon forebears of this child celebrated the ritual of the Yule log, the sacred fire thought to help rekindle the sun's light. Here in the Manse at Staunton, this was a Yuletide of waiting with yearning and fortitude. Unto Jeanie Wilson, a child was to be born, a child whom many men in all parts of the world one day were to call blessed.

For Jeanie and Joseph, steeped in the record and the lore of The Nativity, it was inevitable that they should wonder whether the child might be born on Christmas day. The service, sermon and communion commemorating Christ's nativity were ended. The faces of Joseph's flock had an earnest warmth. At the door after service, friendly ladies of the congregation murmured polite solicitous inquiries on being greeted by Dr. Wilson, his manner more brusque than usual, a little impatient, for he was anxious to be home. The old church on the hillside would remain closed for a few days—these short brisk days that still seem to pass so slowly.

Christmas Day itself passed, notable only for the parents' effort to give something of its traditional pleasures to the two little girls of the house, and to mark the Day in kindly fashion for the good servants. For Jeanie and Joseph in this waiting time, expectancy had become the dominant thread in their days and nights. It was the "Dark of the Moon"—when nights are still and good for sleeping, when animals and humankind are not restless and roaming about—a time when quiet repose is everywhere. On the farms about Staunton the cattle lay still, asleep; horses were quiet in their stalls; the chickens were on their roosts with heads under wings and feet tucked snugly under breast feathers.

Came the twenty-sixth, the twenty-seventh. These were lowering gray days. December's swift dusk shrouded garden and town. With each slowly passing hour, Joseph's solicitude deepened. Jeanie, he well knew, was not overly robust. Two of the dominant traits out of his heritage came to the fore in those days and nights of waiting—his domesticity and his masterly competence. He was a man truly to husband his wife, the mother of his bairns. Love of home and own family, and courage, were bred into him, as into everyone of the Ulster breed through the generations of incredible vicissitudes that had hardened that breed and eliminated the weak in the counties of northern Ireland. And Joseph Ruggles Wilson had been the most loved son of a stern but deeply devoted mother.

So, as Jeanie moved about now and then, tending the children, still directing her household, but returning to her room and bed at more and more frequent intervals in these days after Christmas, Joseph followed her movements with watchful eye. He saw to it that the fires were kept burning brightly, especially the one in the bedroom. Occasionally there was a caller, courteously but formally received by Dr. Wilson in the parlor across the hall. And Dr. Tate, the family physician, stopped frequently to assure the minister that he held himself in readiness to come instantly when his professional services were needed.

The daylight hours of the twenty-seventh slowly passed. Though near the shortest day of the year, it seemed unusually long. The evening meal was served to the doctor and the two little girls in the basement dining room. Soon he was back in the bedroom with Jeanie, who by now definitely felt labor approaching. With the first undeniable twinges, a servant was dispatched quickly to bring Dr. Tate. Mothers did their childbearing at home in those days.

It is certain that a man of Joseph's temperament could not sit still at such a time. As labor advanced, it is likely that his wife heard him intermittently pacing the hall upstairs, heard him sit down in his reading chair, pick up a book and then shortly lay it down, get up and pace again. It is certain that the familiar aroma of strong tobacco smoke from his pipe floated down the stairwell.

As the hours before midnight wore on, there was profound stillness over the Blue Ridge, the Alleghenies, and throughout the Valley, and in this godly town everyone was abed. The garden of the Manse lay dark and still, the life of fruit trees and flowers asleep in seeds and roots. And in the Manse, an intense silence, a waiting silence. Dr. Tate spent now and then a little time with Joseph, purveying indefinite bulletins, but for the most part he waited alone. Only when he heard Jeanie's servant go scurrying down the basement stairs to the kitchen to fetch a bowl and a big container of hot water, did Joseph abandon both book and pipe. Then the pacing became continuous. Unconsciously, he began to sing, quietly:

> O God, our help in ages past,
> Our hope in years to come;
> Be Thou our guard while troubles last,
> And our eternal home.

The Sudden Cry

Then, in the "wee sma' hours" of the new day, there came to his ears, from the bedroom at the bottom of the stairs, that sudden cry of a child just born. Awaiting nobody's summons, nor thinking of the dignity befitting a minister—he just "goes aclatterin' " down the stairs, to be greeted at the bottom by the exuberant servant: "Doctor says, Sir, you got a fine boy chile!"

We may be sure that Joseph's heart leaped with pride and gratitude as he tiptoed swiftly to the bedside where Dr. Tate stood, looked at the tiny bit of humanity there beside his wife, touched her hand and her forehead and fervently said a low-voiced prayer.

At some later hour, he wrote in the family Bible, in a hand not too steady, beneath the names and birth dates of Marion and Annie, the following: "In Staunton, Virginia, on the 28th December, 1855 [sic] at 12:3/4 o'clock at night, Thomas Woodrow." This entry in the Bible reading 1855 seems evidence enough that the father was somewhat distraught from fatigue during the days of waiting, especially the last six dark tense hours of strain and expectancy; for December 28th, 1856, as the true date of President Wilson's birth, has been verified from many sources. Below another entry in the family Bible reads: "baptized April 15 by Rev. J. H. Smith of Charlottesville."

It is significant that this, the first son, for whose coming Joseph must have longed even more than did his wife, was named, not for his notable father, nor for grandfather James Wilson, but for the mother's father Thomas Woodrow. This betokens Joseph's deep respect for Jeanie, his admiration for her father, and a great affection and generosity of spirit, rather than vanity or pride, though pride there surely was, for the child was "a beautiful boy," described "as noble of mien." The minister, who truly possessed ample self-esteem, might well have taken the event pridefully. Possibly one consideration weighing heavily with both parents in the matter of naming was the fact that Joseph Ruggles was not a family name, but that of an admired friend of his father's. When a second son came he was given Joseph's name. This is clear evidence that in christening the first boy-child Thomas Woodrow, Joseph was foregoing the natural inclination of a father to have the first son bear his own name.

Jeanie was a mature mother. She had married late for those days—in her twenty-first year. Now she was thirty, and she already had borne two children, both girls. Her husband's call to the First Presbyterian Church at Staunton, the awakening of a new sense of a mission there, must have aroused in her an even greater feeling of religious devotion and dedication. Whatever the complex of causes, it is significant that she "united with the Church" during the month before conceiving in her womb the child that was to become a leader of great spiritual power in America and the world; but it is certain that with Jeanie, Thomas Woodrow's daughter, this decision was a matter of deep conviction, independently arrived at.

When we read her ardent letters, at a slightly later date, expressing (in what to modern ears seem somewhat extravagant terms) her delight that a beloved brother has "joined himself to the Church," we have a sure clue to the deep feeling with which she linked this her own step with the blessing now vouchsafed to her by a watching Providence. And as the waiting time was ended, and she and Joseph gazed in joy and devout thanksgiving upon the son so ardently desired, it is not to be doubted that their sense of "a family united in Christ Jesus" was far from being the least part of their gratitude.

Stepping Across the Dark

> What could his birthday give,
> Giving all he could,
> Except—
> Stepping across the Dark—

An interesting pattern of what may or may not be coincidences occurred as the robust infant, destined in his lifetime to become the most widely acclaimed leader of his time in the world, was born. He entered his first day in its dimmest hour (near midnight); and that day (December 28th) was near the darkest of the year (the winter solstice); it was the dark of the moon; and, last but not least, it was a year when solar radiation earthward was at low in the "sunspot cycle." Astrophysically, this baby who was christened Thomas Woodrow, started life at scratch—or just beyond "scratch."

Figure (2) symbolizes the cosmic moment of birth.

90

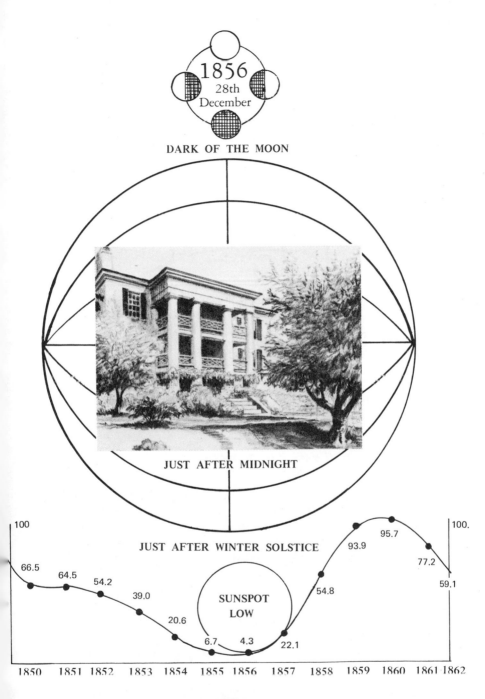

DARK OF THE MOON

JUST AFTER MIDNIGHT

JUST AFTER WINTER SOLSTICE

SUNSPOT LOW

Figure 2

THE MOMENT OF BIRTH

That this birth was just *beyond* "scratch" is another interesting and striking coincidence. The time was just *after* the minimum of sunspot flares; these were again on the increase, beginning a new cycle. It was six days *after* winter solstice: the sun's warmth was slowly returning northward from its autumnal retirement to the Tropics. It was just *after* the dark of the moon: solar energy reflected from the moon was on the increase, as a larger and larger portion of the moon was exposed from out the earth's shadow. And it was just *after* midnight, when the sun's faster light vibrations already are bending earthward through the outer atmosphere. The insurge and upsurge of light and energy were on the ascendant as the small organism took hold on life with his first breath and cry. Electromagnetic energies were "on the up and up," giving the infant a slight but definite boost at the very start. The diurnal boost would continue unabated for nearly twelve hours, until noon of the twenty-eighth.

After that ordeal "just after midnight," there came for Jeanie and the infant blessed sleep. As the new day dawned, Jeanie's energies were reviving, and the baby's likewise. Her eyes welcomed the morning light as she responded to his gropings for the breast. Morning is a time of new hope, especially after an ordeal in the night time. For the whole household that was the dawning of a welcome day. The prevailing mood would, in that family, have been well expressed by lines from two old hymns:

> Now that daylight fills the sky
> We lift our hearts to God on high. . . .

> O blest Creator of the light
> Who mak'st the day with radiance bright. . . .

The reflected light from the moon would wax for fourteen days and nights. In this exceptionally cold winter, the ground was white with snow during these nights of early January. The waxing moon would be high in the heavens in the early hours of the night. When skies were clear the light on the snow was brilliant, and it is likely that a period of clear weather during a week or so preceded the "Great Snowstorm" which descended upon Staunton on the seventeenth of January. This brightness of the still, wintry night-world about the Manse must have gladdened the eyes of the mother, often awake in the "wee sma' " hours, tending and feeding her baby. It was like an extension of the blessed dawning of that first day of her recovery. And the waxing moon, the release from anxiety, the natural pride and gratitude over his wee first son, were likewise good tonic for the spirit of Joseph, and his moods were ever contagious for Jeanie.

The sun's direct light would be on the increase for nearly six months (until the summer solstice, June 21-22). Actually, now in the "dead of winter," the lengthening of days following the winter solstice was barely perceptible. Yet before January was ended, and quite definitely in February, the dawning was discernible more and more early, and when genial days came, the sunlight was markedly warmer. Spring might still be distant, but it certainly was "around the corner." There were days, as everywhere in Virginia in winter, when it was warm enough for the mother to sit with her precious bundle in a sheltered sunny spot in the garden behind the Manse; afternoons when the baby's crib would be moved into the sunshine that flooded the west window of the nursery. By mid-February, warmish spells would come with a southerly breeze, when the sun had real warmth in it; and these came increasingly in March, alternating with gusty spells when winter seemed determined to reassert his dominance. It surely was with longing that Jeanie sensed and welcomed these harbingers of the approach of spring, and with joy that she greeted it as it came with a rush after mid-April.

All things considered, it is evident that in the first twelve months of growth spent by this infant in Staunton he would have benefited not only from spring, summer and autumn of the Valley's abundance, but from the steadily mounting effectiveness of those influences which our sun, master of our physical life on this planet, was to exert. The hydrogen eruptions on the sun would increase for nearly four years after December, 1856.

A fuller discussion of the rate of hydrogen emission from the sun, or "sunspots," and its relevance to the subject in hand will be found under "The Sun has its Seasons", *The Astrophysical Frame of Reference,* beginning on page 216.

Actually the rise and fall of solar radiation is not a *steady* waxing or waning, as is implied in the graphs which accompany those discussions. These were drawn in terms of the *average* numbers of sunspots recorded year by year. For the years 1856 and 1857, we have here drawn a graph (Figure 3) in terms of the actual number of sunspots recorded for those months. We take the single months of December, 1856, and January, 1857, to illustrate the sharp differences that occur. In December, 1856, there were 7.2 sunspots recorded; in January, 1857, there were 13.7,

Figure 3

NUMBER OF SUNSPOTS

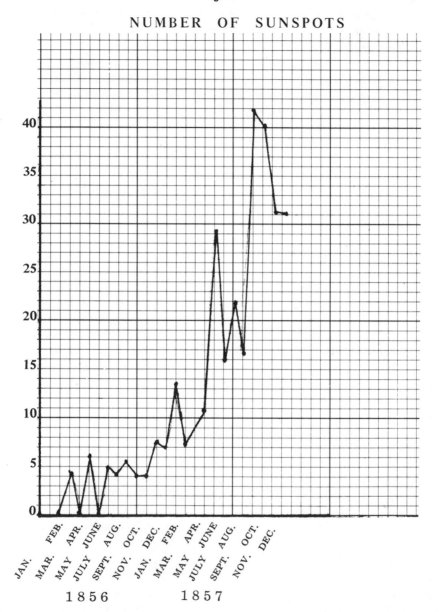

The graph in Figure 2 is a smoothed line plotted in terms of the mean (average) Sunspot numbers per year. (From Stetson, 1947, p. 239)

Figure 3 above, which is plotted in terms of mean sunspot numbers per month, indicates the variability of the averages month by month.

almost twice as many. The sharp rise in January very likely may have been responsible for the great snowstorm of January 27, since turbulence in the atmosphere, which causes such storms, is a matter of abrupt changes in the ionosphere (the area beyond the atmosphere), which is exposed directly to solar radiation. The doubling of the amount of radiation in January undoubtedly would have resulted in increased storminess in that month. We may assume that the fewer discharges in December, preceding the January storm, and likewise following it in February, indicates that these months of December and February had fewer storms, despite the wintry cold that prevailed. This, however, is pure speculation. Unfortunately we have no precise day-to-day records of weather changes at Staunton in 1856 to 1857.

The Winter Cold

The elemental forces of our earth and of the universe were so poised in this winter of 1856-57 that in the Valley of Virginia it was one that would be long remembered for its severity. The three-storied Manse, with its large halls and stairwell, substantial and well planned though it was, was not as easy to keep warm as a snug cottage would have been. There was a fireplace in every room, each with a grate for coal. But the minister's salary was meager. We may infer that the only grate that was constantly replenished was in the bedroom where stood the big bedstead with the crib close by. During the daytime, an open fire was on the kitchen hearth, and the warmth from this drifted up to the first floor. In Dr. Wilson's study on the second floor, the fire would have been lighted only when he read or worked on his sermons.

But that hard winter must have agreed with the new baby, for he was reported to be sound and healthy, which betokens the care and skill exercised by his mother. For her, however, it must have been truly a long and stern ordeal, as January followed the day of delivery, February followed the month of recovery, and in this extraordinary year March dragged on with winter still blanketing the town and the hills, while beyond them the distant mountains glistened whitely when the sun shone but more often were obscured by gray clouds or more snowfall. It would be long before plowed land and greening winter wheat would greet her eyes, or the really genial days, come April; and even in May, that year, there would be frost.

We find in Joseph A. Waddell's *Annals of Augusta County* the story of the Great Snowstorm of January, 1857, at Staunton, just nineteen days after the birth of the baby. Sunday, the 18th of January, must have been a Sabbath when Dr. Wilson preached to a very small congregation and trudged his way uphill to the Manse after the service as quickly as he could get away. It is well that the house contained sufficient provender to last out the storm; and that the baby was not dependent on a "formula" as he probably would have been today, but was nursed by his mother; nor dependent on milk from the country, either, for none would be delivered for many days.

Here is Waddell's account of that January storm:[1]

> We must not omit to mention the great snowstorm of January, 1857, which is still often referred to in conversation . . . and by the newspapers. Snow began to fall about seven o'clock Saturday night, the 17th, and continued without cessation for twenty-four hours. All day Sunday, the 18th, the mercury stood at zero and the wind blew in a gale from apparently every point in the compass driving the snow into the houses through every crack, piling it up several feet deep in some places, and in others sweeping the earth bare.
>
> The running of trains of the Virginia Central Railroad was suspended for ten days, and as this was the one telegraph line to Staunton, the people of the town and county were cut out of communication with the outside world, but never did good fellowship and all the social virtues prevail so generally in the community.
>
> Two issues of the Staunton newspapers were brought out during the embargo, and the editors were put to the trumps for copy. At length after dark Tuesday evening, the 27th, the town was startled and elated by the unaccustomed sound of an engine's whistle and a large part of the population rushed to the depot to hear the news. . . .

A great snowfall releases enormous amounts of positive ions into the air. And the increase of ultraviolet light and formation of ozone, due to the sunlight shining on snow after the storm clears, is also great. This must have been a time, then, when the life energies of the mother and her baby were vitalized to a high degree, and when the joy of living was at a high pitch in the Manse. The period after the storm was literally one of those times when the air was tingling with electrical energy — when hair clung to combs in the brushing, woolen blankets and clothing crackled when handled or shaken out, when the minister's fingers felt needled as he shook hands with wellwishers, and his horse's shod hoofs struck sparks on the cobble paving of the streets about town when cleared of snow.

The naturalist Murrill, describing another hard winter in Staunton, that of 1896, refers to this famous winter of 1857, giving further evidence of the severity of these episodes of snow and continuing cold in Augusta County. He writes:[2]

> The winter of 1895-6 was remarkably cold and snowy. The lowest temperature recorded at Staunton was 18 below zero. It began to snow on Dec. 26 and land peeped out from beneath its white blanket on February 22. Not since 1857 had the ground been covered continuously for fifty-eight days.

If, as Dr. Huntington states in *Seasons of Birth*, "The most distinguished people show a tendency toward birth in cold weather,"[3] and if, as is a well known fact, initial vigor and tonus of the body are assured by vigorous climatic conditions, then Thomas Woodrow Wilson chose an excellent year and season in which to be born.

We have been considering external factors affecting Jeanie and her child. In the midst of the circumstances of this environment, the small human creature, as the nervous system and mind gradually assert themselves, will deliberately achieve personal awareness, thereby becoming a self. This process, like the physical development of the embryo and foetus, is a process of extraversion, of the groping of the nervous system and its appendages toward an apprehension of external phenomena, a drama of integration of faculties of the brain, which is the legatee of inherited proclivities, aptitudes patterned in the ancestral heritage.

> Mind! meditate on the eternal Spirit;
>   remember past deeds.
> Mind! remember past deeds;
>   remember, Mind! remember.
>
> —Isa (Eesha) Upanishad[4]

The Enlivening Spring

Spring in the plateau Valley of Virginia, though late in 1857, came with a swift and lilting rush. The flowering seemed almost to lift miraculously out of snow, so suddenly did it come; and the meadows and orchards were greening and blossoming while chill breezes yet blew down off the snow-patched Blue Ridge, and the peaks of the Alleghenies to the west were still hazed over with winter mist. Strong enlivening sun and invigorating mountain breeze—what a combination to speed the first growth of a winter-born baby! The same impulses that set early lambs to gamboling ecstatically in the hillside pastures must have brought a fresh stirring to small human arms and legs as the baby lay in his cradle, and a new uncomprehended joy, to be expressed only in smiles and soft crowing noises, invaded his being.

We may be sure that, as the warmer and more dependable days came, he was taken out often into the garden, to be watched and tended by adoring small sisters, supervised by the vigilant and stern admonitions of his Negro nurse. The nostalgic love of the Southern scene, and the Southern spring, which was to follow the mature man through all other scenes and throughout a lifetime, must have been laid then and there, under the crepe-myrtle and climbing roses of his sunny native garden. Just as that first spring brought returning health to Jeanie and stimulus to every fiber and organ of the new little human body she was nourishing, it also must have wrought its enlivening magic in the spirit of that small creature slowly learning to become a person.

As for the father, feeling the expansive warmth of the sun, seeing throughout the verdant countryside, wherever his pastoral calls took him, the promise of another season of nature's abundance—if the man's emotions are to be judged by the outpourings of his personal letters, there must have been in his heart a jubilant pride mingled with deep thankfulness for God's providence, and especially for this rich bounty of the land in which they dwelt. That abundance, he doubtless realized, had prepared Jeanie for her ordeal and given her strength to make such a good recovery after bearing the child in the hard winter. And that boy, he must have mused: "a fine healthy fellow," indeed . . . "a beautiful boy," as his mother had been writing to her kinfolk. Indeed *I* am proud of him! The substance of this land of plenty is truly giving him soundness of body. *In corpore sano, mens sana.* . . .

But there is more here than what the good earth can give. Man lives not by bread alone. That lad, Joseph must have vowed, shall have all that we can give him. All in good time. "Unto us a child is born, unto us a son is given." 'Twill be soon enough to feed the mind when the mind of itself begins to show hunger. Now it is the hands that reach out, and the mouth that is always seeking. But the eyes and the brow—they do give promise! It is not impossible that this child may become a great preacher, one whose voice will minister to all America, perhaps through America to the less privileged peoples of the world.

Knowing Joseph's subsequent adoration of this little son, knowing his ambition and his carefully wrought and persistently followed plans for him from earliest years onward, surely one might thus sum up his ardent musings at this time?

A Gifted Child

Certain it is that Dr. Wilson sensed in his infant son that rare quality that marked him as a "gifted child." That what he felt there in the Manse at Staunton gradually became conviction, when Tommy was still a small boy at Augusta, Georgia, a few years later, is indicated by the father's vigorous and determined stimulation and tutoring of the boy's mind while he was still a child there and later in Columbia, South Carolina, where they went to live.

Joseph was not a man to keep such a conviction to himself, but Jeanie would not have needed to be told of it. Both the quality of intense awareness and sensitivity which made her so much of a homebody—so "exclusive," as many of her neighbors thought her—that and her Scotch-English breeding, marked her as a woman who must have pondered much in her heart over this beautiful child she had brought into the world, with pain, in the small hours of the morning on the coldest night of a bitter cold winter. He was a child who throve, as a healthy infant with a sound body would, in this benign milieu of the Valley of Virginia, with the easing of winter, the swift onset of spring, and the following richness of summer typical of the area.

She heard Joseph's exuberant comments now and then. She was proud of her child, with a possessive woman's pride, which, in one of her temperament, is expressed in silence, in the mind's nourishing the heart with little pleasures and a deep and abundant joy. Joseph would talk, though not boastfully. She shared all his pride. And all the while she treasured instinctively in heart and mind the sense that greatness lay ahead for this precious boy that was hers, for whom she had laboured and suffered. Joseph was happily exuberant—Jeanie must have known *in her heart* more than he could have comprehended, things she could not impart even to him, and certainly would not have shared with any other living soul, even had she not been extremely shy and reserved in expressing her feelings. Probably she also was a bit embarrassed, even apprehensive, over Joseph's talk—for "The Lord giveth and the Lord taketh away. . . ." It was a time when infants, even the most healthy, could be lost to the prideful. Pride, she felt, can be a sin.

Hers was the duty, the joy and the labor of suckling the baby. He was big, his hunger for the breast seemed insatiable. Could she sustain

99

him? She had seen her baby brother die in Carlisle; and then her own mother, from the effects of physical exhaustion in that dreadful bleak winter in New York City when she herself was a child of nine and exhausted by the midwinter voyage from England. Oh, there surely was joy, *and faith*, in her heart, *a-plenty*—but was it happiness troubled at first and not infrequently with foreboding?

Yet "a fine healthy fellow" he was, she wrote to her father in late April when the baby was four months old, and "what is best of all, he is just as *good* as he can be. . . ." An old friend of the family wrote describing the infant, when a few months old, as "very plump and fat and remarkably quiet." His Grandfather Woodrow remarked, on first seeing him, "That baby is dignified enough to be moderator of the [Presbyterian] General Assembly!"[5] Perhaps Grandfather Woodrow did not take account of the fact that all infants of a few months old are quiet and passive, unless some defect of health or environment makes them fretful; but that he, the father of eight, should remark upon it makes it significant.

There is no evidence from the boyhood years, spent later in Georgia and South Carolina, that an early anxiety of his mother was justified, or that these descriptions of his infancy in Staunton were to be belied by later events. The plumpness presumably came from the father's side, for the Wilsons were massive. The quietness and "dignity" no doubt reflected the quality and passivity characteristic of the less exuberant, more fragile and sensitive Woodrow-Williamson inheritance. But he was not to become a "delicate" little boy. Quiet and dreamy at times, he loved to lie on the floor and be read to. In his play a creator of imaginative adventures and an organizer of his playmates for participation in these "adventures," he was always ready for excited vigorous games when his father abandoned lessons and gave vent to his own exuberant spirit. No, the training of mind and spirit was never to the neglect or at the expense of his physical wellbeing. And even in the less dynamic climate and ravaged state of post-Civil-War Georgia he was to retain his native endowment and remain a sound and healthy child, slowly and soundly developing the special gifts of his heritage.

Development of the Personality

All growth is largely a matter of "aging." During the nine prenatal months, the growth was physical. Week by week after birth, and accompanying the physical, the aging process would become one of experience and behavioral reaction to it. Researchers in human behavior have noted that the now well-established cyclic nature of personality-development in children from the age of two years to adolescence is equally operative—but at a much more rapid rate of change—in infants during the supremely important first 18 to 24 months of the new free life.

So, as aging begins at birth, behavior also "grows," to quote Drs. Gesell and Ilg.[6] And that growth follows a reasonable and measurably predictable pattern, as does the growing body—predictable within the limits set by normal or abnormal environment and experience.

Normal and Abnormal

The story of this life whose inception we are studying, is, on the physical side, that of the struggle of a sound and normal organism (one that was high-powered, sensitive, and in extreme crises nervously vulnerable) to sustain a creative, vigorous and ardent mind in its thrust and surge, through times and through a career in which cumulative tensions and frustrations inevitably mounted steadily. The opposition which Wilson's aggressive leadership was to engender also engendered abnormal fields of resistance which only a superman could have surmounted. His was not a super-organism, only a superior one with very real handicaps and limitations.

Climatically, the setting of his life and labors, largely in southerly lowland localities from childhood to old age, was not normal for his Staunton-born Kelto-Nordic Scotch-American organism. Boyhood in Augusta, Georgia, during the Civil War and Reconstruction; youth in the Carolinas, at Columbia and Wilmington; mature years in tidewater areas such as Princeton, Baltimore, Washington and Paris—these scenes of an arduous career were favorable for the mind but not for the body that was Woodrow Wilson's.

Dietetically, his regimen in youth and maturity, and until Dr. Grayson came to his rescue in 1912, would not be the best for this particular organism. The Southern menus of his mother (when, after the period of Civil War deficiency, something of the old richness of cookery was restored) were doubtless delicious; and those of his wife Ellen, who for his sake studied the art of cookery from one of the foremost dietary experts of the day in Philadelphia, were, it is said, both delicious and to a large degree wholesome. But definitely, neither had substantiality of the sort to produce a physical vigor like that of his Scotch forbears.

Both the climatic and dietetic factors probably combined to accentuate the episodes of physical depletion which developed in late youth—coupled with an inherited neural sensitivity this was to culminate, due to fatigue and extreme and continuous overexertion, in the cerebral hemophlegia of his 65th year. Low altitudes and warm humid climate do not harden nerve fibre—they soften it—and the consequent susceptibility was to increase through the years even though Woodrow Wilson regularly sought relief from these disabling climatic influences in summer, during the good years of his middle life.

After maturity, the unrelenting habit of overwork (more than was "normal" for his body) was to result in cumulative fatigue and periods of enforced rest. The effect of these episodes, none too serious in itself, was accentuated by a series of abnormal situations precipitated by or resulting from his ambition and his pyramiding career, and by the suppression of his normal mode of living, self-expression and achievement (private, domestic, artistic, literary, scholarly, social) which the career entailed. All this combined with the factors already mentioned to accelerate the process of aging.

Yet this aging was not abnormal; he lived to be 68. On the contrary, hard striving developed to the maximum every normal faculty and energy of the organism, through articulate and dynamic action, enabling that good body to transcend, throughout his maturity and right up to the very end, every minor abnormality. Rarely has a man so gifted—who regarded himself always as utterly expendable, who never spared himself, who weathered so many supreme crises—lived so sound, so normal, so whole and so happy a life. His sound heritage, his advantageous place and season of birth, his early nurturing, all combined to give both the foundation and the impetus for this development.

The Body and the Person

The time at Staunton was a period during which this small human organism was almost wholly vegetative. The vegetative or autonomic nervous system motivates the vital functions of the body and is there and ready, after the first breath, to come into full play with all the intricate movements of a living body controlled by nerves, acting through organs, glands and muscles. This vegetative system remains primal throughout life. The seat of intelligence, the central nervous system in brain pinioned on spine, is there, but at birth is still dormant. Its rude or happy awakening and education must await the stimuli and experience that cannot commence until the organism is exposed to the contacts arising out of its activity as a living, sentient creature.

As neural psychologists point out, organic cravings, at the start of the life process, are the sole originators of activity. The infant human being, like the small puppy, at first sucks, squirms or cries only because its stomach is empty (or too full) or its digestive processes impeded and causing physical distress, or because of some other reaction of the vegetative nervous system to cold, heat or pain. These nervous responses of pleasure and pain and the cravings they arouse become more complex as the life experience proceeds, but, as Allport puts it:[7]

> The vegetative nervous system, where these cravings originate, is thought to be more primitive and more essential than the central nervous system which is primarily an agency of adjustment. The vegetative system is the master, the cerebro-spinal is the servant; the former compels adjustment, the latter effects adjustment.

Even though we develop the thesis that the innate qualities inherent in this child, which made him a great thinker and leader, were a matter of heredity plus heritage, and interpret the evidence as indicating that the endowment so received was but a vehicle for the ardent spirit that ceaselessly animated this person, we give full weight nonetheless to the importance of recognizing the plasticity of this organism that *was* the vehicle for the person who grew to the stature of Woodrow Wilson. The body was the horse, Woodrow Wilson its rider. And he rode it hard.

He was in the beneficent environment of Staunton scarcely more than a year. But this measure of time omits the all-important nine months when he was in his mother's womb and the preceding months when her own body was being nourished by its beneficence. From late March in 1856, when the embryo took root, until December 28, when he was born, the foetus was absorbing through the placenta attached to the wall of the mother's uterus the abundant nutrients of the Valley foodstuffs. This period, plus the year in the physically and emotionally wholesome climate of the Staunton Manse after he was born, launched a sound and vital body on its career. His attachment in later years to his birthplace was reasonable and right, for that spot of good earth, in its bounty, gave a lifelong blessing.

As we have observed elsewhere with respect to Hippocrates' insight into the effect of atmospheric conditions on the human organism, there is much in modern science that is but an elaboration of classical conceptions. We now know more, thanks to better means of observation and to the accumulation of accurate and adequate records, but what we know is engrafted upon the rootstocks of knowledge of our Graeco-Roman intellectual forebears.

Heading his chapter on "Foundations of Personality," Allport quotes Cicero:[8]

> Nature, then, has generated and fashioned man's body in such a way that some parts of it were perfect at birth, others were formed as its age increased, without much use of external and adventitious aids. Now in other respects she made the mind as perfect as the body, endowing it with sense capable of perceiving things, so that little or no assistance of any sort was needful to supplement them. But that faculty which is highest and most excellent in man she left lacking . . . she furnished merely the rudiments; nothing more.

Allport himself defines the human endowment at birth with more precision:[9]

> The three principal raw materials of personality, *physique*, the endowment of *intelligence*, and *temperament*, are genetically determined through structural inheritance, and are only slightly altered by conditions existing subsequent to birth. They are the effective agencies of heredity entering the process of growth at every stage to influence the development of traits and attitudes. Sometimes they accelerate the molding influence of the environment; sometimes they place limitations upon it; but always their force is felt.

If man's crowning gift or endowment—intelligence or the capacity for intelligence—is innately there at birth, what more can be added to complete the whole man? The answer is: direction, growth and experience. The career of the man this child was destined to become is an exemplification of the fact that growth is channeled and character crystallized by three major factors: milieu, relationships and genius. The degree to which genius is important depends upon how much genius is there. Woodrow Wilson's life is one in which innate qualities of genius are of prime importance—his genius and that of two others. He became a leader, statesman and prophet because of the interplay of his own unique spiritual genius with many to whom he was related. But in the years of his growth and maturation, although many were stimulators and sharers along the way, there were two who were his great companions—first his father, and later his wife, Ellen.

This is not a matter of our judgment, but of Woodrow Wilson's own. To his father, in mature life, he wrote:[10]

> As you know, one of the chief things about which I feel most warranted in rejoicing is that I am your son. I realize the benefit of being your son more and more as my talents and experience grow; I recognize the strength growing in me as of the nature of your strength, I become more and more conscious of the hereditary strength which I possess, the capital of principle, of literary force and skill, of capacity for first-hand thought . . . You have given me a love that grows, that is stronger in me now that I am a man than it was when I was a boy, and which will be stronger in me when I am an old man than it is now . . . a love resting upon abiding foundations of service, recognizing you as in a certain very real sense the author of all I have to be grateful for. . . .

To his wife, Ellen Axson Wilson, he wrote in 1889:[11]

> I never discovered my real self till you brought your sweet love and sympathy into my life. You have 'drawn me out,' as I have often told you, as I never would have been drawn out had you not been so daring as to love and marry me. Your love has brought to me self-revelation of the most remarkable kind.

Just when a human organism becomes a person is a moot question. The moment probably is that time when self-consciousness first dawns upon the mind of an infant. Altogether an illusion is the almost universal thought of parents that a baby's gaze—sometimes placid, sometimes bright with interest, often stormy—is one of recognition. Facial expressions, before mental activity begins, are the random reflexes of the autonomic nervous system resulting from a variety of physical stimuli, internal or external. They do not denote conscious delight, affection, anger or fear. These are the responses of the thinking person, and (according to Allport, whose study of personality we are following) for all its intricate neuro-psychic equipment, incipient talents and capacities, "the newborn infant lacks personality," and does not inherit it.[12]

Throughout the first six months of an infant's life, his senses only gradually begin to achieve true awareness of his surroundings or any identification with the person or sound seen or heard. In the remaining six months of the first year, the behavioral growth is more rapid. From almost complete passivity in the reception of objects or attention the child begins actively to seek contacts, devise means of attracting attention, react delightedly to play, such as the time-honored "peek-a-boo," and show curiosity concerning half-hidden objects. These actions and reactions will be comparable but uniquely different for each infant. The development of personality has begun.

Upon this development, during his first year of experience of the outer world, certain aspects of the life in the Manse at Staunton would have made their indelible impress. Here the basis would have been laid (to be reinforced in subsequent years by life in "the Manse" elsewhere) for that assured sense of status, that reliance upon intellect engendered by an intellectual environment, that dependence upon affection and that passion for privacy which were to mark so strongly the temperament of Woodrow Wilson throughout his life—all this quite unconsciously absorbed by the small personality now actively developing. The jealously guarded privacy of family life in the Manse, with few intimates; the pleasant comfort of life there, ministered to by devoted mother and kindly servants; the honored place in the community which occupancy of the Manse indicated—all these factors, their significance not yet comprehended by the infant and growing child, were as important in the formation of his personality as were the locale and climate.

After describing a variety of studies of infants, Allport draws four important conclusions "from the evidence now in hand":

1) The growth of personality though not yet formed, "may be said to begin at birth."

2) The developing personality, however, showing itself in "spontaneous activity" and in "emotional expression," is in both instances reflecting inherited factors.

3) This growth process "probably" does not involve real "learning" during the first three months of postnatal life; distinctive personality responses come after the sixth month.

4) These earliest distinctive qualities "tend to persist," and from them, later personality traits can be predicted.[13]

The studies of psychologists are a matter of contemporaneous appraisal plus retrospect in terms of childhood years shortly following infancy. What may we say in retrospect of the infant that became Woodrow Wilson, in the light of knowledge of his whole life span? Paraphrasing Allport's four conclusions we may say:

1) That the baby born in the Manse on December 28, 1856, was on the threshold of an adjustment to his environment, which at long last would lead to his willingly laying down his life for his fellow men. In

other words, the stage was set for the growth of the directive intelligence which would completely supersede the primal vegetative creature which for a short time he would continue to be.

2) That the intensity and capacity for deep, consistently channeled emotion through his maturing and mature years must have been there from the beginning. The remarked-on quiescence of this baby was the stillness of a powerful temperament poised for early flight.

3) That by the second half of the first year, the cheer, animation and heartiness of Joseph and the benign care of Jeanie already were working their magic of heart and mind on the budding intelligence and latent temperament of their little son.

4) That those qualities so distinctive of Woodrow Wilson the man—extraversion, one-pointedness, self-containment and attachment—must have been apparent from the beginning, had there been an observer interested to record them.

Warp and Weft

We want an exact definition of what this child was, because the man he became was cut sharp and true in shape and substance, whole cloth out of the warp of his breed, with a weft out of the times and places that gave a pattern to his forbears, to his kith and kin, and to him. To know the Wilsons and the Woodrows and their congeners, and when and where and how they lived—to know not casually, in generalities, but with precision—we must examine the past in detail, for everything about Woodrow Wilson was precise, wrought in character by heredity, heritage and experience. Experience began at Staunton. But heredity and heritage reach back through Ohio and Pennsylvania to Ulster in Northern Ireland and to Scotland.

BACKGROUND IN IRELAND

The Wilson Search

When Ray Stannard Baker, to whom Woodrow Wilson entrusted all his public and private papers before his death, set out to write an account of the President's ancestry for the first volume of *Woodrow Wilson, Life and Letters,* he found a remarkable scarcity of exact information concerning the Wilson family origins, as compared with that concerning the Woodrows.

James Wilson, the President's grandfather, had arrived in Philadelphia in 1807 as a youth of 20, emigrating from Ulster (in North Ireland, it was thought "near Londonderry") and going straight to a printer's job on William Duane's newspaper, the *Aurora*. Beyond these meager facts of his origin, the records concerned with the quite notable activities of his life in America are silent, and those among his descendants who were still living, in the 1920s, apparently knew or remembered little to augment them. There were no traditions extant as to *why* he, or his future bride Ann Adams, had come, although the hard conditions in Ulster following "the Ninety Eight"—the Irish rebellion of 1798—would be reason enough. Nor were there any stories to suggest what had been their occupation or station of life in the old country. The two circumstances in which his most famous grandson, Thomas Woodrow Wilson, gloried were that James Wilson was, in his lifetime in America, ever in the forefront of the fight for liberty of thought and action, and that he was of that "tough Scotch-Irish breed" which put fire and a hard joy into the fight whatever be involved, whether physical life itself or political and religious principle. But *was* he of the Scotch-Irish breed? Might not the Wilson surname have come into Ulster during the early period of the London Plantation along with the English colonists of that time? And might not the doughty James Wilson, despite his fiery yet genially expansive temperament, so typical of the Ulsterman, turn out, on closer inquiry, to be a great disappointment to those of his descendants who had prided themselves on their Irish as well as their Scottish blood? This was a possibility to be reckoned with.

In so reckoning, various decisive facts emerged. Long before so-called "family names" had come into use as hereditary designations (and this was, in the British Isles, not until after the Norman Conquest), it had been the custom to give descriptive designations to individuals, both for local convenience and for greater exactitude on the tithe and rent rolls. This descriptive term might indicate occupation, locality, relationship to a liege lord or demesne, or it might (particularly for baptismal records) be simply "son of." This "son of Will," "Will's son," "son of William" or "William's son" became sometimes Williamson, sometimes Wilson, as the name later came to be formalized into a true surname. In Ireland and Scotland the Gaelic prefix *mac*, meaning "son of," or *O*, meaning in descent from, was the more usual designation. But as English influence spread northward in the centuries between the Saxon conquest of England and the Norman invasion, and the Lowlands of Scotland (as distinct from the unconquered Highlands) took on more and more of the English ways, the old Gaelic began to give place to English forms, particularly in the makeup of names. So by the time established surnames became the fashion, there were as many "sons of" Andrew and Robert and Will as there were "Macs" on the record books of Scotland. It is interesting to discover that by the seventeenth and eighteenth centuries *Wilson* was one of the twelve principal family names in all Scotland in point of numerical prominence.

If James Wilson's paternal forebears were not among the North Irish who migrated to Scotland and returned, but had been continuously settled in Ireland from their beginnings, there is still good reason for giving credence to their Irish rather than English ancestry, despite the form of the name. For as early as 1465, the Parliament of Ireland in Dublin enacted a requirement that all Irish living "within the Pale" (that is within the territorial limits of the Anglo-Norman conquest of Ireland at that time) should take English names and as far as possible "live like Englishmen." Although the latter part of the requirement was scarcely successful, large numbers of natives did Anglicize their names—either by changing *mac* or *o* to *son*, or, in the case of occupational designations, by taking the phonetic English equivalent (such as Carpenter or Carter, instead of MacIntire or McCarthy).[1] In any event, Wilsons who regard themselves as authentic Irishmen are scattered plentifully all over Ireland today.

This became clear when the effort was made, during the preparation of Baker's biography, to push back the borders of knowledge a little further in North Ireland, for investigators in genealogical libraries and public records soon found themselves, it is said, floundering in "an ocean of Wilsons," from which they withdrew with no tangible leads in any direction. And so, for twenty years, the matter had rested (so far as publication was concerned) on the western side of the water: James Wilson and his wife Ann Adams came from Ulster—"it was thought near Londonderry," "possibly county Down or Antrim."

Then in the summer of 1956—the Woodrow Wilson Centennial year—with new biographies and appraisals in the making, a young scientific scholar with peculiarly appropriate qualifications was sent upon a new search. David H. Kelley, graduate at Harvard University, veteran of the second World War and of subsequent archaeological expeditions, a trained genealogist and (perhaps even more significant) an Irishman by blood with a warm approach to people, was chosen to go overseas to Ulster to see what he might unearth in the long buried Wilson background. The story of "the search" came back in fascinating day-by-day jottings and reports.

Mr. Kelley went directly to Dublin to start his paper search in the Genealogical Office. There, and later in Belfast, in the famous Linenhall Library, the Public Records Office and Presbyterian Historical Society, he found himself quickly engulfed in that "ocean of Wilsons" about which earlier searchers had complained. Anyone familiar with genealogical search knows the meticulous hours that must be spent in checking references, running down dates and clues, following false scents. Days passed and references accumulated, none of them definite. But in Belfast he soon discovered that he was eliciting warm interest in his search.

The first tangible lead came when a helpful clerk in the Public Records Office telephoned to a Reverend Robert Allen, at the Presbyterian Historical Society, who she felt might know where James Wilson had come from, and he had replied, without hesitation: County Tyrone—"completely away from any district I had been considering," wrote Kelley. On the heels of this lead came another. Mr. Vitty of the Linenhall Library hailed him on the street to say that he had heard of a gentleman reputed to have full information on James Wilson. Did Mr. Kelley wish to write to him? Though not the "full" information hoped for, this contact proved to be another straw blowing in the new direction. The gentleman replied regretting that he could not be of much positive help, but adding "For myself, I always understood James Wilson was a native of Strabane, County Tyrone."

The next day, on the way to the bus station, his friend from the Public Records Office saw and beckoned him. She had been talking with her uncle the previous evening about the Wilson search, and he had said "Why yes, Wilson came from Strabane in Tyrone." He also recounted to her an amusing yarn. When Woodrow Wilson was first elected President there was such wild elation in Strabane that there was a good deal of property damage, and somebody got the idea of sending the bill to the United States Government, and that it was duly paid. Whatever the rights or wrongs of this tale, Strabane now seemed to be a strong claimant for Wilson honors.

That evening, checking the files of the Belfast *Evening Telegraph* for possible additional clues, an article on Woodrow Wilson came to light (it was republished later in a pamphlet called *Ulster Links with the White House*). This article stated that James Wilson, the President's grandfather, was a native of Dergalt, near Strabane, and had worked in a printshop at Strabane before emigrating.

So the straws drifting toward County Tyrone accumulated, and interest in that aspect of the search became brisker with the freshening winds of anecdote and speculation. Mr. Kelley learned that the Dukedom of Abercorn had encompassed the town of Strabane and its countryside since the earliest days of the seventeenth century "Plantation." Knowing that in the Woodrow Wilson family there had been a tradition of some vague connection with the Abercorn title, he wrote to the present incumbent at "Baronscourt" near Strabane with the suggestion that the family of this "James Wilson of Tyrone" might have been a tenant of the Dukes of Abercorn. The Duke's reply was disappointing, for he wrote that all the records of his estates in the Strabane area were destroyed by fire in 1912, but he too had always understood that James Wilson came from the Strabane area.

Other inquiries brought more heartening returns. An introduction to the Reverend Mr. McClelland, minister of the First Presbyterian Church of Strabane, from a fellow cleric in the Belfast area whose interest Mr. Kelley had aroused, elicited a friendly reply, with the assurance that "the Wilsons" still lived on the old farm at Dergalt where James, the President's grandfather, had been born. This, wrote Dave Kelley, "made the trip to Strabane very exciting."

The Strabane Story

County Tyrone is in the very heart of Ulster—east of Donegal, west of Antrim and Down, south of the rugged north coastline of Derry. Its

111

varied area of stream and plain, stony crag, bog and wooded glen abounds in ruins and relics and, for the Ulsterman, is rich in cherished remembrances out of Ulster's long and stormy history.

The thriving market town of Strabane (pronounced Strahbahn, which in Gaelic means The Fair Holm, or The Fair River Meadow) is set amid rich river-bottom lands, but with mountains or hills everywhere forming the distant and nearer prospect. The town lies on the river Mourne, which at this point forms the eastern border of county Donegal and the barrier between Ulster and the Republic of Eire. It is today the most important of the towns of Tyrone, both in size and in the perspective of history. It still preserves, in the center of town, many ancient features which must look much as they did in James Wilson's time, but many more, such as the old castle, are long since gone, though "Castle Street" remains. Not even the present Presbyterian Church on Meeting House Street is old; being neither the original "Meeting House" of mud and thatch built in 1693, nor even its late successor, destroyed by fire in 1938. It was to the new church parsonage that Mr. Kelley went to meet the Reverend Mr. McClelland, who had volunteered to give whatever guidance he could.

Mr. Kelley's next visit was to the Main Street, to the home of Robert Wilson, who had moved to town with his family from the family farm at Dergalt, and had opened a grocery. "Oh, aye," Mr. Wilson said cheerfully and matter-of-factly, he was a relative of President Wilson, although how close the relationship might be he could not say, for he possessed no family records. He was most cordial, however, and invited the visitor in to tea. After tea, he took Mr. Kelley to Gray's, the old printshop where, according to Strabane tradition, James Wilson had his apprenticeship. The Gray family had given up the printing business only about five years before, but the Maginnises still carried on the tradition. Mr. Kelley was shown the old printing press, bought long ago in Edinburgh, which still sat in a backroom up some old, badly worn flagstone steps. Here James Wilson, he was again assured, had learned the printing trade.

Actually the press is identical with the "Columbia" press invented and manufactured in Philadelphia a few years after James Wilson left Ulster, and though it soon supplanted the old wooden handpresses, James Wilson must have learned his trade on a more primitive style of press. But again unfortunately, Gray's file of records did not go back as far as a hundred and fifty years.

112

Strabane, County Tyrone, in Northern Ireland

–Lorna E. Freeman

However, one bit of history emerged which in itself seemed to offer strong associative corroboration of James Wilson's apprenticeship at Gray's. This was that John Dunlap, famous printer of the Declaration of Independence, also had been apprenticed at Gray's, and had gone to Philadelphia at the summons of his uncle William Dunlap, also formerly of Strabane, to take charge of his printshop there. John Dunlap inaugurated a newspaper, the *Pennsylvania Packet and General Advertizer* in 1771, which some ten years later became the first daily newspaper in the United States, now the *Philadelphia Inquirer*. He was the first printer to Congress, and printed both the Declaration of Independence and the Constitution. He retired in 1785 and died on November 27, 1812. Thus there already was a traditional connection between Gray's and America, when James Wilson came to his apprenticeship and every reason why he should follow it. When he arrived in Philadelphia in 1807, the "grand old man" of Philadelphia printing, a native of Strabane and former apprentice of the same printshop, was still alive.

On another day, the Reverend Mr. McClelland took Mr. Kelley out through the lovely countryside of small rounded hills and level meadow and farm lands between meandering streams, to meet the Wilsons of Dergalt and see the farm where James Wilson spent his boyhood. Here again he met with cordial hospitality and keen interest in a visitor from overseas. The thatched cottage into which he was invited for talk and tea was the old family farmhouse James Wilson had known, though added to by later generations. But indoors, James would not have recognized the "wireless set" or the wall decorations—photographs in color of little Prince Charles and Princess Anne, and black and white reproductions of Gene Autry and other Hollywood "royalty."

The two bachelor brothers and the two spinster sisters still at home, product of generations raised on this same Irish soil, were alert and modern in their interests, Dave Kelley wrote, but true country people in their attachment to the land. He was reminded of an old saying of his own father's: "The true Irish, that never leave the cow's tail."

The days that followed were crowded with the various lines of pursuit a researcher must follow in order to be assured that no possible source of exact data has been overlooked. Crowded old graveyards were searched—wherever possible among the tangle of underbrush—but the worn stones offered no legible names of the parents or brothers of James the emigrant. Parish and school records were examined, but there again the chief enemy of exact history—fire—had destroyed everything

114

before 1800. The Presbyterian baptismal records carried the Wilsons of Dergalt back almost far enough, but not quite into James's or his parents' day.

Although so-called "documentary proof" seemed elusive, there was ample certitude in the community recollection, as in the family tradition. Mr. Kelley met and interviewed people who "had it from the old folks"—James Bradley of the Urban District Council, Eugene Gormley, stationer and local historian, Edward McIntire, librarian of Lifford (across the river in the Free State), Wilson and Sims, lawyers of Strabane, the parson at Ballymagorry manse, and many others, including all the Wilsons and relatives of Wilsons that he could discover. He was referred to many a printed page concerning Strabane, official and otherwise, which pointed with special pride to this particular James Wilson among others of the town's notable sons.[2] In the end, this part of his investigations concluded, David Kelley left the green hills of Tyrone with the conviction that this without doubt was the land that had nurtured Woodrow Wilson's paternal grandfather and his forebears.

Woodrow Wilson, throughout his life, showed great interest in his Scottish Woodrow heritage. But not, so far as we know, in the Scotch-Irish Wilson background. Why was this? At the time of his election it certainly was known across the water that his grandfather had been James Wilson of Strabane. Yet Ray Stannard Baker, the official biographer, who knew only that James Wilson came from somewhere "near Londonderry," failed to learn more than this either from Wilson himself or from his correspondence with other family members, although there is documentary evidence that the town council of Strabane sent to Woodrow Wilson, from "the town of your ancestors . . ." a message of congratulation which he acknowledged.

Woodrow Wilson admired his father so intensely that it seems strange that his interest in his father's parents would be negative.

Two facts may have bearing on this. Joseph Ruggles Wilson was antipathetic to his brothers after the Civil War, because of a quarrel over the rightness of the secession of the Southern States. In the home of Joseph Ruggles Wilson, this undoubtedly made the subject of his family painful and embarrassing to the father, and hence to his loyal and admiring son.

A second reason for Woodrow Wilson's lack of interest in the Ulster relationship may have been that during World War I, the whole situation in Ireland, both North and South, in relation to Great Britain and

115

the Allies, was reprehensible. Both Sinn Fein and Ulster Irish leadership had a pro-German attitude, and, after the war was ended, deValera tried to persuade or force Wilson and the United States to sanction the Irish rebellion. Some Irish-Americans were among the hyphenates who were something of a problem during the war; and in the late stages of the negotiations in Paris, when American-British relationships were none too happy, a group of Irish-Americans visiting Dublin indulged in a broadside of gratuitous insults to England which angered Wilson greatly. Altogether, there were many reasons why Woodrow Wilson should not have wanted to stress his kinship with the Irish, even the Ulster Irish, in his late years.

Subsequent Visit to Strabane

In the summer of 1957, the authors visited Northern Ireland in order to know the terrain and the present-day Wilsons at first hand and arrive at their own conclusions. It had been a summer of unusual rain, even for Ireland, and the first glimpse of the Strabane countryside in late July was one of extraordinary verdure and richness. Strabane itself was gray and venerable looking, under a gray or changeable sky. The "Abercorn Arms" inn in Castle Street, much frequented by parties come for sport fishing in the famous rivers Mourne and Foyle, offered a quaint return to the past century. Only the motorcar traffic on the streets, the commodities in shop windows, and the varied costume of the crowding city dwellers on the sidewalks spoke of modernity—these, and the pleasant flat of the Robert Wilsons to which we were invited for a Sunday afternoon tea.

Mr. Robert Wilson had welcomed these unheralded visitors with the utmost cordiality, and with pleasant recollections of Mr. Kelley's visit the summer before. Mrs. Wilson could not have been more hospitable in her kindness and in her amply furnished tea table. The two daughters and two sons, handsome children all in their low teens or younger, were shyly friendly and soon lost their constraint in the warmth of the family gathering. They were Elizabeth and Margaret, John Knox and Thomas Woodrow Ian Wilson, aged twelve.

This younger lad had been named by his paternal grandmother, except for the "Ian" which his mother had added, feeling that the other might be a right heavy load for young shoulders. But though it had led to a few fisticuffs when first he entered school and the older boys had nicknamed him "President Wilson," that difficulty was soon settled,

116

and Woodrow he had elected to remain, the "Ian" unused as the intended safety valve for troubled sensibilities. An unassuming boy, quickwitted and likeable, funloving, he is modestly proud of his famous name. Later, when acquaintance had sufficiently ripened, he shyly offered the visitors his photograph, which he signed simply, in a firm round careful script, "Woodrow Wilson."

Mrs. Robert Wilson's two sisters, Winifred and Kathleen, had been summoned from Belfast to meet the visitors from America. They too, the Colhoun family, belonged to the Tyrone rural area and had been born and reared near Strabane. Woodrow's young aunts, Winifred and Kathleen had moved away to the more cosmopolitan world of the Ulster capital, but they remained firmly centered in the Tyrone home life. Attractive landscape paintings from Aunt Winnie's hand adorned the Wilsons' living room, hung above piano and fireplace, and the presence of the two sisters that afternoon, with their vivid interest and vivacity, brought added warmth to the family circle. (They were to offer the most wholehearted, spontaneous and delightful hospitality of their own home later on their return to Belfast. The visitors were treated to so much kindness that they left Ireland with the warm feeling of old family acquaintances.)

In Strabane, our walks through town and along roads that led up over gentle hills overlooking the countryside were augmented by drives with the Robert Wilsons in their car to see the wild beauties of the Gortin Glen, a view of the ruined castle of Newtownstewart, and along the winding River Mourne, placid in the open, tumbling through the glens. "And over there's Bessy Bell," said Mr. Wilson, pointing to a hill, steeper and more individual than the others. "Bessy Bell!" Reminder of Staunton in far-off Virginia! And was there a "Mary Gray"? "Oh, aye— just there, a bit further on." And small Margaret chimed in:

> Bessy Bell and Mary Gray
> Were twa bonnie lassies;
> They built their house on yon burn brae
> An' cower'd it o'er wi' rashes.

The Wilsons remembered no more than this of the old ballad. They were astonished to learn that it was known in Staunton, and that two hills of like name are within sight of the Manse where their distant cousin was born. They counted it a quaint coincidence—that James Wilson in Ireland and his grandson in Virginia both should have been born within the sphere, so to speak, of these legendary hill-sprites' habitations.

On another evening—the late light evening of the Northern Ireland summer—instead of to the upland regions of brown bog (where "turf" was being cut and piled for peat-burning) and fells yellow with brae-weed flowers and dotted here and there with the purple of heather just beginning to blossom, we were taken on a visit to the family at the Dergalt Farm.

The Family at Dergalt Farm

This is a thirty-acre farm whose fields run back up a gentle slope, where crops of potatoes and "corn" (oats) are rotated with hay and grazing in fields of from four to six acres framed in rough stone, sod and hedge fencing. Cropping on these acres occupies the full time of the two Wilson brothers, William and Lowther, who with their sisters Susan and Margaret and the younger brother Robert were the present generation of owners. Robert, who now gives his time fully to his prosperous grocery business in Strabane, also was born here and, like the elders, had his elementary schooling in Dergalt school.

The approach to the farm gives a sense of its antiquity. It is along a stone-surfaced narrow winding lane between vertical banks at least five feet high on either side, just wide enough for Robert's grocer's van to pass through. The original cottage, now the kitchen-living room, looks as old as the ancient home of the Stewarts on the adjoining farm, where we paused for a visit on our way in. That Stewart homestead, we were told, is 500 years old. Mrs. Stewart is an elder sister in the present generation of Dergalt Wilsons. In the Stewart cottage, cooking was still done over an open peat fire in the great fireplace, with its big iron pot hanging from a crane, and its raised hearth with nooks in each corner where shoes and woolens are put to dry. This house and its farm have been in the Stewart family from time immemorial.

How long the Wilson farmhouse at Dergalt has belonged to the Wilsons no one knows, but Robert Wilson, the grocer, knows that his great-grandfather Wilson was born there. Allowing 30 years for each generation behind Robert, this takes it back about 130 years: (Robert, in 1957, was about 40 years old.) In other words this takes it to 1820, which approximates the time when James Wilson was living at Steubenville, Ohio, and it may be presumed that Robert's great-great-grandfather, who was farming this land then, was a brother of the James who migrated to America in 1807.

The brothers William and Lowther and Robert showed us their new

The Wilson Farmstead at Dergalt

–Lorna E. Freeman

poultry house, where one of the sisters kept a large flock of laying hens; and a new byre (cowstable) where they wintered their "oxen" (steers), but which at this season housed a flock of young turkeys. We strolled up a lane between fields and viewed the stand of thriving potatoes, while discussing the problems of weather, spraying, manuring, rotation, cultivation and harvesting. After having admired the rich black soil and the flourishing crops—especially a pasture rich with white clover which they call "Devon rambler" (in America "ladino")—we walked back to the house. Passing through the barnyard, we observed the big double plow and cultivator that they attach to their tractor.

The kitchen-living room of the old cottage is certainly very old. Its floor is clay. Its walls, several feet thick, are of fieldstone mortared and plastered with clay and whitewashed. Joists whose ends rest on top of the walls are rough-hewn and by no means straight timbers, and the rafters and ridge pole are similar, though smaller. On the upper side of the rafters is an irregular basketwork of trimmed thorn stems, and on top of these, a solid layer of dry matted heather-roots still imbedded in the surface turf, placed here many generations ago and looking almost as smooth and hard as plaster. This is the base upon which the thatch is laid. It is black from centuries of smoke from peat burning in the fireplace.

That broad fireplace stands today as through many generations, but the old grate no longer is in it, nor the crane or cooking pot. Instead, fitting snugly in the neatly whitewashed recess was a large white-enamel-faced stove which burns either peat or coal. Emblazoned across the stove's face was its tradename—quaintly and appropriately—"The President." (No mention was made of this coincidence.)

The boiling water for our tea, served with a hearty country graciousness that was truly Irish, was heated over peat. The delicious great slices of brown "wheaten" bread, thickly covered with home-churned butter, had been baked in this great oven, as had the big apple turnover that was cut and handed round when all the family and guests were gathered in the living room for late refreshments and the children had been persuaded to abandon their games outdoors in the ten o'clock dusk. The menfolk, over tea, continued their talk of farming and of family history; and the women exchanged questions and answers on how gardening and preserving and "deep-freezing" of produce was done in America and in Ireland, with comments on schools and "wireless" programs and such, all with the warm interest of old acquaintance spiced by novelty. There is a friendliness, competence, and sense of solid happiness about both sisters—fair Miss Susan and dark apple-cheeked Miss Mary—that warms the heart of the beholder.

Yes, this cottage is certainly hundreds of years old. As to the land, it seems that no papers cover the title to it. But there is no reason whatever to believe that it was not the Wilson family's holding even long before James Wilson was born there. "Tied to the cow's tail," however, is very much a figure of speech now. Dairying has little place in the economy of these folk, and even grazing beef cattle is secondary to cropping the rich fields in a thoroughly modern manner. In other words, although the homestead is very old and represents the authentic Irish rural tradition, as do its residents, the farming definitely is up to date. William, evidently the manager, is a real countryman, but as a farm operator a modern expert. As one followed his intelligent responses, searching questions and thoughtful comments, one saw clearly how a man of James Wilson's type and gifts could grow up in and emerge from just such a household.

The same quality of vigor and drive, of solid rootage in old principles, along with a readiness to accept the new, to pioneer into new lands, new ventures or, as here at home, new methods—this is marked in these modern brothers, as in their relative of a hundred and fifty years ago. William and Lowther with their modern planning and equipment and grasp of new ways, Robert a successful small urban entrepreneur and man of growing consequence in the town, and another brother, Archibald, who had gone farther afield, have much in common still with the young farm lad James, who apprenticed himself to the printing trade in Strabane and then, when times were hard, took his new skill overseas and forged a distinguished career for himself and for his sons, as pioneer, politician, legislator and founder of a chain of journals of opinion in the new nation. With him, as with the Wilsons who remained in the old country, their Presbyterianism remained a fighting faith.

That James Wilson in the early nineteenth Century was, as described by contemporaries, very much of Robert's solid energetic compact build and florid complexion, but with the Irish blue eyes. In Robert's younger son, Woodrow, the persistence of the blond strain, which is Keltic, is most interesting. His father is brown-eyed and has brown hair. But two of his uncles and three of his aunts on his father's side have hazel-gray eyes and a fair complexion, as does young Woodrow himself.

According to the family history, as we have pieced it together, the present Robert Wilson of Strabane is third cousin of Eleanor Wilson McAdoo, President Wilson's daughter.

American Family	Dergalt Family
James Wilson	James' brother
his son	his son
Joseph Ruggles Wilson	William Wilson
his son	his son
Thomas Woodrow Wilson, second cousin of	Thomas Wilson
his daughter	his son
Eleanor Wilson McAdoo, third cousin of	Robert Wilson

Thomas Woodrow Ian Wilson, therefore, is third cousin-once-removed of Eleanor, and, as youngest son of youngest son, is of the generation that would be the grand-nephew of President Woodrow Wilson, whose namesake he is.

The Ulster Migrations

James Wilson was but one of a breed that swarmed to America out of Ulster in the eighteenth and nineteenth centuries to escape persecution and oppression in the old country—religious, social, political and economic oppression and prejudice of the worst sort. Certainly these were primary factors in shaping the idealism and passionate devotion to social and political justice that distinguished his grandson who was to become, at the climax of an era of economic imperialism, first the spokesman for equalitarian representative government for all classes and interests in the United States, then for self-determination for all peoples everywhere.

The Presbyterian Wilsons of Tyrone had seen no dearth of persecution while they clung tenaciously to their acres near Strabane through shifting episodes of Roman Catholic and Church-of-England domination. The English Crown grant to the Scottish Earl of Abercorn dates from 1613, when the area that now comprises Counties Tyrone and Donegal was a land of harsh desolation, due to the clan wars of the Irish O'Neills and O'Donnells. In this peer's domain, the Dergalt farm lay. It is but a few miles from the boundary which today separates Catholic Eire, the Free State, from the western border of Protestant Ulster. The Wilsons and their neighbors are no strangers to the strife that still flares in a persistent pattern of provocation and outrage across these peaceful-

122

seeming streams and vales, where night and day patrols of the constabulary are routine, augmented in times of special stress by an armed citizen guard, in which every man of the district at some time—and perhaps frequently—does service. So persistent are the age-old animosities, and the more recent ones arising out of the Partition and the avowed determination of the South to reunite the country under the Free State rule.

But in that long-ago time, when mercilessly over a century, the tides of English invasion and religious and economic conquest flowed and ebbed and flowed again, we may reasonably infer that the little thatched farmhouse where James Wilson was born had remained a modest bastion wherein the generations of this Irish family lived on, as farming families have done the world over, through the periodic uprush of war and rarer interludes of peace. They knew where to send the women and children to safe hideouts in the hills when the men gathered to defend the land, and always had the stubborn courage to return to pillaged homes and fields for a fresh beginning.

We do not know when the Dergalt farm of the Wilsons became a freehold, nor in what faraway year it first came into the possession of the family for which it has so long been a cherished home.[3] But there is no reason to suppose that if the Wilsons already were tenants of these fields when the Barony of Abercorn was created they would have been evicted, either then or later. In those days, the new landlord's problem was to attract enough tenants to farm his lands. And subsequently, whether because the Irishmen of the North were a tougher breed than their brothers of the South or because the grantees were of a more reasonable disposition, Ulster folk did not suffer quite the dreadful sequence of grinding poverty, mounting rents and evictions in any degree approaching the scandalous history of South Ireland under absentee English Rule.

It is good to know that the Dergalt home in which James Wilson was born, and which had belonged to this family through so many generations, has been taken over and restored by the National Trust in Northern Ireland.[4] There, in 1957, we were aware that the old farmhouse and the present generation of Wilsons living there epitomized the tenacity and permanence of Northern Ireland's rural folk and their culture.

At the turn of the eighteenth century, when America had been proven to be the greatest and best new horizon for Ulstermen, James

Wilson left home as a late migrant to share in and help make the better life of that young nation. The kinsman of his generation, whoever he was, who inherited the home and the land, continued to stick it out on the old farmstead, to improve the fields and enlarge the house, for love of home and love of Tyrone and the living that was theirs by right of succession and survival.

Strabane was still politically volcanic when James Wilson was a youth. Presumably he had been baptized by the Reverend James Porter, then minister of the Strabane Presbyterian Church and still remembered there for his virulent political satire, "Billy Bluff and the Squire." As a leader in the 1798 revolution, the Reverend Mr. Porter was arrested and convicted on a trumped-up charge of robbery and hanged before his parsonage and church. James, a boy of eleven then, surely remembered these events vividly. His apprenticeship in Strabane in Gray's printshop, where William Dunlap and John, nephew of William, had worked before him and whence he followed the Dunlaps to Philadelphia to begin his own picturesque career as a printing crusader, may not be unrelated to that event in 1798. For the minister who succeeded Mr. Porter in Strabane and who would have been James' religious mentor in his formative years, was the Reverend William Dunlap, probably a cousin of the John then living in Philadelphia. The minister, and hence his flock, would have been in touch at first hand with events and opportunities in the new land.

What Lay Behind

To understand James Wilson's reasons for leaving Ireland, we must consider the times in which he grew up. The rebellion of 1798, bloody though it was, was but a late episode in the long history of repression of the nonconformist faith in all Ulster, and in Strabane, whose site was strategic. In order to perpetuate their worship, ordinations had to be performed in secret. Marriages consummated by dissenting churchmen were declared invalid. Despite Irish resistance to the Cromwellian conquest and hatred for his rule in the North as in the South, repression during this perhaps was less sharp than before. But with the Restoration of the English Crown, and during the whole of the reign of Charles II (1660-80), this repression became persecution. All meetings were forbidden, and the hired soldiery of the English were ordered to prevent any but Church-of-England assembly. Strabane's first recorded nonconformist minister was the Reverend Robert Wilson, installed in 1659, formally deposed for his nonconformity by order of the Crown in 1661 at the beginning of the Restoration, yet continuing secretly to serve his congregation until 1689, when he died a valiant Protestant defender during the Catholic James Second's siege of Derry.[5] Whether this Robert was a forebear of James is unknown, but it is reasonable to infer that he was, as Robert is the name of one of the living members of the Dergalt farm Wilsons. Strabane's first meeting house of dissenters, no doubt one of plaster and thatch with an earthen floor, dared not be built until 1693, after the fall of James II and the advent of the Protestant William of Orange.

But this episode of tolerance was likewise ephemeral. A Presbyterian clergyman-historian of today describes the chief grievances that led nonconformist Ulstermen and their families to migrate to America in great numbers after 1708. Not only was the validity of Presbyterian marriages still denied and Presbyterians forced to pay tithe to the Established Church, but also, he adds:[6]

> Dissenters were barred from teaching in schools. They were compelled to serve as churchwardens (in the Established Church). They were often not allowed to bury their dead without the funeral service (performed by the priest) of the Established Church. Moreover, in the reign of Queen Anne, the Sacramental Test for all officeholders (that is, acknowledgement of the Episcopal Sacraments which non-conformists denied) was restored, and there was considerable interference with Presbyterian ministers and Presbyterian worship.

To this must be added a sequence of material hardships and social and political injustices. Here we may well quote at some length from the writings of two Ulstermen of our own time:[7]

> There were six years of drought between (i.e., including the years) 1714 and 1719. There was disease that caused a high death-rate in sheep in 1716. There was an outbreak of small-pox in 1718. There was a scarcity of silver and copper coin that hampered trade. The woollen industry had languished, and the linen trade was not flourishing. There were three very bad harvests in 1725, 1726, and 1727, so that in 1728 the price of food was higher than in living memory, and the minister of Templepatrick declared that there was not seed enough to sow the ground. There was a great frost in 1739 followed by famine and disease, and Gordon states that in 1740 the mortality caused by scanty and improper food was very high. There was a failure of the potato crop in 1756-7. Then there were the very high rents

and the consequent increase in tithes. By the last quarter of the 18th century, in County Antrim, for example, the leases on Lord Donegall's estate expired, and the rents were then so greatly advanced that thousands of tenants were unable to pay them. The tenants were evicted in great numbers, and these Antrim evictions resulted in a wholesale emigration to North America. . . . We can truly say, then, of these Ulster emigrants in the 18th century, that it was not of their own free will they left their native soil.

What one wonders is: how did they pay for passage to America, and how did they subsist after arrival, until they had built a new life? The answer to this probably is that they were helped by their relatives who had preceded them.

All this was taking place just before our American Revolution. Strabane and its neighboring communities were vividly aware of it. Hayward writes:[8]

In the War of Independence the record of Congress was not good. It would not give Washington enough troops, nor would it properly clothe or equip those he had. And here the sons of Ulster (in America) came forward again, this time on the civil side, and subscribed large sums of money to provide Washington with what he so sorely needed. Blair MacClenaghan gave 50,000 dollars, James Mease and his uncle John gave 25,000 dollars apiece, and John Dunlap did the same; these men came from Strabane in the County of Tyrone.

There were other like contributions from various localities in Ulster.

The younger men from Ulster who were in America volunteered, thousands upon thousands of them, to fight in the armies of General Washington. In the War of Independence "the foremost, the most irreconcilable, the most determined in pushing the quarrel to the last extremity, were those whom the Bishops (of the State Church of Ireland) and Lord Donegall and company had been pleased to drive out of Ulster."[9] Older colonists, sons of earlier emigrants from Ulster, in numbers far greater than their proportion in the population would lead us to expect, were in the forefront of the critical war for men's minds in the New World. There were other Americans of Keltic breed, but not from Ulster, who also were most determined and who risked their all, like Thomas Jefferson, whose ancestors were Welsh and Scottish. And there were too, let us remember, the Washingtons and Lees, and their peers of the Tidewater, whose forebears were English gentry, Anglo-Norman in breed—the officers who led the Scots and Scotch-Irish

126

frontiersmen, and who risked in the venture their heads, their families, their estates and all vested interests, economic, social and cultural.

Again we quote from Hayward:[10]

> One of the greatest events in the history of the world, and by far the greatest single event in the history of the United States of America, was the drawing up and signing of the *Declaration of Independence*. That document is in the handwriting of Ulsterman Charles Thompson of Maghera, Perpetual Secretary to the Continental Congress, whose parents were born and bred in the County Down. This world-shaking document was printed from Thompson's transcription by another Ulsterman, John Dunlap of Strabane, and it was first read in public by Colonel John Nixon, whose father came from Ulster. Of the other signatories of this great charter of freedom and democracy, Whipple, Paine, MacKean, Nelson, Thornton, Taylor and Rutledge were all sons of Ulster families.

Without detracting from the honor due to the scribe, the printer and the signers, all courageously committing treason against the King, the penalty for which was death, it is yet worth recalling before leaving the subject, that it was Thomas Jefferson who *composed* the Document.

All these ferments, at home and abroad, were in the air when James Wilson was child and youth. These, in their more violent aspect, culminated (so far as concerned him) in "The Ninety Eight," an abortive but bloody political rebellion which even crossed religious lines in a combined effort to dislodge the English tyranny so recently vanquished in the American Colonies. Carefully planned but prematurely touched off by hotheads, it came to naught save an intensification of English ruthlessness, which in turn was to remain long an incentive to further political unrest and an example of hopelessness. To James Wilson, as to many other young men at the beginning of the nineteenth century, this sense of hopelessness of the cause of independence at home must have led to the determination to emigrate to the new "Land of the Free," westward across the Atlantic.

The Wilsons are Irish

There is no doubt whatever that the heritage of Joseph Ruggles Wilson, father of the President, though complex—as is that of all the Ulster breeds—was predominantly Gaelic North-Irish.

"Tied to the cow's tail," the old saying often repeated with a twinkle in the eye of elders who like to feel they are native Irish, bespeaks a rural derivation—and, it may be said, the true Irish of olden time *were* herdsmen. It was the Anglo-Normans who brought to Ireland the town. Even as late as 1505 a visiting Englishman wrote this of the Irish of that time: "There is one use amongst them, to keep their cattle and to live themselves the most part of the year in boolies [a temporary dwelling of boughs, covered with turf], pasturing upon the mountain and waste wild places, and removing still to fresh land as they have depastured the former".[11] This is one reason why Irish Scots and Scotch-Irish were among the foremost of the pioneering breeds in the Western Hemisphere. Edmund Spenser, from whose account this quotation is taken, was describing not the ancient Irish of antiquity but those living in Erin in the years just after the earliest settlement of Englishmen in America, on Roanoke Island in 1585. By the next century, these Irish themselves were following "the pioneer trail" to the new continent.

"A strain of Irish blood"

On one occasion before his election as governor of New Jersey, Woodrow Wilson indulged in what evidently was for him a whimsical flight of fancy. He was charming a group of "The Sons of St. Patrick" with a bit of Irish humor shrewdly calculated to titillate the sentiments of his audience, which included members of the Tammany Hall political dynasty. He said: "I am myself happy to believe that there runs in my veins a very considerable strain of Irish blood. I can't prove it from documents, but I have internal evidence. There is something delightful in me that every now and then takes the strain off my Scotch conscience...."[12] Actually we now have external evidence a-plenty to substantiate his "internal evidence." He came by the rollicking Irish spirit that charmed not only the "Sons of St. Patrick" but a considerable majority of the American voting public in his first exhilarating years of political campaigning, directly through his father and his father's father, for the Wilsons of Tyrone County were true North Irish. Certain it is that the rollicking spirit came not from his father's mother, the stern, austerely religious Ann Adams, nor from the scholarly Woodrows. Among earlier biographers it was William Allen White[13] who recognized that Woodrow Wilson was right in thinking himself as Irish, but with Mr. White it was a matter of inference. Now we may add to inference some testimonials from history.

Tirowen

In ancient Keltic times, the northernmost area of Ireland, spanning what now are Counties Donegal, Derry and Tyrone, was called Tirowen. From this was derived the name of that central portion now called Tyrone, where Strabane and Dergalt are located. This area, even to the present day, is inhabited by folk primarily Keltic in type, in contrast to more Nordic types in east and west Ulster.[14] Infusion of blood from Norwegian and Danish invaders by way of the great inlet Lough (Loch) Foyle, and up the river Foyle, was counteracted by the return from Scotland and the western isles of descendants of those Ulstermen who had invaded Pictland and established the kingdom of Scotland. Counties Down and Antrim then were dominated by Anglo-Normans who came first as followers of John de Courcy in the twelfth century. Englishmen also came as colonists to Londonderry, which was set up as a town and plantation area north of Strabane in the seventeenth century. It is certain that many of these English settlers intermarried with the Gaelic Irish of Tyrone County. Crossbreeding in the Wilsons is evident in the brown eyes of one brother and sister and the hazel-gray eyes of another brother and two sisters.

The land roundabout the Fair River Meadow, which later became the town of Strabane, was a favored territory, lying close to the River Mourne where it enters the Foyle. It also was the most strategic inland point in the far north, for here was the best ford giving access to the westward lands of Tirowen. Here cattle grazed in times of peace, and here men feuded, invaded and fought when their chieftains or their restless spirits or hunger or spite incited them to ravage and plunder. So the "fair meadow" was by no means always a place of bucolic tranquility. Indeed this favored spot, by the ford, was destined to be the focus of fierce battles between the O'Neills of a later time and the O'Donnells who entrenched themselves in the western mountains across the river and became their relentless rivals, after the unity wrought by the first O'Neill fell apart. It also was destined, at the Dergalt farm near Strabane, to nourish the forebears in the male line of a man of Ulster breed named Woodrow Wilson, who would fight the good fight for a league of all nations of the earth—an American Presbyterian whose mind and heart may have laid the foundation of a golden age for mankind when war shall be no more, and men of all breeds and faiths shall be equal on earth, as before God.

Strabane as a place of settled life came into existence after the manner of the founding of many Irish towns—following construction of a monastery. The first monastery was built soon after St. Patrick's lifetime on lands given by Earc, widow of the chieftain Muiredach and grandmother of St. Columcille. There were others as the years and the centuries passed, under other famous abbots of the Keltic church, such as St. Cairnach, St. Lughaidh (one of St. Columba's disciples and a descendant of the O'Neill), St. Adaman and St. Colgan. The fortunes of these establishments waxed and waned. In the fourteenth century, a group of Franciscan Friars came from the continent to found their monastery on Church Brae. Mission-minded abbots always had an eye for utility of location as for beauty—and around the religious community gathered the first secular settlement that was to become a village. From the twelfth century on, clan feuds between Tirconaill and Tirowen—the O'Connells and the O'Neills—had ravaged the countryside, making necessary the addition of a castle to the village scene. Thus Strabane developed as a fortified town.

At the beginning of the seventeenth century, when monasticism, under interdiction by the Reformed Church of England, was dead, a new castle was erected here by the first Baron Abercorn of the newly created Barony of Strabane. This was the true beginning of the "modern" town. James I of England, having accomplished the conquest of West Ulster, had granted the Fair Meadow and its lands to James Hamilton, son of the Scottish Earl of Abercorn, of Paisley. That this area on the east bank of the Mourne was mainly Gaelic and already inhabited by thrifty hard-working folk, partly explains the fact that no town plan typical of the Plantation settlements of the London Companies of Derry was designed for Strabane. The other reason is that this was a private royal grant and not a company undertaking. The Baron Abercorn, on his own initiative, set about creating an orderly community with "a strong fair castle," a school, and eighty houses, of stone and timber, to house one hundred and twenty families.[15] In 1613, the town was chartered as a royal borough.

On the site of the present flax market, in Strabane, there previously had stood the Castle of the O'Neill, in its strategic place next the ford where today the bridge crosses the Mourne to Lifford. Across the Mourne and down the Foyle had also stood the castle of the first of the O'Donnells to become a fierce rival of the O'Neills, as the Golden Age faded and gave way to unbridled strife between warring chiefs—strife which culminated in the crescendo of internecine wars that well-nigh

130

bled Tirowen white. A final surge of that Keltic fighting madness had obliterated Strabane momentarily, when Hugh O'Donnell swept into the town with a party of raiders in 1583 and completely destroyed it by fire.

That was just two years before the ill-fated first settlement on Roanoke Island in the New World. Scarcely twenty-five years later, in 1607—the year in which the English colonists were establishing their town on Jamestown Island in Virginia—the tottering elements of West Ulster independence gave way. In that year, the last of the Irish earls of Tyrone, Hugh O'Neill, defeated and dispossessed by the English invaders and with a price on his head, passed through Strabane. He was on his way to join Rory O'Donnell, earl of Tirconaill, defeated and outlawed also. These two erstwhile enemies, in consequence of the long clan feuding which had laid their desolated country wide open to foreign invasion, were on their way to Rathmullan where lay the ship that was to take these last of the dominant lords of North Ireland from their homeland, never to return. This "Flight of the Earls," still mourned in song and story, was the final act in the centuries-long drama in which England had wholly prevailed, and the Baron Abercorn built his "fair castle" and new town round about it.

Yet again, in the rebellion of 1641, when the Roman Catholic town-folk and peasants of Ireland were driven to violence in an attempt to put an end to persecution under Charles I, the wildfire of strife engulfed the town. Strabane was burned and the castle of the Barony reduced to ruins. During these wild years, many Protestants were killed in cold blood as well as in the fighting. A like fate befell many Catholics when the town was retaken by Cromwellian troops in 1656, and again by the Irish in 1688 in resistance to the new Roman Catholic King James II.

Through all these calamities affecting the town's landlords and the clergy and townsmen, we may presume with some certainty that a farm family like that at Dergalt suffered little but hard times and occasional pillage, except for its young masculine hotbloods who doubtless rallied round their minister and their church, imbued with the loyalty and the love of a good fight that is so essentially Irish. In intervals of peace, especially after the defeat of James II and the comparative tolerance enjoyed in the Protestant reign of William and Mary, life could regain a measure of wellbeing for self-supporting dwellers on the land. And in the town, the Strabane markets slowly grew to the position of eminence they were to enjoy most markedly in the late eighteenth and nineteenth centuries, with their great horse and cattle fairs, the busy wheat and flax trading centers, and the early linen mills.

Strabane is a prosperous market town still, but gone are the picturesque fairs, the mills and the tanneries, and the old commodities of trade. It is a humdrum modern mart in an ancient and geographically lovely setting.

Whence Grandmother Adams?

Ann Adams, mother of the Reverend Joseph Ruggles Wilson, has not taken form in the biographies of her famous grandson with as much clarity as her husband has, although family tradition has endowed her with a forceful and indomitable character, a militant Presbyterianism and a fixed purposiveness (which her portrait in middle life entirely substantiates). This is perhaps natural, since her husband was a public personage, writing much and much written about, while she herself was the help-meet and mother, however "masterful" in that domain.

Nevertheless, her recollections, coming down through the generations, serve as chief guide to those in search of Wilson and Adams family origins in the old country.

Because young James Wilson and Ann Adams came over to Philadelphia on the same ship from North Ireland, it has been assumed that they came from the same locality. And because Ann Adams told her children she lived on the coast, so near that they could see the linen drying on the lines in Scotland across the channel, it has been assumed that the place of origin must have been either County Down or County Antrim—for *both* Wilson and Adams. Thus it came as an entire surprise to David Kelley during his 1956 Ulster search to find, as we have seen, the Wilson clues all pointing to County Tyrone, in the midlands.

With the Dergalt farm in the barony of Strabane, County Tyrone, quite well established in local tradition as the birthplace of the James Wilson who went to America in 1807 and became the grandfather of the wartime President, it was disturbing to the investigator (even allowing for probable journalistic inaccuracies thus long after the event) to read a newspaper account published in Belfast during President Woodrow Wilson's incumbency stating that that same James Wilson had married, in Philadelphia, a *Miss Annie Mills*, also from north Ireland! What had become of Ann *Adams*, who married James Wilson in 1808 and bore him ten children?

132

Donaghadee, County Down, Northern Ireland   *Lorna E. Freeman*

Mr. Kelley already had come to the conclusion that of the various but not too numerous Adams families listed in the Public Records Office of Ulster and in the Presbyterian Historical Society of Belfast, only two or three such families lived in areas where the coast of Scotland could have been seen across the North (or St. Patrick's) Channel, outlet between the Irish Sea and the Atlantic Ocean. Of these, the most likely were the Adams families of Donaghadee and of the Ballycopeland-Millisle area in County Down. Could an explanation of that newspaper statement possibly lie in the chance deletion of "Adams" from an old report reading "Annie Adams of Millisle?"

Donaghadee formerly was the principal Ulster port for Scotland, and still has port facilities remarkable in a town of its size. At the turn of the eighteenth century, it would have been a quite feasible point of embarkation for America, by vessel sailing north past the Scottish Firth of Clyde and out to sea through the strait still traversed today by all Atlantic-bound ships from Glasgow and Greenock. But whatever the worth of that supposition, it is clear that Donaghadee is (except for Ballycastle in County Antrim, across the narrow outlet from the Mull of Kintyre) the one point in North Ireland nearest to Scotland, only nineteen miles across the Channel.

Donaghadee is still a quaintly charming small town. Set in the midst of the seaward range of the old town, and quite dominating it,

133

are the green remains of a moat and bailey erected as part of the stronghold of William de Coupland, one of the knights who accompanied de Courcy at the time of the first Anglo-Norman invasion of Ulster in the twelfth century. Now it looks simply like an abrupt artificially raised grassy hill with a winding path leading around it to its summit, and at its top is a crenelated red stone tower of more recent construction. From the tower, one can look over the slate roofs of the ancient town, or out along the rocky curve of the little harbor, to sea. The flat Scottish coast does seem remarkably close. As to "linen on the line," perhaps that was a picturesque exaggeration. Perhaps, on the other hand, shipowners and sailormen's wives used telescopes from this vantage point to spy out their ships. It was a seafaring region, and most men added "mariner" to their other callings.

If Ann Adams Wilson *was* indulging in a bit of Irish exaggeration for the benefit of her children, years later in America, at least we know enough of her sternly righteous nature to be sure that she was not prevaricating. If she so clearly remembered (no doubt with a tinge of nostalgia for the countryside of her youth) that her family had lived within sight of Scotland, then that can be taken as "gospel truth." Probably it had been also a nostalgic saying of her own mother's, as *she* looked across to an older homeland on the Scottish coast and believed with wistful faith that she could see the linen blowing! For all that part of County Down came to be populated largely by Scots, after the fall of the Irish chieftain Con O'Neill and the loss of his lands in Down.

The Donaghadee-Millisle area, at the period of Ann Adams' birth, had an extremely heavy representation of Scottish settlers, first established in Northern Ireland around Carrickfergus in the early sixteenth century and steadily reinforced during later decades, despite the efforts of the encroaching English in the reigns of Henry VIII and his daughter Elizabeth to repulse or contain them. If Ann Adams, then, belonged to the long-established Adams family of this general area—in fact, of either Antrim or Down—she almost certainly was nearly pure Scot by descent, for most of the English colonists of the seventeenth century "Plantation Period" were concentrated elsewhere.

At first glance, there might be some question of the justification for that statement, since the surname *Adams* or *Adamson* is perhaps as numerous among families of English descent as among Scots. With the spreading of Christianity throughout the British Isles, Biblical names were popular as baptismal names wherever the faith became strongly

134

established. As baptismal and tithing rolls became numerous enough to require it, further identification was made by adding "son of . . . " to the "given" name. Often "son of Adam" was written Adamson, or more simply still, Adam's (son being implied). Still further on, when it became the fashion (or more necessary for purposes of public record) to have a second name, the descriptive designation became fixed as a family surname. Even though at this point, for example, a certain Andrew might not actually be the *son* of Adam, but rather Andrew-son-of-Adam's son-Robert, nevertheless his father's patronym became the accepted appellation and was so handed down through later generations.[16]

Before this, and before the penetration of English power, many "Adam's sons" were recorded in the parish records of Scotland. Later, with the waning of the Latin clerical influence in favor of the Gaelic or Saxon tongue, *filius* was changed in the records to *mac* or *son*, or as we have seen, simply *'s*, with the apostrophe elided.

There was a famous Duncan Adam in the reign of Robert Bruce, and his sons founded their families variously as MacAdam, Adams and Adamson, all using the same armorial bearings.[17] Among these Scottish Adams families of all social degrees, it is likely those of less pretentious origin that became the chief adherents of the stern religious teachings of John Knox, after 1560. From them, later in that turbulent century, the first Presbyterian missioners crossed the Channel into Antrim and Down. Once established there, in what became virtually a Scottish colony (though under English rule), the most plausible theory is that these settlers would have continued to marry "within the fold" of their own fighting faith, and that the heritage they handed down was in essence pure Scottish, both in blood and in faith.

Woodrow Wilson's religious heritage came to him strongly from both sides of his lineage, but on the Wilson side it was through his grandmother Ann Adams. She herself was intensely and sternly religious. This trait she transmitted to Joseph Ruggles Wilson, her youngest son, who studied for the ministry, and it appeared also in her grandson Woodrow Wilson, whose face strikingly resembled hers in shape of eyes, nose, mouth and chin, and the lines of the cheeks. The same indomitable quality is in these two faces, and these features likewise distinguish Joseph Ruggles Wilson's portraits. The forthright rugged Scottish look of the well-known Wilson "fighting face" unquestionably came to the President from grandmother Ann Adams, and it had been hers by right of succession from her own forebears. The Scottish Adams family of County Down, as ministers, teachers and men of letters, were the spiritual leaders of their community, while the Irish Wilsons of County Tyrone, settled on a farmstead, became a successful farming family whose younger son James turned his interests and abilities to the printing profession and to politics.

Late in his Wilson investigations at Strabane, David Kelley found a statement which in some degree corroborated his surmise that the reported "Miss Annie Mills" actually was "Miss Annie Adams [of?] Mills." But this statement was equally puzzling. It read that James Wilson married "Miss Annie Adams of *Sion* Mills." As Sion Mills is only a few miles from Strabane it may be that the Strabane folk, seeing a reference to "Miss Annie Adams . . . Mills" would have inferred that she belonged to that area. Nothing beyond that single statement has been found to corroborate it, and one is inclined to think that if James and Ann had been near neighbors—as near as Sion Mills and Dergalt Farm— they most likely would have been married at home before embarking on this journey to the New World. But the evidence points to their having made their acquaintance on shipboard, and they were not married until a year later in Philadelphia, after James was established in the printing trade.[18] However, if it was Annie Adams of Sion Mills whom James Wilson married, then it is clear that she must have moved there lately with her parents or relatives from the locality on the eastern coast where, as a girl, she could remember seeing the shores of western Scotland across the Channel.

Arthur Walworth, author of *Woodrow Wilson, I: American Prophet, II: World Prophet*, visited Strabane in 1967. While there, he heard that members of an Adams family were still living at Zion Mills. He met two of them, and the elder stated that it is a tradition in their family that the Ann Adams who married James Wilson was a member of their family who had lived at Zion Mills. Despite the absence of documentary evidence, it would seem that the tradition itself has reasonable significance.

Sion Mills was not set up as a linen weaving establishment until about 1840, but it is possible that a small settlement of weavers was there before then. An Archibald Wilson is recorded as having come from Island Magee to County Tyrone before 1745 to follow his trade as a linen weaver, indicating a movement of workers to the westward at that time. It may be that an Adams family of Down was among them,

136

and that Ann was of that family. In this case, she and James Wilson probably would have sailed from Londonderry, perhaps a more likely theory than that he would have gone from County Tyrone to Donaghadee to emigrate.

Of County Down?

Mr. Kelley's researches in Belfast, and in the Donaghadee coastal area itself, all point to this region as the most likely center from which Ann Adams Wilson sprang. The Adamses of the coast were many and notable as devout Presbyterians, being churchmen and ministers, mariners, landowners and patriots in the Rising of 1798—but always Presbyterians. They were extremely prolific. "The old Templepatrick cemetery, between Ballycopeland and Donaghadee, was full of Adamses, the old stones often reused by later members of the family, and sometimes the older stones being entirely obscured by new ones erected right in front of them."[19] Of the many present-day Adamses whom David Kelley met, it was not unusual to find that they belonged to families of twelve, fourteen, or even seventeen offspring. So the records to be searched were voluminous, even though Adams as a family name, present in County Down at least as early as 1660, is concentrated mainly in this coastal region.

On foot and by bus, he investigated the nearby areas of Newtownards, Grey Abbey and Ballyblack, wherever he got wind of an Adams, hoping to learn from either gravestones or living descendants the exact information he sought. William Adams of Craigboy had a daughter Ann, but she was born in 1820. A half-legendary character, "Old Jack of Killaughey," might well have been a brother of the Ann who went to America, but no positive proof remains. And, nowhere among the genealogical records he uncovered did there appear any mention of the parents of an Ann, born in 1789, who emigrated to America in 1807. Nor, among the families now extant whom Mr. Kelley contacted in Belfast, Millisle, Ballyblack and Newtownards—is there any tradition of a connection with America's wartime President—as in the case of the Wilsons of Strabane.

Thus Ann Adams remains more or less the mystery she was at the beginning of the search. Except for the reality of the beautiful little town of Donaghadee, set among rolling green hills beside the sea, its graystone houses slate-roofed or thatched, built in continuous lines along curving streets. Donaghadee, with its harbor and its hill-top observation tower, and the even higher Craigboy hill a mile or so along the coast—the one stretch of coastal Ireland where one *might* see the linen drying in Scotland, across nineteen miles of sea.

This section of County Down, at the northeastern point of the Ards peninsula which the deep bay (or lough) of Belfast creates, not only was a center of old Scotch-Irish resettlement and of the Presbyterian faith, but one of the chief centers of the Rising of 1798, when the United Irishmen turned in rebellion against religious persecution and the evils of English landlordism. There, it is said, the "rebels" were nearly all "cloven-footed Presbyterians," their ministers preaching "rank treason"; but also among them were "rascally Papists" who suffered equally with the Dissenters in that era, from the English overlords and the heavy-handed intolerance of the (Anglican) Established Church. The rebel cause was fought bravely, but it was insufficiently planned and unwisely triggered—indeed, quickly snuffed out, though not without much terror and bloodshed on both sides.

Ann Adams, who would have been seven or eight years old at the time, could not well have escaped witnessing much violence, particularly as members of her family name are known to have been prominently involved in the particularly gruesome fighting. A frightened alien authority, taken unaware, was determined to quell the uprising before its dangerous potential could explode into an unquenchable flame. And they had reason to fear, for inspired by the French and American revolutions, the Irish leaders already had made their pleas to both nations for aid, and this the English knew. The French were expected to land forces at Donaghadee at any moment, and, it was thought, already were landing arms. Hence there was ruthless slaughter of the ill-armed rebels, the hanging of leaders in the public squares, the display of heads on pikes, all measures of intimidation. Many a hero rose to an eminence of almost legendary local fame, and heroines too, such as she who was commemorated in the historical account *Betsy Gray, or Hearts of Down: A Tale of Ninety-Eight*, written by W. G. Lyttle a century later. Perhaps the deathless Betsy Gray, murdered with her brother and her sweetheart by the soldiery after the remnant of insurgents had fled, and buried in the field where she fell, was a relative of Ann's. It is a tradition, David Kelley was told by Mrs. Susan Adams, a sprightly lady of 80—daughter of an Adams of Craigboy and wife of Andrew Adams of Ballyblack—that at least the Craigboy Adams were related to Betsy's family at nearby Ballygraine.[20]

Considering all this, there was reason enough for emigration in the years of suppressed hostility and fear that followed, and good reason, no doubt, for the stern unbending nature and the joyless expression of a woman who had witnessed all this in her youth.

The young Ann Adams, the great decision taken and the journey to America well under way, surely would have remembered as a link with the New World toward which she sailed, the tale the old folks had liked to tell, of the time when excitement overran the coast of Antrim and Down in 1778. Then it was that John Paul Jones, intrepid American naval commander, won his first victory over the English, right here in Belfast Lough. A gallant and thrilling tale it was, since it discomfited the hated English overlords. But nonetheless it had been fearsome to the countryside to see an alien ship sail suddenly in from the open sea and open fire on the great stone ramparts of Carrickfergus Castle on the north headland of the Lough, to hear the continuing reverberations of battle as the *Ranger*, with starry flag flying at her masthead, turned a murderous broadside upon the British naval defender and quickly put his vessel, the *Drake*, out of the fray.[21] It was a daring exploit and one long recounted in Ulster. Its immediate consequence had been the formation, for local defense, of the Ulster Volunteers, forerunner of the "United Irish" of "The Ninety Eight."

If there were other memories—and there must have been—memories of the fertile farm lands amid "the little rounded hills of Down," the small, intimately charming countryside and the everchanging sea, then these in after years must have been relentlessly buried in the heart of Ann Wilson, wife of the vigorous, genial, politically minded editor whose career had led him and his family to prominence in the midlands of the vast new continent in which they made their home. Such memories seem not to have been handed down to her children.

Who Were the Prehistoric Irish?
An Ethnic Inquiry

Who were these Kelts, this breed that has left its mark so indelibly on the Rhineland, France and Spain, Great Britain and Ireland, and England's overseas offspring, particularly North America, during the past three thousand years? Especially those Gaedhelic (Gaelic, Gallic) Kelts who made Ireland their own and there brought to flower their unique civilization? Who later invaded, conquered and united north Britain, taking with them their Keltic Catholicism and its rich culture, along with their tribal ways, which included fierce pride and clannish-ness, the sword, a herding economy, bagpipes, jigs, and craftsmanship? These are the Gaels of Ireland, with a speech derived from the same source as that of the Kymric folk of Britain, whose language survives still in Wales and Brittany. These Goidels (old Irish Gaedhel) came to Ireland from Gaul in the centuries before Roman conquest. They were tall (and still are in Ulster and Scotland), with light hair and light eyes. Racially they are classified as Nordic, which makes them akin to the Scandinavians with whom they later crossed. The Norse spoke Teutonic languages, however, and culturally were quite different, being kin to the Angles and Saxons who ousted Rome from Britain.

Carleton S. Coon[22] describes the Kelts as a race of conquering migrants with certain basic physical characteristics that are still pro-nounced in the population of Ireland, a composite breed which blended Nordic characteristics with Alpine. Typical Keltic features he lists are low skull vault, long upper and short lower face and jaw (certainly not characteristic of Joseph Ruggles Wilson or his son), brow ridges, high long nose and blond complexion and hair. Racially the Wilson "lantern jaw" evidently is a Nordic attribute that came through Ann Adams, as are likewise the eyes, which were like hers.

The early dispersal of the Kelts over Europe by infiltration and conquest was due to their being horse-riding herdsmen possessing iron weapons. (The continuing dispersal of their pioneering descendants has been due to mobility on foot and with horse, added to an emerging mechanical skill with tools and machines and the creation of industries that process iron and steel and the mobile products thereof.) Their culture emerged from the La Tene civilization in the Swiss corner of France about 500 B.C., to overrun much of nearby Europe. The Rhine-land and bordering areas were theirs before Julius Caesar's Roman legions came. Their area was identified with what had been the first center of Iron Age civilization on the continent a millenium more-or-less before La Tene.

Up the Danube and down the Rhine these Kelts moved and, when they came to the sea, on into Britain and Ireland. (They were boatmen, and still are—from the coasts of Brittany, England, Wales, Scotland and Ireland and now in all the ports and oceans of the world, from bridge and deck to engine room.) The speech of these migrants out of south-eastern Europe was Indo-European, more closely related to ancient Italic (pre-Latin) than to Greek or Teutonic or Slavic, or to Iranian or Indo-Aryan.

These mobile Keltoi, as the Greeks called them (Galii in Latin), had spread overseas to Britain and Ireland before Caesar conquered Gaul (51 B.C.). Various authorities date them as appearing in Ireland from 500 to 200 B.C.[23] They brought with them those same talents and traits known to the Greeks and the Romans, and still known to us today—craftsmanship, fearlessness, hot-headedness, loyalty, a genius for priestcraft, but not for civic- or state-craft. In these last they were less evolved than the Romans, whose political and civic institutions transmitted through France and England were destined ultimately to supplant theirs.

The gift and zeal for church politics that was Dr. Wilson's, and for political science that was his son's, were not part of their Keltic heritage. The Presbyterian Church, with its ordinances and ordering, was the creation of the Scottish civilization of the lairds of the midlands and the south, who were mainly Anglo-Norman and Catholic French in their culture, and of the scholarly churchmen of Glasgow and Edinburgh. The democratic phase of "the auld Kirk," we may say, was the gift of the Keltic Scots, but the institution and its parliamentary procedures were from Rome, by way of Geneva (Calvin to Knox), the French Court, and the Anglo-Saxon and Anglo-Norman kingdoms which prevailed over all of Scotland south of the Highlands.

Irish Scots and Scotch-Irish

The early history of Ireland and Scotland in our era is a tangled one, at first glimpse a puzzle of nomenclature. Early historians in Britain, writing in Latin, referred to Ireland as the Island of *Scotia*. The country north of but contiguous with the Roman province of Britain and now known as Scotland, they named Caledonia or Albania (Alban), and from there the barbaric clansmen of the north interminably raided and looted the Roman garrisons and settlements as they pressed forward their frontier, ultimately as far as the Firth of Forth and the Clyde. Later, Caledonia was at times referred to as *Scotia Minor*, to distinguish it from *Ivernia* (Ireland) which was *Scotia Major*. From the second to the eleventh centuries A.D., the Kelts of the northern provinces of Ireland (Latin Scotia) more or less ruled the whole of Ivernia. From Ulster—Antrim, to be exact—these fighting Gaelic Kelts crossed over the North Channel and the Irish Sea and established colonies in the lowlands of the southwest of what we now call Scotland, while the Romans were still very much occupied in subduing the Brythonic or Kymric Kelts of north and west Britain.[24]

The designation *Scot* was applied first by the Romans to these north Irish from Scotia Major who had invaded Caledonia, and it seems that

141

the earlier inhabitants of this invaded land adopted it as an ethnic and national designation for themselves, taken from the Latin *Scotus*. (The term *Scotch* is specifically applied to the dialect of the Scottish Lowlanders.) The early scholarship in this area was clerical and monastic, and whether Keltic or Roman Catholic, the script was Latin. According to the Oxford Dictionary, *Scotus* was then the ordinary term applied to Irishmen in general. Ireland became Hibernia (Ivernia), northern Britain was extended to include Caledonia or Alban. Later, following the reign of Alfred the Great (c. 900 A.D.) official dynastic relations existed between the separate English and Scottish kingdoms of Britain and Caledonia. Thereafter Scotia became the official designation of Scotland, and no longer appeared as the name of Ireland except in the writings of historians.

The Scots Fare Forth

Not long after they settled Ulster, the Irish Kelts, no doubt when food was scarce, began settling over on the western shores and isles of what was then north Britain, within sight of the hills of Antrim. They found themselves not too unwelcome in the settlements of their Keltic racial and linguistic kin from Wales and the west of England, who were filtering northward along the same coasts. Authentic history of the region begins between 212 and 220 A.D. when, during a time of famine, according to an old manuscript, Ulstermen referred to as "Dal-Riata and Fir-Alben" were on the move, one division going over to western Caledonia, while the other remained in Scotia, specifically Antrim, "whence the [name] Dal-Riata to this day," a clan name known then and since both in what we now know as Scotland and Ireland.

Their settlements in Caledonia increased and multiplied. The Venerable Bede wrote of this migration: "From the name of their commander they are to this day called Dalreudini".[25] But it was two centuries later, in 503 A.D., that large scale invasion of North Britain and Caledonia by Ulstermen (*Scotii*) from Antrim began. Fergus, Angus and Lorne, sons of Erc, sailed forth leading a colony of settlers from the district of Dalriada (the modern spelling of the word), or Antrim. Their descendants ultimately made themselves masters of the whole north country, and the royal line of Scottish kings down to the Stuarts traced its descent from Fergus, son of Erc, through the later Kenneth MacAlpine.

The colonizing Dalriadic settlers in Argyll and the isles, these Irish

Scots, were Christians in the heritage of St. Patrick. They were defeated in 560 by Picts, the ancient Keltic breed of the Highlands. Whereupon in 563 another conquering Ulsterman, St. Columba (himself a follower of St. Patrick), accompanied, like Christ his Lord, by twelve disciples, founded a mission and set about building a monastery on the isle of Iona just off the western Firth of Lorne. This was completed in 565. From Iona, St. Columba soon journeyed into the northern Highlands to Inverness, far on the North Sea Firth of Moray, and there converted to his Christian faith the king of the Picts, as St. Patrick earlier won the Irish king at Tara. Iona long remained the foremost center for the conversion to Keltic Catholicism of the pagan Picts by St. Columba's missioners, who gave no allegiance to the Roman See. This first winning of their minds and their hearts, and the implantation of the institutions of the church then spread through the establishment of abbeys and monasteries endowed by local chieftains.

The second conquest was through a marriage. There had been centuries of battling between Irish-Scotch and English in the southern part of what is now Scotland and the northern part of England; similarly between the Irish-Scots and the Picts in the Highlands, and against invading Norsemen and Danes around the coasts. Then in 860 A.D., Kenneth MacAlpine of Kintyre, king of the Dalriadic Scots of Argyll, made himself king of the Highland Picts of "Scotland." This he accomplished, not by exterminating his enemies but actually, according to the bards, by asserting a right of succession; for his mother was the daughter of the Pictish king, and under Pictish law, inheritance passed in the female line. Kenneth MacAlpine's own daughter he married to a Welsh prince of Strathclyde, thereby giving Scotland (the Highlands) a foothold to the south.

Thus, we may say, the first conquest of Scotland by Ulstermen was by persuasion, and the second by shrewd calculation. So, Scotland was won not by arms but by Irish wits. They still prevail. Belfast is said to be the true capital of Scotland; and every Scot knows that neither culturally, commercially, politically nor militarily could the British Empire (now the Commonwealth) have been created and held together, had it not been for the skills and the wits of Scotsmen.

Return of the Scots

Nearly a thousand years after the founding of St. Columba's monastery at Iona, descendants of the Dalriadic Ulstermen began coming back to Antrim. In that millenium, the Highlands and the Lowlands had together become "Scotland," under one king, Irish Catholicism had merged with the Roman and the realm ruled by the descendants of Kenneth MacAlpine was the peer of England in culture and in power. But the descendants of those first colonists led by Dal-Riata from Antrim, who were living along the western coasts and in the western isles of Scotland, though loyal to the royal house of Stuart—as they well might be, for it was from them it sprang—were relatively untamed, though civilized.

In the time of Henry VIII (1509-1547), native Ivernian Kelts were still predominant in Antrim, the same Irish breed who had conquered Caledonia a thousand years before. On the coasts of Britain to the northeast of Antrim their emigrant kin, the Irish Scots, led a hard life. From the Mull of Kintyre to the Point of Aird in Skye, and westward in the Scottish isles to the outer Hebrides, existence was stark struggle. They became restless along their rockbound coasts and among their lonely isles, like the Norse and Danish sea rovers whose blood also was in their veins. Their lands were seabound and stormy, and from the harsh sea they wrested much of their scanty living, and the rest from wild game, herds and flocks. The poorer among them had only the sea.

Their chiefs, the MacDonnells of the Isles, in the sixteenth century, began leading forays upon North Ireland, the ancient homeland, where England already had staked a claim. By 1539 at least 2,000 Scots had gained a foothold in Ulster, and in 1545 the Lord of the Isles disembarked 4,000 more men at Carrickfergus in Antrim. The English hastened to reinforce the then Earl of Tyrone (Con O'Neill) to keep the wild Scots from overrunning the whole north of Ireland. But all the King's soldiers and all the earl's men could not dislodge these Scots-Irishmen. "Redshanks" they were to the English—these rough clansmen in their kilts.

A second invasion was attempted in greater force some ten years later, but was driven back in 1556, although many already were settled firmly in Down and Antrim. In 1560 Shane O'Neill was able to hire 1,500 of them as fighting men. He was the last of the O'Neills to reign in his own right in Tyrone. Vengefully, out of hatred for Queen Elizabeth who had played him false, he scourged all of eastern Ulster that the English then ruled. But his scourging was done without discrimination, for in 1507 the English allied themselves with other Ulster chiefs whom Shane had plundered, and defeated him. But it was the Scots of Antrim who killed him. Forgetting that but a few years before,

144

in a mad fury, he had sought to drive them out of Ulster and had killed some 700 of their clansmen, he now sought their help. In revenge instead, they reviled him, hacked him to pieces, wrapped the pieces in an old cloak and tossed them contemptuously into a pit.

Thus it was that these Scots from the Isles, descendants of Dalriadic colonists from Ulster, not only returned there to reinforce the ancient breed but themselves put an end to the political supremacy of that breed in the North of Ireland.

Irish Civilization

In describing a land and people, one must know their historical background in terms of the times and the events peculiar to them. In appraising and explaining the character of persons identified with a place this is equally true. Many of Woodrow Wilson's dominant traits were derived through his father from his father's parents, James and Ann Adams Wilson, who were North-Irish. County Tyrone and County Down must be comprehended as parts of Ulster, the one more Irish, the other more Anglo-Norman; Ulster must be comprehended, not as a separate entity but as a province of Ireland before partition; and all Ireland must be comprehended as a country whose people were the product of the Emerald Isle's peculiar environment through the millenia during which Bronze and Iron Age Gaelic herdsmen had flourished and wrought a distinctive and in many ways superior civilization under the inspiration of Druidical and later Christian cultural and spiritual heritage centered at Tara, the seat of the Irish Kings.

Among modern Irishmen, there is a habit of mind that is typical of the southern section of the United States—a nostalgia for a brilliant past sometimes likened to the Golden Age of Greece, an era of nobility, culture, gentility and gracious living, of civic and political leadership, of noble cities in sovereign commonwealths whose economy and prosperity were rooted in native soil. Old Ireland, with its five principalities and its brilliant and distinctive culture under native leadership, is fondly likened to Hellenic civilization. Tara hill is "The Acropolis," Cormac the lawmaker and architect is the Solon (sometimes the Solomon) of Ireland, as was Jefferson of Virginia. In the pagan era the learned men of Ireland were well acquainted with the history of Greece. In fact, the Bronze and Iron Age migrants had come from the fringes of Grecian civilization in the Danube region and Switzerland. After the coming of Christianity, the Irish became an outpost of Gallic Catholic

145

culture, which had its roots in Rome, and the source of this culture, carried afar to pagan lands. But it is to the era of the great Kings of Tara that Irishmen look back as to the Golden Age. This Age we must understand in some measure if we are to understand the Irish heritage.

The pageantry of Ireland underlay the histrionic temperament of Woodrow Wilson. His ideals, his hopes and his ambitions, his writing, teaching, administration and formal relations were dramatized and vitalized by a sense of the living past. At Princeton, he invested his academic robes and always his roles with a lively dignity. In the White House and in the Peace Conference at Versailles, it was never Woodrow Wilson the personally modest individual who spoke and acted, but the man aware that he was the embodiment of authority, the dramatic symbol of The People of The Nation, the passionate epitome of that tragic Moment in History. This was a true and natural attitude of mind and heart, never assumed, never meretricious. It had its roots deep in the cultural soil of Tara.

It must be remembered always that the partition of Ireland, the separation of the Protestant six counties in the North from the Roman Catholic South, is very recent. And it is superficial. All Ireland was one when Tara was the center and focus of its rich and enlightened civilization, during the eras both of pagan prehistory and in Christian monasticism, after St. Patrick established Irish Keltic Catholicism in 433 A.D. All Irishmen, including those of Ulster today, feel in their hearts that Ireland is one and look forward to ultimate reconciliation and reunion.

Tara and Newgrange

Gaelic tradition attributes to Tara an unbroken continuity of 1,700 years up to the Norman conquest (1169). Tara is about 12 miles south of the three great burial tumuli near the River Boyne known as Dowth, Knowth and Newgrange, Bronze Age sites that certainly were sepulchral monuments of ruling chieftains of Ireland. The greatest of these is that called Newgrange, a massive earth-covered tumulus of rough stone, whose corbeled construction is reminiscent of the stonework of Mycenae, although it is made of uncut slabs. The Bronze Age in Ireland is dated by archaeologists from 2,000 to 250 B.C. A mortuary site certainly would not have been the scene of festivities such as we know were celebrated at Tara in its heyday. Therefore, it is entirely logical to suppose that such festivities already were being celebrated at Tara by the Irish chieftains and their followers, as early as the later Bronze Age.

The first assembly at Tara is reputed to have been in the reign of a King named Ollamh Fodhla who lived about 1200-1300 B.C., in the Bronze Age. During this reign, the Newgrange tumulus was erected.[26]

The form and outlines of the earthworks on Tara hill, upon which stood buildings that may be dated historically, have remained through the centuries. Despite quarrying, tillage, fence building and construction of utilitarian structures in the centuries after the site was abandoned as a place for assemblies adjacent to the palaces of the High Kings, these ancient earthworks remain. The word Tara is Anglicized Gaelic Teamhrack (pronounced theouroch, taragh or towrach), which is the genetive of the word meaning "place of assembly on a hill," or "acropolis."

All of the main divisions of the Tara site mentioned in legend and archaeological studies are identified with historically known characters or episodes: Cormack MacAirt, king of Ireland from 227 to 266 A.D.; Loguire, king of Ireland from 428 to 458, thus holding sway at Tara when St. Patrick came in 433; Niall, Loguire's father; Grainne, the daughter of Cormack, whose elopement was the theme of the great Keltic tragedy which is retold in Wagner's *Tristan and Isolde* and Maeterlinck's *Peleas et Melisande*.

The continuity of both the burial tumuli (known as the Palace of Oengus) and the Tara structures with the life of the Scotch and Irish people is evident in the names Angus (Oengus), Cormack, Leary (Loguire or Laoghaire), MacArthur (Mac Airt) and St. Patrick.

On Easter Eve, in the spring of 433, the founder of Keltic Christianity, recently returned from France and Rome, lit a paschal fire on the hill across the valley north of Tara, at Slane on the River Boyne. This act contravened the royal prerogative of lighting a fire on Tara hill to mark the commencement of the Druidical solar festival of Beltane. On Easter morning, St. Patrick crossed the valley and challenged the magicians of the king to a test of power, in which he was victor. King Loguire personally remained pagan, but St. Patrick's wit and skill had opened the way to the rapid spread of the Good Word (Gospel) throughout Ireland. The culture must have been ripe for the message, for it was not more than five years before he was able to convene here, in 438, upon the Acropolis of Ireland (Tara) his synod which established the system under which the civilization of the monastic era flourished.

The Adams and Wilson Heritage

My gifts have come to me down the years
I am the son of huntsmen of old time,
The heir of harsh virtue deemed sublime,
Offspring of fighters and of pioneers,
Inheritor of impassioned hopes and fears,
Some gave me purity, some gave through time
This purged, clean soul, that helped me climb
Godward. From some came joys, from others, tears.[27]

"Tyrone among the Bushes" is a saying known to Ulstermen all over the world, for folk from Tyrone are natural frontiersmen. Their country is so situated that it has in all times remained a frontier, in which the Gaelic racial strain remains dominant. In the Bronze and Iron Ages, their ancestors were horse-riding herdsmen and hunters, not townsmen. Moving on, ever seeking new hunting grounds, new pastures, they drove before them their cattle and sheep and swine, pausing to broadcast and harvest oats and barley on suitable meadows, but never settling down and fencing their lands in "closes," or real farms. Among them were skilled craftsmen in metals and wood and leather. Their families were united in clans and tribes by flexible bonds, typical of free men accustomed to open spaces and wide and new horizons.

In our time, this breed came on across the Atlantic to the Americas, entering through all the Eastern Seaboard ports, and fanned out as pioneers across this continent. In the Valley of Virginia they cleared farms, sowed their grain and herded their livestock, moved on to settle the southwest counties and the frontier territories of Tennessee, Arkansas, Texas, the Southwest. From Scotland and Ireland they have migrated also to Africa, Asia, the Antipodes. Preachers and teachers, printers and politicians and reformers, herders and planters, mechanics and engineers, this folk has bred some of the most indefatigable and tough-sinewed sappers and pioneers of western civilization. As one of this breed, James Wilson migrated to Philadelphia and on to Steubenville; his son came to Staunton, and his grandson, born at Staunton, went to Princeton and Washington. It is a breed ever on the move, and for whom freedom is the breath of life.

The Ulster folk have as an essential element a certain hardness that is related to land and climate. There is much beauty there on bright days, a charm that has a peculiar poignancy because these moods of nature are rare and always evanescent. For half the year the days are short, and the nights long. This gives a precious quality to the long daylight hours in summer. Even in the more genial months there is a deal more of chill damp than warmth, of cloud and rain than sunshine—breezes off the north Atlantic are rarely zephyrs. And from November through March, the nights are very long and weather chill to very cold. This is really a shut-in time.

The folk life at Dergalt in the time of James Wilson's boyhood would have been quite simple. The tools handled on the farm and in the household of that day can be matched in illustrations of medieval rural life—the toothed sickle and flail, three-legged stool, the upright churn, the open hearth with crane and pot for cooking. It was also like the equipment of a frontier household in Colonial America. The aspects of modernization that we see today in County Tyrone are very recent. When James Wilson was a boy, he undoubtedly wore clothing homespun out of Dergalt wool, shoes and boots made of native leather by local cobblers. He would have helped milk, scythe hay, slaughter livestock, and have done his share in the labor of cutting, drying, stacking and hauling of "turf" (peat) for the fires. The conveyances were a "slide car" (a drag on the lower end of shafts), "slipe" (sled) or wheeled cart; and the motive-power donkey or pony. This is one reason Ulstermen adjusted to the harsh and primitive living in New World pioneering more easily and more successfully than the townsmen and countrymen of the English midlands and southern shires.

But James' apprenticeship at Gray's Printshop in early youth doubtless released him from the heavy labor of ploughing and spading. That same predilection for letters and for exercising mind, rather than muscles, was so strong in his grandson that he had a positive aversion to gardening, and exercise was always a duty rather than a pleasure.

Not many years before James Wilson emigrated was the famine time when the potatoes froze in the ground before they could be harvested. This particular famine was only one in a sequence of hard times which tested the powers of endurance of countryfolk even more than of townfolk. Such ordeals have tempered the spirit of the North Irish with an underlying quality of dourness which distinguishes them from the South Irish, who endured many famines but not such cold.

It was political and religious persecution, however, that made that temper grim and relentless. Both parents of Joseph Wilson, in their youth, witnessed the orgy of hatred and bloodshed let loose in "the '98." Both, belonging to "nonconformist" families, had grown up in an atmosphere somewhat like that of a police state, surcharged with contempt and hatred, which produced the violence culminating in that ill-fated rebellion. Ann Adams's photograph reveals that grim and relentless temper. Her husband James Wilson's portrait, while less dour, reveals the hard lines of a relentless fighter. The same quality is latent in the features of their son Joseph in youth, more definite in middle life when he became notable for asperity, a trait which in later years became so caustic that he is reported to have felt it had alienated many friends. Even his grandchildren have said they stood in awe of him in his old age. Joseph's son showed a like temper when hard pressed and in a fighting mood. This trait, though long dormant, led Woodrow Wilson's opponents to label him, when it did emerge, as "intolerant" and "intractable," and that expression, caught by a photographer, gave credence to the epithet.

We have seen the same expression transform the face of a friendly travelling companion in the train from Belfast to Dungannon, the moment "the religious question" (i.e. Presbyterianism vs. Roman Catholicism) came up in connection with a discussion of the prevalent Border depredations of that season. From a humorous cast of great charm and sparkle, the expression changed to a grim and incisive hardness. (We were reminded of a succinct remark of Woodrow Wilson's: "When it comes to religion, argument is adjourned.")

Some days later we were to see, even more dramatically exemplified, that same look of resolute fine-tempered hardness on the faces of the volunteer Border guards, in civvies but with rifles slung over their shoulders, who stopped Robert Wilson's family car as we returned with him to Strabane from being shown the wild beauties of the Gortin Glen. The road here paralleled the River Mourne across whose narrow stream lay Donegal, northern-most county of the Republic of Eire. Sandbagged sentry boxes were at strategic points, as there had been along the railroad. The men of the countryside served their turns as guards, stopping all traffic for identification of occupants, source and destination, and there was nothing "routine" or casual about their quiet method. It was, and needed to be, one of deadly earnest. Within a few weeks after our departure, sentries were killed along this road, the customs house on the bridge from Strabane to Lifford was blasted, a powerhouse on the railroad near the town of Omagh was partly disabled by a bomb, agents of the (South) "Irish Republican Army" were arrested in Londonderry. So do the political and religious feuds of the dangerous years of James Wilson's youth perpetuate themselves, continuing their hard conditioning of the Ulster folk of today.

Esteem, valor, sensitivity to insult or injustice are values and traits distinctively Keltic from the earliest times. These are personal qualities which can be good or bad according to circumstances and temperament. They were important components in the total complex which led the fighting Irish to feud their nation out of a unified existence, but they also are the source and guarantee of the fierce loyalty of Scots and Ulstermen to great causes.

As virtues, those traits were among the most prominent in Joseph Wilson's behavior. When tinged with bitterness, they brought to his character the strong quality of asperity we have mentioned. Inherited by his son, these traits gave to Woodrow Wilson his indomitable esprit, yet perhaps in the end certain antipathies must be reckoned as contributing factors in his failure to realize his highest hopes and his greatest potentialities as a leader.

These qualities, with their undertones and overtones, are so typical that we may best describe our Ulsterman in the words of one of the Irish breed—Richard Hayward, writing on Ulster today in *This is Ireland*:[28]

The typical Ulsterman of to-day is fiercely and aggressively Irish, but he is Irish in a very special way. Indeed, he considers himself quite a separate kind of Irishman, which, as all his historical background would lead us to expect, he is in very sooth. His speech is rougher and more vital than that of his Southern brother; he has less grace but a deal more sincerity; and instead of the familiar Irish wit he is endowed with an immense command of devastating satirical humour. Protestant and Roman Catholic alike, the Ulsterman is a type well-defined and not to be mistaken for any other variety of the human race, but in the Protestant the Ulster peculiarities have become more completely crystallized, the Ulster traits are in sharper focus, the contrasting lights and shades are more violently set one against the other. And so when we speak of an Ulsterman we usually think of a Protestant, and most of the inconsistencies that perplex a stranger in Ulster arise from this vulgar error. Fiercely and vitally Irish, your Ulster Protestant will yet look with deep suspicion on any Irish movement or tendency; he will, for instance, at once detect the hand of Rome in Irish dancing, Irish music, or the Irish language. On Saint Patrick's Day, if he wears a shamrock in his buttonhole, he will wear it with a defiant air. But if you are in doubt about his nationality, say something disparaging about this emblem of Ireland, and you will quickly learn that if an Ulsterman is a special kind of Irishman, he is nevertheless an Irishman— and a very downright and decided and forcible Irishman at that.

But there is another characteristic aspect of the Ulsterman, seemingly at variance with the dour qualities just discussed, actually only the reverse face of the coin. It too was strong in the heritage of the Wilsons.

The Woodrow Wilson generally remembered and pictured is the austere and humorless President of the war years. Few realize that in his childhood, youth and early years of marriage he was, when at leisure, exceptionally gay, blythe, vivacious, full of whimsy, humorous, at times hilarious. This persisted into later life in the privacy of his family. Private gaiety also was characteristic of Joseph Wilson as the happy young husband and father. Besides being an irrepressibly witty conversationalist, he was sportively playful with the boy Tommy, showing a quality of exuberance much like that reported of his own father in active life. As Tommy grew into youth and maturity, he and his father loved to indulge in bouts of repartee that were sheer fun. This kind of fun is typically Irish *and* Scotch. The proclivity in this instance must have come through James Wilson, a genial, sociable soul, despite his somewhat virulent reputation as publicist and politician. Certainly the witty and facetious, sometimes gay, sometimes barbed humor characteristic of Woodrow Wilson did not come from his severe grandmother, Ann Adams, nor from the earnest, serious Woodrows. Probably it was his ability to sway audiences by his spirited attack, vivid imagination, colorful use of anecdote and illustration, as well as the issues he championed, that brought him his great victories at the polls in his first two campaigns, even though in his public utterances he always rested his case on the appeal of facts, reason and moral principle.

But at home with family and intimate friends, this aspect of Woodrow Wilson's heritage had free rein in gaiety and nonsense, playfulness and mimicry. For closely allied to the playful was a histrionic vein, strong in the Irish and strong in him. It was notable in the dramatic style of his story-telling—as it was in the legends, songs and poetry of the ancient Irish bards, and even in the quality and enunciation of Gaelic speech today. It was a strong element in that love of mimicry which relatives and close friends have all remarked on; and which the young folk of his household delightedly remembered as marking those hilarious episodes in which he regaled his family with evening recountings of his day's encounters during the political campaigns. He loved to strike bold or absurd poses, declaim nonsense verse, dance a Highland fling or an Irish jig, take part in the favorite family pastime of charades. And all through his life he loved the theatre, attending for fun and entertainment—in the later years mostly for relaxation from the too serious drama of his life and the world role imposed upon him.

There was also that Keltic love of singing which Joseph and Jeanie had shared, and which Woodrow Wilson inherited. This was a family for whom song was a natural outflowing of the heart, as it is with the Irish and the Scots, and Jeanie's guitar, before there was a piano, was the center of the family musicmaking. The quality and tone of voice in which, later, Woodrow sang to his own children, and in his father's failing days, to the old doctor—that quality in which was couched his genius for lucid speech, a mellow tone with fine timbre which won our country, and almost the world, to his ideals—these are characteristic of his breed. That fine, light timbre we recognize in the voices of Irish and Scottish and Welsh singers today—" . . . a voice so rich, so well modulated, so vibrant with repressed energy that I was enchanted."[29] This was the reaction, on first meeting President Wilson, not of a sentimental admirer, but of one of his Secret Service men who had known little about the President personally. That quality may be heard today in the services at Washington Cathedral, in the voice of Woodrow's grandson, Dean Francis B. Sayre, Jr.

Well known is the lament of Thomas Moore:

> The harp that once through Tara's halls,
>   The soul of music shed,
> Now hangs, as mute on Tara's walls
> As if that soul were fled.

So great was the love of the old Gaelic chiefs for the harp and all it symbolized that poets and musicians travelled always with the Irish kings whenever they made their regal circuit of the island. But one might answer Moore's lament with the reminder that, though Tara's walls and splendor have vanished, her "soul of music" has fled not into oblivion but into the uttermost parts of the earth wherever the Gael has gone to make new homes, new churches, new communities, new festivals of song.

BACKGROUND IN SCOTLAND

The Woodrow Search

Janet Woodrow brought to the children of her marriage with Joseph Wilson a distinctive heritage. Whereas her husband brought fire and force, forged out of the temper of a long line of fighting North-Irish and Irish-Scots, she carried the blood of a gentler yet strong and obstinately enduring breed, the Lowland Scots, enriched by centuries of Anglo-Norman influence in culture, and in blood as well.

The Irish-Scots, as we have seen, had crossed the narrow North Channel from Ulster, and venturing northward up and beyond the Firth of Clyde, by the sixth century A.D. had wrested from the Pictish people much of the southerly part of the Grampian Hills now known as the shire of Argyll. But already during this and the preceding century, the Lowlands to eastward between the Firth of Clyde and the Solway Firth, which separates Cumberland and the Cheviot Hills, had been occupied by the Romanized Britons, driven up from the south of what is now England by successive Saxon invasions after the withdrawal of the Roman power in 407 A.D. Later, in the sixth century, the Angles from the continent had established themselves in the mid-Lowlands to the south and east of the Firth of Clyde, bringing in a new non-Keltic culture. In the seventh century, the then-powerful Anglo-Saxon kingdom of Northumbria, just below the Scottish border, made repeated invasions across the Lowlands in an effort to conquer the wild Highland Picts. They ravaged the countryside as they went, and even after each withdrawal, left their mark behind them, in new ways to be imitated and in the new blood of their casual progeny.

So it was that even before the Norman conquerors of Britain appeared four centuries later, the population of the Scottish Lowlands had become greatly modified over and beyond the simple Pictish and Keltic beginnings, and was ripe for the new Anglo-Norman influences.

Lowland Scots

The people of Lowland Scotland, south of the Clyde on the west and the Firth of Forth on the east, were subjected to and assimilated more non-Keltic culture, including words and names, than those of the Highlands or the Western Isles. They acquired still more of this racial admixture through cross breeding as a consequence of invasion and occupation by the Romans (A.D. 47 to 410), Saxons (A.D. 407 *et seq*.), Normans (A.D. 1066). But in physique, they remained fundamentally Keltic. According to Coon:[1] "A collection of 524 male skulls from a modern Glasgow cemetery, representing the western central part of Scotland, shows a predominance of this Keltic racial type with considerable fidelity. This series is drawn from the region in which the Scots of Deira [Dal Riada] settled when they moved across from [Northern] Ireland and began their conquest and absorption of the Pictish kingdom."

These Scots who invaded the area south of the Clyde, the region from which all the ancestors of Janet Woodrow have been found to have come, were the descendants of Iron-Age Keltic-speaking people who overran Britain *and* Ireland several centuries before the beginning of the Christian era. Their physical type is well established. The typical skull is of moderate size and medium broad, with a low vault that is rounded in profile when viewed from the rear; the forehead is sloping; nose long and prominent; face rather short, and the whole physique relatively tall and rugged. It is essentially Nordic, although not always lighthaired, while the eye is blue, gray or hazel,[2] i.e. not "pure Nordic" (if such exists).

It would be logical to suppose that the type has been modified significantly by the intrusion of Roman, Saxon and Norman traits, but actually it has not, because the racial type of each one of these was almost identical with that of the earliest invaders, Iron-Age Keltic-speaking folk. The invading and occupying Roman legions were recruited in Gaul, whence had come the Iron-Age Kelts themselves. The people of Saxony were of the same physical type. The Norman invaders were from areas of France (Normandy and Brittany) where the same physical type largely prevailed.

Language, of which names are a part, was another matter. A strong Gaelic element remains in the speech of the Glasgow area, and throughout the Lowlands, as exemplified in Burns' poetry, which belongs to the area roundabout Ayre, southwest of Glasgow. But it is not true Gaelic, like that of isolated localities in the western Highlands and the Isles. Anglian, from the era of the Saxon rule that succeeded the Roman; Latin, through channels of the Church of Rome, and then

English and French through Anglo-Norman intrusion and contacts, have largely displaced and transformed the Lowland Scottish speech and names.

The culture of Christian monasticism, both Keltic Catholic from Ireland and Roman Catholic from England and France, first established the mores of the native lowland Scottish settlers, who were semi-nomadic herdsmen. The monasteries gathered primitive towns round them. The Saxons, in turn, brought to the Lowlands a true farming economy based on tillage of the meadowlands near the coast and in the dales. Villages grew where landings were made, and around the forts at strategic points where the Saxon earls established their seats.

Then came the castles of the Norman kings, dukes and barons, and around the greater castles grew small cities or royal burghs, the more important ones, such as Glasgow, identified with a bishopric and a cathedral.

Strathclyde

The forebears of Jeanie Woodrow appear to have been entirely identified, except perhaps for one slight Norman-Highland strain (de Morteyn), with Strathclyde, the western lowland area of Scotland. This area extended in the eighth century from the River Derwent, on the south in Cumberland, northward to the lower ranges of the Highlands beyond.

The northern boundary of Strathclyde was the Firth of Clyde, and the western boundary, above the present city of Edinburgh, ran east along the south shore of Solway Firth to the great forest of Ettrick, which separated Strathclyde from the Anglian kingdom of Berenecia on the east. The area comprised what is now Cumberland and most of Westmoreland (now part of the north of England) and the present Scottish shires of Dumfries, Ayr, Renfrew, Lanark and Peebles. In the southern half of Strathclyde, including Dumfries-shire, the population was of Cymric or Welsh extraction, and in the northern half Cornish. The capital of the kingdom was the castle or fort on the abrupt small mountain of rock which, from the north shore, overlooked the strategic River Clyde and the town of Glasgow. The Scottish Gaelic name of this fort was Dun (meaning fort) Breaton, now Dumbarton. In the Brythonic tongue it was called Alcluith.

The second most important town in the realm of Strathclyde was Caer Luil, now the English Carlisle, through which in later centuries ran the Roman Wall that marked the northernmost conquest of the Roman Legions in the British Isles. With Carlisle, Paisley, Glasgow and Dumbarton all thriving and important towns since and before that era, it is evident that this, more than any other province of Scotland, was one in which urban culture has conditioned the habits and minds of townsmen for many, many generations.

The open seaways, firths and rivers were what made Strathclyde accessible to the Iron-Age Keltic Brythons and Cornishmen who populated the area just before the Romans came. The population assimilated both the blood and culture of invading and settling Irish and equally, Saxon (Anglian) influence from the east. But those same waterways made the country accessible in the tenth century to the raiding, plundering pagan Norsemen, whose predaciousness was ended only by the coming of the Normans to power in Britain. It was not access to the sea which made Strathclyde a rich and thriving realm, but the soil. For the life of the people was basically that of farming (in contrast to fishing in the northeast and west, and in the isles). Oats, barley and wheat, turnips, hops, linen, wool and meat from sheep, milk and flesh from cattle, pigs—these gave the robust population their subsistence in this cool, temperate environment. Strathclyde is the lowland area dominated by the River Clyde, whose headwaters drain the northwest watershed of the Cheviot Hills.

The Patrick Wodrow Line

The Anglo-Norman-Scottish Woodrows, or Wodrows (it is spelled variously in the old records), were centered in and about Glasgow and Paisley for as far back as records go. They were a prolific family, so that at any given period there might be several persons of that surname with identical baptismal names in the area, yet probably only distantly related. This creates certain blocks and hazards in genealogical search or surmise. If Janet Woodrow were indeed descended from the most prominent Woodrow line of Glasgow and Eagleshame (although one link in the chain of evidence is missing), then we know something of her family's circumstances from the sixteenth century onward. That earliest recorded progenitor, Patrick Wodrow, was a vicar of the Established Church (Anglican) after the Roman Catholicism to which he had formerly adhered was interdicted. His vicarage was at Eagleshame, near Glasgow-on-Clyde, and he was a landed proprietor there, married to a daughter of the House of Hamilton, a powerful family of the Scottish Lowlands, but of English origin. He was reputed to have been of Norman blood, probably descended from a follower of one of those Anglo-Norman nobles, who by invitation had established themselves in Scotland in the twelfth century, during the peaceful and enlightened reign of the Scottish King David I.

How early in the sixteenth century Patrick Wodrow was living in or near Glasgow we cannot be sure, but as Roman Catholicism was not officially abolished by Act of the Scottish Parliament until 1560, we assume it must have included a period both before and after this date. He would have been involved then, to some extent at least, in the throes and upheavals attendant upon the Reformation. He certainly would have been cognizant of and his fortunes affected by the flight of the last Roman Catholic bishop of Glasgow Cathedral, who escaped to France before the Act of Interdiction could be applied, taking all the Cathedral treasures and records. He undoubtedly witnessed the subsequent excesses of the "Reformers" who swept through the city, and witnessed also the high drama of the spirited defense of the Cathedral by the craft guilds, who saved that beautiful old edifice from mutilation at the hands of the mob of zealots.

As a child, he may even have known something of the turbulent reign of James V, seventh monarch of the Royal House of Stuart. And if so, he grew to young manhood during the constant terror of the Border Raids—a terror which that last of the strong kings of Scotland succeeded in repressing for a time, only to be defeated by treachery in the great battle of Solway Moss, and to die, it is said, of a broken heart, in 1542. The tempestuous career of James' unhappy daughter, Mary Stuart, must have been known even better to Patrick Wodrow, and at closer range. For after her return from France as Queen of Scots, to become a pawn of the nobles and a gambled-for prize between Papists and Covenanters, her fortunes and those of the clergy, lords and earls who intrigued for and against her were cast not only in the Royal Seat at Edinburgh but largely in and about the castles near to Glasgow— those of Bothwell and Stirling—and Loch Leven at Dumbarton, where she was imprisoned after being dethroned.

Patrick, it would seem, successfully weathered the first transition of the Reformation—that from "Popery" to "Established Church," but whether he himself came under the influence of the magnetic John Knox, or whether he remained in the Episcopal faith to the end, we do not know. It was during this latter half of the sixteenth century that

158

Knox, returning from exile in France and Switzerland, where he had sat at the feet of Jean Calvin in Geneva, set much of Scotland aflame with his militant philosophy of the "New Covenant." But Episcopacy, the "Established Church" of Scotland which officially replaced the Church of Rome in 1560, was not seriously menaced by the "Covenanters" for another eighty years, despite constant struggles for power, temporal as well as spiritual. It would seem unlikely, therefore, that the vicar of Eagleshame, a landed proprietor of that region, should have "turned Covenanter" in the early days of that new sect's rise.[3]

By his son's time, however (that is, of John, heir to the family lands at Eagleshame and Mearns), the Wodrow "conversion" quite likely had taken place. The half-century following the Scottish Reformation was a time in which "the Kirk" and its zealous adherents swept much of Scotland into its fold, and by 1639 was powerful enough to bring about, by parliamentary action, the "abolition" of the Episcopacy as a state religion on the Scottish scene.

At any rate we know that by 1660, at the Restoration of the Stuart line (Charles II), John Wodrow's youngest son Robert (who was chamberlain to the Earl of Eglintoun) was certainly a Presbyterian, for he took part in the illfated Pentlands Rising (1666) of the Covenanters against the King's attempted reestablishment of the Episcopacy in Scotland. By this time certainly, and probably before, the Wodrows of Eagleshame were committed completely to the new Presbyterian faith.

Neither John nor Robert, son and grandson of the Reverend Patrick Wodrow, is reported to have been either "clergyman" (i.e. Episcopal) or "preacher" (Presbyterian). But Robert's fourth son James, born in 1637, became, in 1692, the professor of divinity at Glasgow University, chief seat of Presbyterian learning, and was joined thirteen years later by his eldest son Alexander, as second professor.

At this point, Janet Woodrow Wilson's family line, contrary to Ray Stannard Baker's[4] assumption and that of most subsequent biographies diverges from that of the more famous descendants of Patrick Wodrow of Eagleshame—if, indeed, there was any actual connection with the venerable Patrick himself.

Such a connection (which seems to have been a tradition in Woodrow Wilson's immediate family) is by no means impossible— indeed there are several probabilities. Patrick may have had younger sons who founded families. Patrick's eldest son John, heir to the Eagleshame lands, may have had sons other than his heir, Robert.

Robert, we know, had seven children, of whom Professor James Wodrow of Glasgow University was the fourth, but of these other children of Robert we have no knowledge, except that apparently there was at least one elder son who inherited the family lands, since James did not. This eldest son, or another of the possible brothers of James, could have been progenitor of the line of Paisley Woodrows to which Janet Woodrow belonged. But James, himself, it seems, could not have been. At least there is as yet no discoverable connection between either of his three sons and the earliest recorded ancestor of Janet Woodrow.

Names

In the study of heritage in Scotland the history of the names of forebears has both direct and indirect significance. Put a finger on the surnames in Janet's genealogy historically, and each opens a door.

Woodrow is definitely Anglo-Norman, derived by way of Old English *wudu*, meaning wood, with *refa* to tend, originally signifying a man who was a "wood-reever" or overseer of a forest. Its first use as a surname in Scotland probably goes back to the invasion of the British Isles by the Normans, who had begun using surnames in France just before their invasion of England. At a general council held at Forfar (now Angus) in 1061, Malcolm Ceannmor directed his chief subjects to adopt surnames, after the customs of other nations, from their territorial possessions. In 1175 William the Lion, after his liberation, returned to Scotland bringing with him many of the younger sons of Norman noblemen in England, and to these he gave lands. These, like their elder kinsmen in England, required responsible warders to supervise their woodlands. Today the Woodrows (and Woodruffs or Woodroffs) are legion in Scotland, especially in the Glasgow area. There are even more in England, where it is a common name throughout the land, but especially in and about towns which formerly were woodlands, rather than on the Downs.

The mention of a John Woddroff, a landowner in Glasgow in 1505, proves that the name has been long in this Scottish community. Yet it is Anglo-Norman, there is nothing Gaelic about it, it is not of the Highlands, nor essentially Scottish in any sense. Woodrows are and have been townsfolk, some distinguished, but mostly not—ministers, teachers, scholars; burgesses, doctors, lawyers, merchants, artificers, cordiners, brewers. They were seldom landed gentry, and they were not yeoman farmers or crofters. Nor were they aristocrats, and only infre-

160

quently of the entourage of the ruling caste. The name is not notable for prowess in war or the councils of the great but rather always it is there in force among the busy citizenry responsible for the constant enterprise of the great towns, where craftsmanship, enterprise, civic life and culture, and religion, have persisted steadily through the turmoil of wars, conquests, politics and social, industrial and economic change.

Woodrow Wilson was true to the typology of this breed, entirely the townsman, a modest scholar, educator, church member, a vigorous "artificer," devoting his energies wholeheartedly to civics and national progress until an unforeseen climax in civilization summoned him against his will to exercise his competence as commander-in-chief of a nation at war. This he did with such conscientious and competent industry that by the logic of events, the name Woodrow now is more notable in history than if he had been an aristocrat, warrior, great churchman, professional politician or organizer of labor, industry or business.

Documentary Woodrow Evidence

Jeanie Woodrow's great-grandfather, the first John in this line about whom we have documentary records, lived in Paisley. According to the Scottish Registry Office, he married Jean Sclater, also of Paisley, in 1751. Their son John, born in 1765, fourteen years after their marriage, was registered as an artificer, and so probably was the father John. The mother's name indicates that she came of a family of artificers, probably originally from a western shire where slate was mined, for the name is occupational in derivation. Sclater (Sclatere) is a middle-English word meaning a "slater" or man who lays slates on roofs. The name occurs in records from the fourteenth century down in Aberdeen, Forfarshire (Angus), Perthshire, Glasgow, Edinburgh. There were slaters in all the large towns where buildings were slated, from early times. But the name is especially common in the west and in the north, right up to the Orkneys and Shetlands, where slate is mined and worked. The name is English, but the workers in slate in these areas were Gaels, so we may conclude that before local slaters intermarried with Anglo-Normans (like the Woodrows), they were Scottish and Pictish Gaels. Jean Sclater certainly was a very definite character as a person, otherwise her name probably would not have been perpetuated three generations after her time in the memory of the Woodrows who were her descendants, as evidenced in calling Janet "Jeanie."

The name Janet appears in the next generation, in the marriage (1789) of John Woodrow, son of John of Paisley, to Janet Morton, a newcomer to that town. Morton is a name now widespread over Scotland and we have encountered it equally in Ireland. But it is definitely early Norman, from Fifeshire, where the lands of Myrton or Myretown (afterwards Morton) in the parish of Kemback belonged to "an old and considerable family . . . who took their surname from their lands."[5] One, Thomas Myrtone, was chaplain to the King of Scots in 1422. A Lowland Scots-Norman family of the same name, becoming Morton from de Mortun, appears in Dumfriesshire from the beginning of the thirteenth century. Very likely this Janet who came to Paisley was from the southlands, probably from Ayrshire.[6] (Woodrow Wilson, whose distinguished penmanship shows in his signature down to his last days, probably did not know that Alexander Morton, born in 1820 in Ayrshire, possibly a very distant cousin, was the inventor of the machine used for pointing, tempering and grinding steel pens.)

Thomas Woodrow, Janet's father, was the second of twin sons born to John (second in our documented genealogy) and Janet Morton. This Thomas married Marion Williamson, daughter of Marion Wright and Robert Williamson of Glasgow. Loyalty to forebears appears here again, for Jeanie's youngest sister was named Marion, for her mother; and her brother James, the distinguished minister-scientist, also named a daughter Marion. This last Marion Woodrow became the genealogist and family historian of this branch of Woodrows in America. Another Woodrow had come to America before the Revolution—Andrew, eldest son of the Reverend Robert Woodrow (1679-1734), minister of Eastwood (a suburb of Glasgow), church historian and librarian of the University. This Andrew emigrated to Virginia in 1768 and fought for the liberation of the Colonies.[7]

Wright, the maiden name of Jeanie Woodrow's maternal grandmother, is another name that indicates an origin in craftsmanship. It is common in lowland Scotland and the north of England. In Old English *wyrhta* was a skilled worker, particularly in wood, but also in other materials (shipwright, wheel-, wain-, glass-, cheese-).[8] Before appearing as a surname, it was an occupational designation: see Rauf le Wrighte (a burgess of Stirling) and Thomas le Wrichte of Lanarkshire (1296).[9] So here is another line of artificers of Anglo-Norman exigence that is engrafted onto the Woodrow stock.

Robert Williamson, Jeanie's maternal grandfather, enters into the family story as a Glasgow townsman distinguished by a stubborn moral fiber similar to that of the Woodrow breed, and notable in an episode of local church history which directly affected the destiny of Thomas Woodrow, his son-in-law, and Woodrow Wilson, his great-grandson. An account of this episode was given by a grandson of Robert Williamson in a letter to the Glasgow *Herald* dated 10 April, 1917. Mr. Williamson, a Presbyterian of comparatively humble position but of sterling principle, was interested in missionary work. He so far forgot himself as to attend a sermon-lecture in an "Auld Kirk" (i.e. unreformed), preached by the Reverend Dr. Balfour in honor of the newly formed Glasgow Missionary Society. Subsequent public censure by the authorities of the Cameronian Reformed Church, of which he had been a member, citing his "sinful and offensive conduct" in worshipping in an unreformed church, led to his refusal to submit to this disciplinary censure and to his withdrawal from the so-called "Free" congregation. It led also to considerable commotion in Presbyterian Church circles, and to the subsequent founding of a still newer and more "Free" congregation by himself and his adherents. The point of interest for us in this story of rigid conformity and non-conformity lies in the fact that young Thomas Woodrow of Paisley joined the new congregation, and there met and later married Marion, daughter of Robert Williamson, its founder. This was in 1820. Fifteen years later, she accompanied her husband on a missionary enterprise to North America.

The Artificer Tradition

According to his son Thomas, John Woodrow of Paisley (second John in our genealogy) was a manufacturer. In lists of burgesses of Glasgow in the seventeenth and eighteenth centuries appear many Woodrows, all with such Christian names as John, James, William, Thomas, Robert, and occasionally Henry or Adam. Their occupations show them all to have been busy, responsible, city men, which, of course, is what a burger is. They were gardeners, grocers, maltmen, merchants, cordiners, tanners, tailors, bookbinders, servitors, manufacturers and schoolteachers. The list of burgesses would have omitted doctors, ministers and professors, such as Robert the historian, whose duties precluded routine civic service, but we know from other lists that in these professions the Woodrows were likewise busy. In view of the frequency of the occurrence of the name in past centuries, it is rather surprising to discover that in the Glasgow telephone directory of 1957

163

the name is listed only sixteen times (contrasting with more than 1,400 Wilsons)!

Of Williamsons in recent directories there are nearly two hundred, in all types of occupations (ministers, doctors, scientists); in technical and skilled enterprise, from dairying to radio and musical instruments, to contracting and engineering; in trade, selling groceries and meat and fish, wine, tobacco and snuff, books and stationery, clothing, tickets to far places and traveller's checks.

Mr. Kelley's study of Sclaters in industrial Paisley shows them to have been workmen, farmers, grocers, wrights, masons, cordiners, warpers and starchers, merchants, teachers and doctors. And the Mortons of Paisley are of the same busy middle class—bakers, grocers, shoemakers and manufacturers.

From all that has been said about the succession of Woodrows and the women they married, from whom Jeanie was born, there emerges a composite picture of a prototype which perfectly matches the nature of her son as the Woodrow side of his character matured and bore fruit in the course of his sixty-eight years. Woodrow Wilson was a townsman, industrious, responsible, with a mind matured by urban culture, wits sharpened by discipline in a competitive society, morals rooted in earnest Presbyterianism, and heart whole and warm because he belonged to a family which, as in generation after preceding generation, had been united and devoted. That high civic sense which forced him into active politics was the flowering of lines of steady, busy, loyal Anglo-Norman-Keltic citizens and churchmen in Glasgow and Clydesdale through many centuries. The thrift of mind that made him completely one-pointed arose from a shrewdness and calculation of the sort typical of the class and breed of the Woodrows, Williamsons, Mortons, Wrights and Sclaters from whom he sprang. Because he was an industrious artificer (in words and ideas) and persistent in enterprise, after the manner of his forebears, he achieved mastership of the political science and art of his country and times. Those energetic urban virtues enabled him, as President, to improve the laws of his country, to serve so ably as an executive, to lead so firmly in war, and to draft, with a sure knowledge of issues, the Covenant of the League of Nations, which survives today in the United Nations Charter.

This brings to focus what we mean when we say that Woodrow Wilson was what he was and did what he did *because of his BREED*.

In point of time, Janet Woodrow's grandfather John of Paisley conceivably could have been the son of the famous doctor of medicine who flourished in Glasgow in the early eighteenth century, but *that* Dr. John Wodrow (or Woodrow) had no son John among his several children, all duly registered at birth. Dr. John's elder half-brother Robert, the even more famous doctor of divinity, scholar and historian, did have a son John, but that John died in infancy. Consequently both John and Robert, the sons of Professor James Wodrow of late seventeenth century fame, seem to be ruled out as direct forbears of the Paisley Woodrows, so far as present evidence goes.

The names of Woodrow Wilson's recent ancestors in Scotland are recorded in the following genealogy:[10]

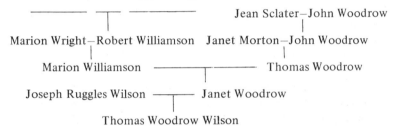

This doubtless would have been a blow to Woodrow Wilson, grandson of the Reverend Thomas Woodrow, for he took pride in his Woodrow ancestry, and special pride in his supposed descent through Robert, eminent scholar and divine. If he actually was not so descended, the tradition in the family carried almost as much psychological effect as if he had been. For that reason it seems important at this point to describe that famous Robert in the frame and idealogical context of his times.

"Robert the Scholar"

The Reverend Robert Wodrow, second son of Professor James Wodrow, not only was a preacher and author of "The History of the Sufferings of the Church in Scotland" (i.e. the Presbyterian "Kirk"), but also a man of wide interests and acute observation. In his voluminous journals, he recorded his interests in Scottish family lineages, in ancient Pictish kings, and in the natural sciences, particularly geology, botany and zoology. His fascination with learning, his career as librarian at the University of Glasgow and master of arts of that University, as author and as preacher of the Word, made of him a man after Woodrow

Wilson's own heart, though in many respects their characters seem to have been quite dissimilar.

Born in 1679 (to ecclesiastical and scholarly privilege), Robert Wodrow inherited the new splendors of the Renaissance, with many of its widening intellectual vistas. But it likewise was an age of ferment, an age in which the freeing of men's spirits was soon followed by the restless and reckless ranging of men's minds. As a Reformist churchman who, in his father's time and his own, had known the strife and intrigue and terror of three religious sects contending for power over men's lives and souls, the thirty years of his own ministry showed him the dangers and pitfalls of the very Revival of Learning into which his own omnivorous interests naturally led him.

He saw clearly that The Faith had a new and more subtly dangerous foe. No longer were either the specter of revived Catholicism or the "idolatrous" Anglican. impositions of the Restoration the chief threat to the Kirk in his view, nor the brutal and callous terrorism of the Stuart kings the worst fate its adherents could suffer. The Covenanters had proven themselves strong enough to resist the one and rise triumphant above the other, but he trembled as he saw the new foe more and more blatantly abroad in the land, taking an ever stronger part in the battle for men's souls. This new "limb of Antichrist" was atheism, and it was the product of the rebirth of pagan (euphemistically termed "Classical") learning and morality. He saw it at work in the *Journal des Savans* (which, it is known from his letters, he read with keen but frightened curiosity) and other speculative writings of the day. He knew of it through reports of the fashionable "Hell-fire Club" of London, imitated by "secret Atheisticall Clubs" in Edinburgh. He saw the enemy at work among the divinity students of Glasgow, who questioned many of the more rigorous tenets of the Faith, and in young ministers known as "the Bright Youths," who relied more upon smart "oratorical" preaching than upon "sound doctrine."

Robert Woodrow had seen enough of mass hysteria, of intrigue and betrayal and insecurity, of beheadings and hangings and burnings in the name of "heresy"–enough, indeed, of bloodthirsty violence on both sides—to make of him the timid soul that some historians describe; and this is an aspect of his nature that Woodrow Wilson could not have understood and probably did not suspect. But if Robert trembled, it was not before the temporal powers of kings and their vengeance, nor before the sort of physical fate that must have been for him a possibility throughout his lifetime, but before the terrifying and unpredictable spirit of the age, at work, it seemed, upon men's minds to the destruction of their souls. Whether or not Robert the Scholar enters into our Woodrow heritage by close blood ties, these profoundly important forces affecting him, and molding the Covenanter heritage of Woodrow Wilson, have great significance if we are to understand that heritage.

The fact that Robert the Scholar was ordained by the Paisley Presbytery and spent the remaining 30 years of his life as a preacher within that Presbytery (Eastwood, between Paisley and Glasgow, was his seat) doubtless lent color to the assumption that he was the direct progenitor of the Paisley branch of the Wodrows with whom we are concerned. But Paisley is only seven miles from Glasgow, and in the entire area of Glasgow and her outlying suburbs, there are today numerous Woodrows or Wodrows who recognize no near relationship between their several family lines. It would not have been an unusual circumstance that a Glasgow Wodrow, a graduate of the University, should have been "settled" for the ministry in nearby Paisley, or somewhere within the area included in the Paisley Presbytery, irrespective of any family connections there.

Ancient Paisley

Paisley, on the White Cart River near its juncture with the Clyde, was a twelfth century abbey village, growing up around the Cluniac Monastery established there in 1163, some thirty years after the building of the beautiful Cathedral of St. Mungo at Glasgow. The monastery, founded by Walter Fitzalan, High Steward of Scotland, was dedicated to St. Mirrin, a sixth century missionary, contemporary with the Irish St. Columba of the Isles who brought Keltic Christianity to Pictland (which became Scotland), from where it spread to northern Britain.

Three hundred years later the town was, according to the historian Marwick:[11]

> ... erected by King James IV into a free burgh or barony, with power to the inhabitants to buy and sell in the burgh, wines, wax, woolen and linen cloth, wholesale or retail, and all other goods and wares coming to it, to have bakers, brewers, butchers, etc., and workmen in various craft, a market cross, a weekly market on Monday, and two public fairs yearly, one on St. Mirrin's Day, with tolls and the other privileges enjoyed by any other burgh or barony in Scotland.

The Abbey, about whose ruins much of the new town of Paisley has grown up, was raised to that status in 1219. After nearly a century its peaceful existence was destroyed by Anglo-Norman invasion during the wars of Edward I of England against Robert Bruce. There it lay in semi-ruin until, near the end of that century, it was restored, to enjoy two hundred and fifty years more of busy contemplative life before its final destruction as a religious center during the excesses which accompanied the Reformation.

The latter years of the Abbey's existence were linked closely with the fortunes of the powerful Anglo-Norman Hamiltons. Young Claud Hamilton had been named abbot in 1553 at the age of ten—only a few short years before the interdiction of Roman Catholicism in Scotland when the plundering of the abbeys began, following the example of Henry VIII's Reformation in England. But in this instance, probably due to the family's prominence, the abbey tenure was raised to a temporal lordship, the erstwhile abbot became Lord of Paisley, and the abbey lands, after his marriage and death, passed to his son as the nucleus of the earldom created by James I (of England and Scotland) for that second Lord Paisley. Thus we first meet an Earl of Abercorn, that name so closely tied in with the Plantation of Ulster, particularly in County Tyrone where, as Earl of Abercorn and Baron of Strabane, the Lords incumbent from about 1715 onward would have claimed the fealty of James Wilson's forbears. Today Paisley is still the seat of the earls of Abercorn, and many Hamiltons are buried in the abbey church, as are likewise one royal Stuart (Robert III) and Margery, daughter of Robert Bruce.

A drawing of Paisley[12] in 1820 shows a half-dozen factories with tall chimneys in the dale south of the abbey, evidently along the River Cart, and shows the canal along the thoroughfares named Cawseway Side and Canal Street. Appropriately, since the barony had belonged from its founding to the earls—now dukes—of Abercorn (the Hamiltons who descended from the first Lord of Paisley), the street passing the abbey and running northeast is Abercorn Street, which is bisected by Hamilton Street. This was the Hamilton family who likewise were landed proprietors on High Street in Glasgow, where they gave the college its first buildings and landholding there on the Molendinar Burn.

Paisley history is written again in the names of two other streets east of the abbey, Cotton Street and Gauze Street. Cotton goods, thread and gauze were manufactured products for which Paisley has been famous from early times. In Thomas Woodrow's era the town was especially noted, not only for linen-lawn and silk-gauze, but also for the very popular "Paisley shawls," adapted in color and design from the fine woolen Cashmere shawls of India, and described by a writer of the day as distinguished by "a style of elegance and ingenuity elsewhere totally unrivalled."[13]

The Roman general Agricola, on one of his northernmost excursions into "Caledonia," as the Romans named Pictland, had discovered this to be a strategic area, and in the year A.D. 84, had built a fort on the west bank of the White Cart and named it Vanduara. From there were carried on sporadic forays against the wild Pictish tribes who dwelt in the Highlands. But for the most part, there are few lasting evidences of Roman occupation north of Hadrian's Wall, which formed the historic border between Britain and "Caledonia" and served, until the withdrawal of the Legions in the fifth century, to repel the assaults of "the northern barbarians."

Ancient Glasgow

Not until after the mid-sixth century did further Roman influence penetrate to this particular region, and then it was the influence of Christianity, that new religious teaching which had become centered in Christianized Rome. But it was a Keltic form of Christianity, outgrowth of the missions of St. Patrick and St. Columba of the Isles. Tradition has it that St. Ninian from Galloway was the first missionary to the heathen in Clydesdale, where he occupied a cell by the Molendinar Burn.

Later the Cymric King of Strathclyde—the domain around the Firth of Clyde in which Glasgow now stands—summoned the Keltic St. Mungo (sometimes called Kentigern) to convert the pagan Britons and Anglians who had infiltrated this region. St. Mungo founded his religious settlement at what he named "The Dear Green Spot"—Celtic Glas ("green") ghu ("dear")—in the valley between the Molendinar and the Clyde, near St. Ninian's early cell. St. Mungo became that settlement's patron saint, and to this day the city fathers use St. Mungo's motto as "the Corporation's" own: "Let Glasgow Flourish by the Preaching of the Word."

This beginning was prophetic, for Glasgow was to become the religious center of the Lowlands. Under King Malcolm the Third, in the latter half of the eleventh century, St. Mungo's little church became a bishop's seat, with its diocese extending from the River Clyde south to the Solway Firth and east to the Lothians. In the early twelfth century, King David I granted land for the bishop's castle and demesne, and by 1136 the first Cathedral had been erected as the bishop's ecclesiastical seat.

In the era of David I of Scotland (1124-1165), the major Anglo-Norman infiltration of the Lowlands began—an era of cultural development under a wise king, who saw the need of inviting the peaceful penetration of both nobles and artisans as teachers of government and the arts of life. Later in that same century, David's successor, William the Lion, took cognizance of the secular needs of the area.

> Between 1175 and 1178 King William the Lion granted to God and St. Kentigern, and Joceline, bishop of Glasgow, and his successors, a charter by which he empowered the bishops to have a burgh at Glasgow, with a market on Thursday, well and honorably, quietly and fully, with all the freedoms and customs which any of his burghs enjoyed. To all the burgesses who might reside in this burgh thus created, he granted his "firm peace" in going and returning through his whole land; and he prohibited everyone from troubling and molesting them or their goods or from inflicting any injury upon them, under pain of his full forfeiture.[14]

Shortly thereafter, King William granted another charter empowering the burgesses to hold a fair at Glasgow yearly for eight days "with his firm and full peace, and with all the liberties and rights granted or belonging to any fairs in Scotland." This annual fair continues to this day.

The town grew up around the market. Its income was derived from the practice of "uptaking a ladleful of each sack of corns or victual coming to the market." This toll was levied at the tollgate where the road entered the town. The town was required to erect a market cross by the Tollbooth. This was at the convergence of High Street and Watergate or Salt-market, Gallowgate and Trongate, where probably, when the charter was granted, booths and primitive dwellings of burghers already were standing. The Tollbooth also became the place where municipal business was transacted, and in time a jail, a courthouse and a hall for the council of burgesses were erected.

So came into existence the rudiments of what was to become the largest city in Scotland. This development awaited, however, the Virginia tobacco trade in the seventeenth and eighteenth centuries, and the industrial revolution in the eighteenth and nineteenth. The wealth that accrued from the tobacco trade enabled the city and its merchants to develop the quays and shipyards which have made modern Glasgow and the Clyde one of the world's greatest centers of marine engineering and shipbuilding, and of commerce to all quarters of the globe.

But despite its growing economic predominance in the earlier centuries, and particularly since the dedication of the beautiful "new" Cathedral in 1197, after the earlier one had been destroyed by fire, Glasgow was to retain its preeminence as a religious center. Throughout the long epoch of Papal supremacy, the lordly Cathedral of St. Mungo, built atop his tomb and adjacent to the walled castle of the bishops at the head of the High Street, dominated the Glasgow scene as it dominated the city's life. And even on into the seventeenth century, when its University became one of the chief centers of the Reformed Church of the Covenanters of Scotland, the dominant influence of the Cathedral, though no longer a bishop's seat, remained.

Glasgow's famous University was founded in the mid-fifteenth century under Papal authority. But its greatest scholastic reputation was earned in the eighteenth century as the seat of "modern learning" and of Presbyterian faith and doctrinal training. Here, toward the end of its period of greatest reputation, Woodrow Wilson's grandfather Thomas Woodrow came as a student, as many a Woodrow had done before him.

There are, as of this eighteenth century period of flowering, interesting contemporary sidelights upon the university and the city, purportedly written by a travelling Englishman of quality while touring Scotland. This gentleman's travel observations were compiled, at that time anonymously, under the title of "Peter's Letters to his Kinfolk" and were published in four volumes. The reader was permitted to gain the impression that "Peter" brought with him the supercilious attitude of a cultivated Englishman toward the "rude northerners" with their "ungenteel" ways. In particular, the "barbarous" syllables of the provincial dialect which distorted the speech "even of the learned," was described as greatly offensive to his ears. He paid tribute, however, to the "grand and impressive city" with its fine Trongate—"one of the very finest things, I venture to say, in all Europe"; to the "noble and magnificent" Gothic cathedral, despite "its nakedness within, and all its desolation without" since the Reformation; and particularly to the University, whose buildings he felt to be reminiscent of the Oxford Quadrangles, and at once more ancient and more pleasing than those of

Edinburgh, all enhanced as they were by lovely gardens and "a beautiful and classical" museum.

This "skeptic" was moved to unexpected and sincere homage, by the power and eloquence of the Presbyterian divines, and the "wonderfully strict" piety of the populace of Glasgow in their Sabbath observances. Particularly the eloquence of the famous preacher Dr. Chalmers commanded his respect, swaying, as it did, "all around him with its imperial rule"—and this, said the author, despite an awkwardness of gesture and an uncouth tongue. "In presence of such a spirit, subjection is a triumph—and I was proud to feel my hardened nerves creep and vibrate, and my blood freeze and boil while he spake—as they were wont to do in the early innocent years."[15] By the time the third edition of his work was published, anonymity had vanished: "Peter" was a native Glaswegian and a graduate of the University, John Gibson Lockhart, later a friend of Robert Burns and Sir Walter Scott, and a biographer of note.

University and Town

The rural and small-town Irish heritage of Woodrow Wilson's paternal forebears has been outlined in the context of Gaelic and Keltic history and environment in County Tyrone, Ulster. The urban environment of Paisley and Glasgow in which his mother's parents and grandparents were conditioned was so utterly different that it has been necessary to go into the history of those communities, and now of the University of Glasgow, their chief center of culture, in some detail. Many of the dominant characteristics which made Woodrow Wilson what he was and which determined his career, thereby affecting human destiny, came straight out of the Paisley and Glasgow heritage.

"Thomas Woodrow, f.n. 2 dus Joannis Artif. Paisley—M.A. 1819."[16] So was recorded in 1819 the granting of the degree of master of arts to Thomas, second-born son of John Wodrow, artificer of Paisley, in the matriculation albums of the University of Glasgow, extant in the modern library.

The circumstances of "Joannis, Artif." would appear to have been at least moderately affluent, inasmuch as his second son was supported for a four-year course of study in the University at an age when young men without fortune ordinarily would have been engaged in making their own living. Quite probably he already had been working and saving his earnings toward this earnestly desired goal, for Thomas was twenty-three years old at the time of his matriculation—an age regarded as relatively mature in those days, and certainly a far cry from the early matriculations of the sixteenth and seventeenth centuries, which frequently occurred as young as twelve or fourteen years.

The decision to become a divinity student in this religiously troubled second decade of the nineteenth century in Scotland indicated a mature purpose, and likewise a devout upbringing in the Paisley home. It was an era when dissension between "the old moderatism" and the new "evangelical reform" movement within the Presbyterian Church of Scotland reflected the growth of Conservative and Whig agitation in the whole British social and political scene, as well as the disturbing world factors of the Napoleonic wars and the Industrial Revolution. Unrest and upheaval were in the air, and in the minds and hearts of most young churchmen. These disturbances were as nothing beside the fires of religious controversy which had raged here during most of the seventeenth century, with their frequent accompaniments of bloodletting in "the Killing Times" following the Restoration (i.e. the restoration of the Monarchy under Charles II, following the period of the Cromwellian "Protectorate"). But the new dissensions nonetheless were vivid and real, involving as they did much pain and struggle and courage in the individual decisions which had to be made; and before the half-century was reached, the decisive step known as the "Disruption" was to be taken within the Church as a whole, when the "Auld Kirk" and the new "Free Kirk" painfully and pridefully went their separate ways.

At the beginning of the nineteenth century, the fortunes of the ancient University of Glasgow were fluctuating with the times. In some degree, the institution's former fame was now lessened, particularly in comparison with the enormous prestige it had enjoyed as a scholarly center during the preceding century. In a new age of political reform, it stood officially for conservatism, though not militantly so.[17] Undeniably it did stand in need of reform, as rectors and visitors over a period of some years had contended. This was due chiefly to the long-entrenched position the faculty enjoyed, together with their steadfast opposition to any change. Very likely this situation, together with the consequent atmosphere of dissension prevailing in University politics and policy, accounted for the fact that the students were more "liberal" than the faculty, in both political and religious views. We know from his subsequent attitudes and activities that Thomas Woodrow found himself in accord with this liberal trend, at least in religious matters, while the University, before many years had passed, was to accomplish its own liberal "Reform" and regain its former prestige, through the fame both of its faculty and its graduates.

The beginning of the nineteenth century was not the first time in its long history that the University's fortunes had fluctuated with the uncertainties of a new age. Founded when the fifteenth century was halfway advanced, this new *"studium generalum"* was launched into an unquiet world, in a time of the decay of long-established institutions and the stirrings of a vigorous new culture waiting to be born. It was an age which saw, on the Continent and in England, the growing power of the secular prince *vis-a-vis* the Papal authority, and a revival of interest in classical learning and art. Yet it was mid-century before these latter stirrings, termed the Renaissance, reached Scotland, and there, for nearly a century to come, the old relationship between Crown and Pope was to remain undisturbed, despite the slow spreading of the movement for ecclesiastical reform.

Perhaps this last factor may help to account for the firm establishment of this infant center of learning at Glasgow, and for its consistent growth and flourishing through centuries of secular and religious strife, despite the storms of revolution and counter-revolution, of Reformation, Covenant, Restoration and Reestablishment, of Revolution and "Kirk Triumphant," Disruption and Reunion.[18] For it was founded upon the solid rock of religious authority and Christian faith, and this prevailed—whatever the changing source of that authority or the varying complexion of that faith—all through the turbulent centuries. Though superficially, the University's fortunes may have fluctuated with the onset of each of the more violent political shocks, its firm establishment never wavered; and it is not the fluctuations that astonish us, but rather the overall constancy of its aggrandizement and growth.

Beginnings of the "Studium"

In 1450, James II of Scotland, Honorary Canon of Glasgow Cathedral, commissioned William Turnbull, doctor of canon law and bishop of Glasgow, to secure from Pope Nicholas I the authority to establish a *studium generalum* under the Church's supervision in Glasgow. The church barony of Glasgow, with St. Mungo's Cathedral at its center, was one of the three oldest and best established of the bishoprics of Scotland, and it was thought desirable that it should include a seat of learning comparable to those at Edinburgh and Aberdeen.

174

Bishop Turnbull had been attached previously to the Papal Court in Rome, as proctor for James I and chamberlain to the Pope, and he found no difficulty in obtaining what he sought. In the Bull of authorization thus issued, on January 7, 1451, the Pope granted all the privileges and honors enjoyed by the famous University of Bologna, where he himself had studied. But the subsequent development of the University at Glasgow indicates that its technical structure followed on the pattern of the more broadly based University of Louvain in Belgium, which had become and for a century continued to be "the model university of modern Europe."[19]

In 1453, James granted a charter to the newborn institution under the "King's firm seal of peace and protection," with exemption of officers and faculty from taxation.[20] This charter was reconfirmed by each succeeding Stuart King—or Queen—during the following two centuries.

Learning, in that day, was still essentially for and by the clergy, but with increasing attention given to promising young members of the laity, upon whom the benefits of a certain amount of secular as well as theological instruction were bestowed. Students and staff alike were selected and supervised by the Church hierarchy. Of the sixteen rectors who immediately followed David Cadzow, the first, all were canons of the Church, and all held ecclesiastical "livings" for whose spiritual administration they were responsible, in addition to their educational duty to the University, and which supplied most of their livelihood.

The beginnings were very small indeed. The "city" of those days was itself small. It centered around the Cathedral of St. Mungo, with its cluster of ecclesiastical buildings and its castellated bishop's palace, set on the hill at the head of the High Street, which ran for a mile or so to the shallow upper reaches of the River Clyde. Further down the High Street was the priory of the Black Friars, about halfway between the Cathedral and Market Cross. Most of the other town buildings and dwellings fronted on the two sides of this street, backed by meadows and on the east by a small stream, the Molendinar Burn, flowing into the Clyde.

Now properly founded, but lacking an endowment, this new scholarly enterprise was dependent entirely upon the Bishopric for its existence, and it began its career in a modest house of the Church's providing in Rattoun Raw (now spelled "Rotten Row") just off the High Street and opposite Weaver Lane. These premises, known as the

The "Auld Pedagogy," Glasgow University

"Auld Pedagogy," where the University was accommodated for the first ten years of its life, remained standing long afterward, and an etching of the ruined facade is still extant.[21] There the Dominican friars, or friar preachers as they were called, from the Blackfriars monastery nearby, lectured in theology and in canon law, and there the masters in the "Faculty of Arts" read from a Latin text in Aristotelian logic or Euclidean mathematics, while their students wrote down from this dictation the versions that were to serve them as textbooks in those years before the art of printing came to Scotland.

Not until nine years after the Papal Bull of establishment and seven years after its chartering, was a specific grant of land and buildings made to the new institution, on January 6, 1460. As of that date the *Munimenta Alme*[22] of the University records the charter of James, first Lord Hamilton, by which "a tenement lying to the east side of the High Street," together with four acres near the Black Friars and beside the Molendinar Burn, were conveyed to the bailies (i.e. stewards) of the burgh of Glasgow, who were to give "seizin of the same to Master Duncan Bunche, Vicar of Wiston, Principal Regent of the Faculty of Arts. . . ."

For this gift of a "tenement" (or block of residential buildings) and meadow acreage, the donor exacted a most complete and minutely detailed interest, to be paid, it appears, *ad infinitum*. The conveyance above recorded was followed by a document of two pages in Latin. The gist of it reads:

> . . . under condition that twice in every day, at the close of their noontide and evening meals, the Regents and Students shall rise and pray for the souls of the Lord of Hamilton, the Founder of the College, of the Lady Euphame Countess of Douglas and Lady of Bothwell his wife, and of their ancestors, heirs, and successors; that every Regent and Student in priest's orders, shall in their masses openly commend the souls of James Lord Hamilton and Euphame his wife, the founders of the college, to the prayers of the bystanders: that if a chapel or oratory shall be built in the College, the Regents and Students shall assemble there on every Saturday after Vespers, and shall on their bended knees sing the anthem of the Blessed Virgin, *Ave Gloriosa Virginuum Regina*, with a collect and remembrance for the souls of the founders of the college; that until such chapel or oratory be built, the aforesaid anthem and remembrance shall be repeated "submissa voce" before an altar in the Church of the Friars Preachers; that every year on the day of the death of the Lord

Hamilton, and on the day of the death of the Lady Euphame his wife, the founders of the college, the Regents and Students shall repair to the Cathedral Church, where every Regent in priest's orders shall say mass for the dead, and every Regent not in priest's orders shall read the non-sacrificial office for the departed, and all the students shall make orisons for the souls of the Founders; and lastly, that every Regent shall give faithful counsel in affairs of the Founders and their successors, so often as he shall be asked.[23]

It would be interesting if one could know for how long this compounding interest of prayers and benedictions continued unabated and unabbreviated by the grateful recipients. One also wonders whether all the accumulation of later grants and endowments, as the years passed, carried with them obligations of a similar sort to swell the duties of a hard-pressed teaching and preaching order.

These succeeding grants included lands, or the "tack" (lease) of or revenue from lands, privileges of use of buildings, assignment of a portion of the Trongate customs levies, and gifts toward the appointment or support of faculty members. These grants or benefices came from all walks of life—the Crown, the gentry, the clergy, the burgesses or representatives of the Burgh—and though few of the gifts were large, in terms of modern grants or necessities, they kept body and soul together, one might say, during the rather precarious first century of the University's existence. And this may not be an inapt phrase, in view of the fact that in a number of instances the assignment recorded was for "a chalder (measure) of meal" (in return for fishing rights), or the grant of "16 bolls (32 bushels) of oatmeal yearly" for the support of a bursar during a course of philosophy.

Survival through Stress

The University was thus intact and growing slowly, but not in very strong state to withstand the first violent shock which came upon it at the end of its first century—the crumbling of the entire edifice of the Church hierarchy in Scotland, along with that of the Roman Catholic authority under which it had been established, and the dispersal of the religious orders from which it (the University) had drawn its chief scholastic support. In other words—came the Reformation.

Despite chaotic conditions following upon England's latest invasion and the death of the last of her strong kings (James V, 1542), despite years of struggle for supremacy among her nobles, and despite the growing spread of the "heretical" movement among the people, Scotland actually did not feel the full force of the religious Reformation until forty years after Martin Luther in Europe and twenty-five years after Henry VIII broke with Rome and declared himself head of the Church of England. In 1599, John Knox, encouraged by the political turmoil at the Scottish Court, returned to Scotland from Geneva and launched upon a fiery reform campaign among nobles and commoners almost equally ripe for change. In 1560 the Scottish Parliament decreed the abolition of the Roman Church in Scotland.

The transition in Scotland came not with the ponderous and slow authoritarian deliberation by which the abbeys and monasteries of England were expropriated and despoiled, and the religious hierarchy, by "due legal process," severed from its Papal roots (either through apostasy or death). In the centers of Scottish culture, its gathering venom burst suddenly, from the populace, and expended itself in violence upon the bishops and clergy, and upon the ecclesiastical buildings with their beautiful ornamentation and ritual treasures, in a fury of destruction. In Glasgow, the ancient Cathedral of St. Mungo was partially mutilated and, it is said, only saved from utter destruction at the hands of the mob by the determined artisans of the town who came to its defense. Forewarned, James Beaton or Bethune, last Roman Catholic Archbishop of Glasgow, already had left his castle, under protection of the French guard provided by the Queen Regent Mary of Guise, to rescue the most valuable of the sacred emblems and relics. With him went most of the medieval charters and records of Church and Burgh—including the University's most precious document, the Papal Bull of 1451, and the rector's mace of delegated Papal authority.

Fearful hearts saw in this loss a symbol and angry augury of the University's downfall. But, whether its very weakness and seeming inconsequence protected it, or whether the wise leaders who emerged from the initial hurly-burly deliberately determined to foster this scholarly center and shape it to their own needs and uses, the University escaped the wholesale destruction. Quoting Mackie:[24] "The lamp of learning, though it flickered uncertainly for a while, was not utterly extinguished, and before long shone forth in a bright and enduring flame." And to cap it, perhaps symbolically still, the mace was recovered later. But never the Papal Bull.

Thomas Woodrow, three hundred years later in 1800, was the inheritor of this religious Reformation of 1560 and of all its subsequent vicissitudes, developments and divergencies. The passionate convictions, the stubborn adherence to principles once taken, the proud consciousness of possessing "the Truth," the rankling memories of intolerance and suffering in "the Killing Times," the strong sense of the prerogative of individual secession in matters of conscience—all this legacy of three centuries was in the blood of his race and family, and showed itself clearly in his own life and the lives of his descendants. These likewise were the heritage of the University in which his scholarly and doctrinal powers were molded.

The "Reformation Settlement" set up by the General Assembly of the new "Kirk" provided a thorough plan of education, in which "the study of theology should be the apex of all good learning"—the rigorously framed and enforced new Protestant theology, of course. With revenues now diverted from the old Church, often into the private treasury of nobles, to whom many of the ecclesiastical lands reverted rather than to the Burgh, ambitious plans were slow in being carried out. The town magistrates did give some aid to the college *hospicium*, including a foundation for the attendance of twelve poor students and a new constitution for the University. Also there was a definite advantage accruing in the allocation to the college by charter, first by Queen Mary in 1563 and more extensively by the Town Council in 1572, of those properties "as yet indemolissit" which had been expropriated from the Black Friars when their luckless order was driven out.

Not until 1674, however, did the upward turn begin and the institution enter upon that phase of growth which was to bring it international fame as a center of Protestant learning.

Advance

Thomas Woodrow, in his studies of church history, would have been well acquainted with the notable figure of Andrew Melville, scholar and redoubtable Presbyterian, who had studied previously at the University of Poictiers and at Geneva, and who proved himself to be a man of great courage *vis-a-vis* certain predatory members of the nobility and likewise versus the authoritarian Episcopal tendencies of the Scottish Regency, which followed upon the abdication of Mary Queen of Scots. Melville in 1574 was named principal of the College (i.e. the active administrator under the rector) by the General Assembly of the Kirk, and his wise and vigorous leadership gave the needed impetus toward scholarly and disciplinary advance. His solid contributions to the insti-

180

tution, in spiritual tone, augmented resources, general reorganization and a growing student body, were to long outlast his time and ensure effective continuance of both the scholarly tradition and the new Presbyterian enthusiasm.

The traditional scholarship and a renewed physical prosperity might have persisted even through the turmoil of the oncoming century, for, as has been noted before, all the Stuart Kings either were generous or complacent toward the University, and neither James VI (and Ist of England) nor his son Charles I was an exception, despite their ardor for the Episcopacy and their constant state of friction with the Kirk. But the Presbyterian tone and enthusiasm, had it not already been founded solidly, well might have faltered under the determination of that James to strengthen the bishops and make them an instrument of power for the Crown, even to the point of giving them dominion over purely academic affairs, as the Roman Catholic bishops had had before the Reformation.

As it was, the role of the bishops, increasingly obnoxious to "the true Faith," strengthened the temper of faculty and students alike and the University relaxed nothing of its new spirit. This remained true even later, while benefiting greatly from the royal favor of Charles I during the early years of his reign, through new gifts and the restoration of ecclesiastical lands which had been alienated to the nobles at the Reformation. After 1638, with the Presbyterian Rising, the so-called Bishops' Wars and the formulation of the National Covenant, the College benefited equally from the renewed ascendancy of the Kirk, in freedom of policy, a fresh sectarian zeal and a reinvigorated department of (Presbyterian) theology.

During this hey-day of the restored power of the Kirk, religion again was playing an enormous part in the life of the University and of its students—differing only in minor detail from the part played therein during the Middle Ages. The diatribes and disputations now concerned a much greater variety of heretics, including papists, all bishops reformed or otherwise (i.e. Lutheran or Church of England), and all · "Arminians, Socinians, Anabaptists and other enemies of the truth." Indeed, under the zealous governance of the Kirk, the Department of Divinity was being augmented greatly at the expense of other departments, and so many young ministers were being trained thus that the Glasgow reputation and influence became very strong throughout Scotland.[25] This new importance doubtless explains why Glasgow, as a center second only to Edinburgh, was the seat of sessions of the General Assembly of the Kirk and focus of Covenanter mobilization in later times of crisis and strife.

Growth

Certain material progress was notable during this mid-seventeenth century. The reputation of the College was high. An English benefactor of the time, who established a close link between Glasgow and Balliol College, Oxford, said of Glasgow University: "It is justly esteemed by all learned men to bee the best in that kinde that ever was yett extant."[26] The student body was growing constantly, drawn mostly from good homes, among the Scottish nobility as well as the "commons," and likewise from among the families of "Reformers" in England and Ireland. In 1646, forty-one apartments were available to students, and, with an average of 125 students registered, these apartments must have been densely populated. Mackie[27] notes from historical sources that the scions of noble houses or of the gentry often attended in twos or threes, either kith or kin (each with private "pedagogue" and page, who lodged elsewhere), so that this crowding was not a token of undue familiarity among strangers or unequals!

Not even the disastrous Plague which visited Glasgow during this period seems to have checked its flourishing progress substantially, although it did necessitate removal of courses to a country district for a time. But a plague of another type was to have more effect upon the tranquil life, if not upon the external fortunes of the University, and slowly to alter its scholarly values and emphases. This began with the Cromwellian revolution in England against the absolute authority of Crown and Established Church, culminating in the victory of the Parliamentarians and the execution of Charles I in 1649. This dampening influence continued through the subsequent restoration of the monarchy in the person of Charles II in 1660 and throughout that monarch's cruel and intolerant reign. Indeed, it was not until near the end of the century that the accession of the Protestant Mary, daughter of James II, and her consort William of Orange to the throne of England ended the long era of religious turbulence, oppression and fierce retaliation.

Concerning that long period of turbulence, Thomas Woodrow had especially good reason to be well-informed, particularly because it was recorded in a volume, *A History of the Sufferings of the Church*, which he certainly must have read, since it was written by a scholar and librarian of the University in the early eighteenth century, the celebrated Robert Wodrow—perhaps a family connection. Robert Wodrow was well fitted, in points even beyond his scholarly competence, to write of these matters, since his grandfather was made prisoner in the 1660 Pentlands Rising against the restoration of the Episcopacy, an uncle had been hanged in Edinburgh as a "Covenanting traitor" after the fracas at Rullian Green, and a cousin, taken at the battle of Bothwell Brig, was lost at sea off the Orkneys with 200 other prisoners of the Crown, during shipment to Ireland to the Plantations. And the author's own father "the gentle" James Wodrow, and an elder brother Alexander had been practicing ministers of the Kirk in Glasgow during the oppressive last years of the Roman Catholic James II's reign.[28] (Later both were professors of theology in the University, but before Thomas Woodrow's time.)

Inner Turmoil

Although Scotland had sympathized with the English Parliamentarians in their opposition to the absolutism of the Crown, the Scottish people, nobles and commoners alike, also had opposed the assumption of power by the dictator (self-styled "Protector") Cromwell. After all, the Kings of England, since the death of Elizabeth, were of the Scottish blood royal, and loyalty to their own died hard among Scotsmen, despite religious differences. Equally, distrust of the imposition upon themselves of this authority by an Englishman—the invader Cromwell—had its strong roots in centuries of strife across the border, despite the fundamental religious similarities involved.

So it was that the fabric of the Covenanting faith in Scotland had been rent by the issues of loyalty to Crown and uncompromising abhorrence of Crown policy, and this rending made itself felt in all phases of life—in clan warfare, in politics, in the General Assembly of the Church itself, before Cromwell abolished even that venerable body.

All this turmoil, naturally, was reflected in the life of the University of Glasgow. Its affairs, along with those of the city, governed by a Cromwellian Commission, were dictated as effectively by outside decree as ever they had been during the monastic regime or the Crown's Episcopate. Its faculty and students had responded to the general divisions and dissensions of "Moderates" and "Remonstrants," and there was general unrest.

Only in its physical fortunes had the University shown consistent progress during these troubled times, and this was thanks in equal measure to the willingness of the new Government to placate dissident local opinion through liberality and to the adroitness of a local "dictator," who when named principal by the Commissioners was willing to gain advantage for the College by flattering and thereby exploiting the Government's complacency.

The ambitious acquiring, borrowing and building program of this rather remarkable Principal Gillespie, resulting in a new College Court in the High Street, new quadrangles, towers and houses for masters and professors, continued until the fall of the Protectorate in 1559 (when, with his customary equivocal skill, he escaped the headsman's axe, but not the prison). Administered dictatorially over strong faculty disapproval as it had been, and with serious results to the academic well being of the institution, this program nevertheless gave the University the chief features of the substantial and dignified quarters it was to inhabit until the growing congestion of the area in an industrial age made removal to a new site necessary in the late nineteenth century.

This, in all essentials, was the college in which Thomas Woodrow had his theological training from 1815 to 1819, and which his son James visited years later, while with relatives in Glasgow on his way back to America from studies in the University of Heidelberg.[29]

In outward essentials this similarity existed, but not in inner governance. For during the thirty years after the fall of the Protectorate, the University had been under the direction of the restored Archbishopric of Glasgow, appointed by the Crown, and its professors, of divinity as well as secular studies, either were Episcopalians or Presbyterians required to take the oath of religious conformity, along with the oath of allegiance to the new sovereign, Charles II.

This change in atmosphere inevitably was upsetting, although at first there was little political interference, and Charles II even had acceded to new grants of lands and revenues. Student attendance was good, including many sons of distinguished families, and diaries of the period attest to strict scholarliness, good teaching, thorough examinations and "piety of living"—in other words, the College's growth in reputation still continued despite change within and political uproar without.

Yet there always was a vocal element of religious dissent within the academic walls, and many still wore ostentatiously the blue ribbon of the Covenant. Before the "thirty years of the Bishops" were ended, these student disorders had brought on many breaches in its privileges and a certain amount of abrogation of its funds. These disciplinary measures, in the backward view, seem of little moment in comparison with the wisdom, tolerance and great scholarly contributions made in those times by such men as Gilbert Burnet of the School of Divinity who, although under the rule of the Presbytery, had been exiled for refusing the Covenant, now opposed similar oppressive measures by the Episcopacy which he represented. Indeed it may well be that the moderation with which the Episcopal regime was ordered within the University, in contrast to the violence without, was a big factor in leading to that lessening of the fires of religious controversy which followed during the reign of William and Mary, and to the "new latitudinarianism" which became apparent early in the eighteenth century in the curriculum of the University and in its spiritual practices. This, in turn, led to the great enhancement of its scholarly reputation and achievements during that century.

This is not to say that Presbyterian authoritarianism in the University, once restored, was any less rigorous than before. With the downfall of James II, last of the Jacobite (i.e. Stuart) kings, due to his Roman rather than Anglican Catholic predilections, and the accession to the throne of his eldest daughter Mary, married to the Protestant William of Orange, there came about a complete purging of Anglican prelates from the Scottish scene and from University influence. In Glasgow, never a center of strong Jacobite sentiment, the change took place without undue disturbance, as exiled ministers returned to accept Faculty office.

The principal and some regents resigned, because no incumbent might continue without accepting the Presbyterian form of government dictated by the restored General Assembly of the Kirk. But owing to the strongly felt influence of the throne (dedicated as it was to the prevention of further religious persecutions) and the new moderate atmosphere already referred to, these changes took place without notable rancor, under a church government largely shorn of its previous political absolutism.

Fame

Although any diversions from orthodox theology in divinity teaching were censured and punished by the Presbytery, there nevertheless was now a notable relaxation in religious domination of the Univer-

185

sity. The general curriculum became far more liberal and received much greater emphasis *vis-a-vis* the theological, as the eighteenth century progressed. New chairs were inaugurated and old courses enlarged in mathematics, natural philosophy, civil law, medicine and surgery. The student body was considerably augmented, and in general the University enjoyed in those latter years of the eighteenth century a period of unusual prosperity and academic brilliance.

This was the more remarkable, in view of the political and economic vicissitudes of the times. Britain was shaken deeply by the outbreak of the French Revolution, with its attendant political and economic dangers, after having been bled severely by the American War of Independence and the loss of her Colonies there. That loss was of particularly great moment to the fortunes of Glasgow and the University, for it had caused the complete collapse of the great tobacco trade, on which the civic expansion of the Burgh and its mercantile wealth had depended principally. Yet in the midst of the diversions and enthusiasms of liberal and revolutionary sentiment, causing turmoil within, and the marked lessening of outside financial resources, the University "expanded its concept of learning, adjusted itself to the demands of a new age and produced in every field scholars of the first eminence."[30]

Robert Simson, occupying the chair of mathematics until his death in 1760, attained world renown. William Cullen, professor of medicine, introduced chemistry as a separate study in 1744. His pupil and successor, Joseph Black, noted for the discovery of new chemical laws, was a great aide and advisor between 1756 and 1766 to that young mathematical and nautical instrument maker, James Watt, to be recognized for his engineering inventions by the granting of an LL.D from his University in 1806. It was James Watt, also, who surveyed the Clyde estuary and planned the modern port of Glasgow.

In civil law, John Millar (one of a succession of law students and professors of that name and family) had become so notable a lecturer by 1761 that students flocked to him from England and the Continent, even including graduates of Oxford and Cambridge. (He subsequently became Lord of Sessions in the national law courts in Edinburgh, taking the title Lord Craighill from the name of his estate near Dundee.) In the chair of moral philosophy, the distinguished professor Francis Hutcheson had much to do with molding the thought of his pupil Adam Smith, who later became professor of logic, economics and ethics in the

University and the famous author of "The Wealth of Nations." In the classical department, William Richardson occupied the chair of the humanities with such distinction during the final decades of the eighteenth century that he attracted many students who later came to fame in the nineteenth; while James Moore during those same years was a renowned professor of Greek.

It was in the flourishing eighteenth century also that Robert and Andrew Foulis set up a printing press in the inner quadrangle, producing celebrated folios in Greek and Latin, in addition to the routine printing which long had been a University tradition. The Foulis brothers also fostered an art collection and art instruction in the University. The Library already had become a special interest of the incumbent chancellor, the Duke of Montrose, who secured gifts for books and a building in 1726, thus enhancing the department where Robert Wodrow had been librarian a quarter-century before. Further toward the end of the eighteenth century, the Hunterian Museum was established through the bequest of William Hunter, to preserve the archaeological finds of the region which the fresh interests of the age were turning up. Altogether, the University was keeping pace with the progress of the Age of Learning, as well as with its own sound and ancient traditions.

But it was not the new vistas in science and engineering, upon which the progress of Scotland was to depend, that drew Thomas Woodrow to the University. Rather it was specifically the ecclesiastical tradition—theology, the Church. This indicates a trait that was of fundamental significance in the character of his grandson, Woodrow Wilson. His mind was not much interested in scientific or industrial development as such. Rather, from boyhood on, history, government and politics, in retrospect and in their implications for the present and future, engrossed him. This conservatism was notable in his whole career, but particularly in his youth when his innate character revealed itself.

But even before Thomas Woodrow's time, during these eighteenth century decades of intellectual ferment, the University was departing markedly from certain of its traditions. To the recorder Robert Wodrow and others following him, the giving over of some of the old disciplines and pieties and the adventurous straying into new paths of thought were matters of profound and anxious concern. To several diarists who provide vivid glimpses of student life and thought in Glasgow during those changing times, both the life and the thought seemed full of vigor and fascination. Yet it was to this new and wayward flowering, this intense and in many ways undisciplined and undirected scattering of energies that a period of temporary decline in the University's prestige at the turn of the century was due. It would seem that, along with certain organizational reforms, a short and undistinguished fallow period was necessary before a renewed or regained luster could shed itself upon students and faculty alike in the days of such later-world-renowned figures as—in physics and medicine for instance—Sir William Thompson, Lord Kelvin and Dr. Joseph Lister.

This renascence, however, did not come about until after the student days of Thomas Woodrow and, in some instances not until after the rebuilding of the University on Gilmore Hill, far to the west of the old Burgh center on the High Street, where it was founded and where it had grown and flourished for four hundred years.

Demise and Rebirth

Overlooking the Kelvin River and Kelvingrove Park, just above the dam where once stood old Patrick Mill in the midst of the countryside, is the high ridge formerly known as "The Woodlands." This site was acquired in 1845 for the new University buildings. The congestion of the High Street, extending from the Cathedral to the industrially teeming Clyde and enveloping the old University quadrangles, had been dictating this removal for years—against all the tenacious arguments of tradition and sentiment. Of all the buildings on this time-honored site bequeathed in 1460 by the good James, first Lord Hamilton, only the venerable gateway of the old College was preserved and removed to the new site, where today it still marks the entry to the eminence on which the new buildings stand under their soaring spire. Thomas Woodrow would not have recognized the new College or its environs, but through this massive gateway he had passed many times as a student on the High Street, below the Cathedral of St. Mungo. We do not know whether his famous grandson, on his several sojourns in the British Isles, ever visited Glasgow in one of the tradition-haunting "pilgrimages" which he loved to make, or ever passed under the arch which had shadowed the Woodrow forbears of which he was so proud.

The University of Glasgow
and Higher Education in America

The evolution of the University of Glasgow has been described in detail, partly because it was the alma mater of Thomas Woodrow, but

188

also because of its significance in relation to subsequent educational developments in America. Our particular concern here is with the Presbyterian-founded Princeton University where, at the turn of the twentieth century, Thomas Woodrow's grandson and namesake was first lay president, instituting reforms which were to affect in large measure the subsequent system of higher education throughout the United States.

It was in the Theological School at Princeton that Thomas Woodrow Wilson's father was trained and granted the degree of bachelor of divinity, so it may be said that the heritage of Scottish Presbyterian scholarship came to Woodrow Wilson through both his paternal and maternal lineage. But from the beginning, the impact of Scottish Presbyterian heritage upon American higher education in general was original, direct and continuous, chiefly perhaps through what is now Princeton University.

In 1727, during the era known as "The Great Awakening," William Tennent, a Scottish Presbyterian scholar, had founded what became known as "The Log College," at Neshaminy in Bucks County, Pennsylvania. His four sons, educated there, became ministers and revivalists. The effect of the "revival" movement and the college which nurtured it was to split the Presbyterian organization in the American Colonies into the "Old Side," or conservative group, which remained in control of the Philadelphia Synod, and the "New Side," whose more radical members established a Synod in New York. The radicals were the American equivalent of the "Free" Presbyterian seceders from the Auld Kirk in Scotland.[31]

This "radical" group wanted to establish in the middle Colonies a college under Presbyterian influence which would rank with that of William and Mary in the colonial capital of Virginia, and with "Congregationalist" Harvard and Yale in New England. The preferred central area of Philadelphia being under "Old Side" Synod control, they petitioned the governor of New Jersey for permission to center their educational program there, and in 1746 such a charter was granted by John Hamilton, colonial Governor, the institution to be known as the College of New Jersey.

Its modest beginnings were set in Elizabeth and not until ten years later was a permanent campus near the village of Princeton ready to become the scene of its steady academic growth toward future greatness. Its first and main building was named Nassau Hall in honor of William of Orange and Nassau, Protestant King of England, Scotland

189

and Ireland between 1689 and 1702. At the time of its completion in 1756, it was the largest academic building in the Colonies, a considerable proportion of the funds for its construction having been solicited in the old country. The architect of Independence Hall in Philadelphia was its designer, and Nassau Hall became the handsome center of what has come to be one of the most beautiful campuses in the nation.[32]

When Thomas Woodrow Wilson entered as a freshman in 1875, it was in "Old Nassau" that most of his classes were held, and the college was still the "College of New Jersey." Indeed, not until 1896, during its sesquicentennial celebration, was its designation changed to Princeton University. On this historic occasion, Woodrow Wilson, who had been professor of political science and government there since 1890, was chosen to deliver the main address. Its subject, characteristically, was "Princeton in the Nation's Service."

It is not surprising that young Wilson's natural bent toward political service should have received further incentive during his student days at Princeton, for during the American Revolution the new college under its eminent president John Witherspoon, had achieved strong direction and prominence in that field and contributed notable leaders in public affairs.[33] But during the years of ferment immediately before and during the War between the States and the years of bitterness immediately following, its large Southern clientele had fallen away and its reputation had languished. Tommy Wilson subsequently was among the earliest of the small group of Southerners to return to this Presbyterian collegiate fold, and his return was due to admiration of his father Dr. Wilson and Grandfather Woodrow for the vigorous Scotsman Dr. James McCosh whose presidency, begun soon after the war's close, was making notable academic advances for the college.[34]

The theme and substance of the famous 1896 Address came directly out of the religious and secular history and dedication of the college itself, and out of the author's heritage and heart as well, when he made its stirring keynote—Princeton as "a school of duty," i.e., of principle and service resting upon religion—and said: "There is nothing that gives such pith to public service as religion."[35]

This address led the trustees to appoint Woodrow Wilson president of Princeton six years later. From William Tennent to Dr. Alexander McCosh, and Dr. Francis L. Patton, who immediately preceded Woodrow Wilson as president, the Presbyterian heritage was continuous. Although a layman, Wilson was as fully Presbyterian in heritage, active faith and character as any minister who preceded him. His introduction at Princeton of the preceptorial plan and the "quad" system established a pattern that became accepted first by the other old endowed universities of the eastern seaboard and later by some state colleges.

Indeed, the Scottish and Presbyterian impact on education in the American Colonies, and subsequently the United States, was far from being limited to the establishment of Princeton University, or even to the ramifying influence of its predecessor, William Tennent's "Log College" in Pennsylvania. Scotch and Scotch-Irish immigrants to Maryland, Virginia and the Carolinas from the late seventeenth century onward also brought with them the passion for religious education, and wherever they gained a foothold for settlement and tolerance for their faith, they imported ministers and dominies (schoolmasters) from the old country and established churches and schools. Francis Makemie in Maryland (born in northern Ireland, educated in Scotland) was one of the first and most notable apostles of Presbyterianism in the New World. The Scotch settlement of the Valley of Virginia, before and after the War for Independence, resulted in a flock of educational "academies" up and down the Valley, much like the one of which Woodrow Wilson's father was principal during his ministry at Staunton around 1855. Before that, the Reverend Joseph Wilson had been educated at the "Male Academy" in Steubenville, Ohio, and had been professor of rhetoric at Jefferson College, his alma mater, at Cannonsville, Pennsylvania (both Presbyterian secondary colleges) before he took his degree at Princeton. Following this he was professor of natural philosophy at Hampden-Sydney College in southern Virginia, and much later (1870-1874) head of the Theological Seminary in Columbia, South Carolina, where his wife's brother, Dr. James Woodrow, was a distinguished professor of natural science. During this period, Dr. Wilson's son received his first education away from home, attending Davidson College, a Presbyterian institution in North Carolina, in preparation for entering Princeton University.

An interesting last touch to this sketch of Scottish-American relationships ties back directly to Glasgow University and also may tie in with the County Tyrone connection. William Dunlop, a noted Presbyterian divine, had gone to Carolina as a colonist during the period of Episcopal reestablishment in Scotland, and distinguished himself there.

By 1690, after the Revolution which defeated the last Jacobite King and brought in William and Mary as the sovereigns, the Reverend Mr. Dunlop had returned to Scotland. He became the effective new principal of Glasgow University, his alma mater, when the rule of the bishops was ended. Enjoying royal favor through a service rendered in exposing a plot against the Crown, he was useful in securing a royal grant of three hundred pounds annually for the College in rents from former bishopric lands. In his favored position, too, he doubtless was responsible for the University's practical immunity from political interference during this difficult transition period, in comparison with that endured by other Scottish institutions. The provocative thought here is: To what extent did Dunlop's Glasgow training influence the later establishment of Davidson College in North Carolina, and to what extent may his familiarity with the Southern colonies in America have influenced the later emigration of Glasgow graduates, teachers and divines, toward strengthening and carrying on his and the Scottish tradition in the New World?

Carlisle Ministry

Thomas Woodrow was 26 years old when he received his master of arts degree from the University of Glasgow and soon after was ordained a minister of the Kirk. He already had been active in one of the "reformed" Glasgow congregations, and there had met Marion Williamson, a daughter of Robert Williamson, who had been instrumental in forming that particular body of dissenters from the strict "Auld Kirk" theocracy. Thomas and Marion were married immediately after his graduation.

As the University was producing what seemed to be a plethora of young ministers at that time, there was no immediate vacancy to be filled in the Glasgow-Paisley vicinity, and so no opening for young Thomas near home. But within a year there came a call which was a challenge and an appeal to the "missionary" instinct which later became so strong a factor in his religious feeling. The call, which he accepted, was to the small Annetwell Street Chapel in Carlisle, chief town of the North English County of Cumberland. So it was that in 1820 Thomas Woodrow and his bride "went over the Border."

There was a different environment from the homeland. Paisley and Glasgow had been the center of Presbyterian faith, militant and triumphant for generations, and the University a mecca for Covenanters even from as far as Ulster across St. Patrick's Channel. Carlisle for as many generations had been a northern bastion of the Church of England. Glasgow and Paisley, from the days of the Scottish Reformation onward, had resented the policies of Roman Catholic Mary Stuart; bitterly opposed political union when her son James VI (nearest claimant to the Tudor throne) assumed the crown of Scotland *and* England as James I; subsequently stormed against the Stuart Restoration when Cromwell's regime collapsed; even more violently resisted reestablishment of the Episcopacy, and in consequence suffered the quartering of troops for the enforcing of religious conformity. On the contrary, Carlisle, in one of the northernmost counties of England, from the earliest days of Roman rule had known and existed in dread of the savage Pictish, later Scottish, raids across the Border. Twice its citadel had been captured, once by the Scottish King David I at the end of his reign, and once during the Cromwellian Civil War; while often it had been besieged unsuccessfully (as by Robert Bruce) by leaders zealous for that age-old dearest wish of the Scots—the joining of their Lowlands and southerly pastoral uplands with the contiguous area immediately below the River Tweed and the Solway Firth.

For these historic reasons, cross-Border antipathies of circumstance and feeling were slow to moderate, and in 1820 (little more than a century after the actual political amalgamation of Scotland and England into one kingdom through the union of their parliaments, 1707), the Scottish Woodrows from Paisley, settling in the little old town still largely enclosed within its Wall, found themselves quite literally in a strange land.

Not the least of the strangeness lay in the fact that the ministry to which young Thomas Woodrow had been called was a comparatively new and struggling congregation. He was only the fourth "stated minister" to serve this modest chapel of Dissenters. Annetwell Street Chapel, as it was known, the one such congregation of the Dissenting faith in Carlisle, had come into formal but precarious existence by 1786 under the patronage of Lady Glenorchy, who owned the building and for some years had fostered the preaching cause of the "Secession Church" throughout the northern counties of England. Before this date, upon which the "solemn Covenant" was entered into between the eleven worshippers then constituting its membership, there had been meetings for several years in Lady Glenorchy's private chapel whenever visiting preachers from Glasgow or elsewhere could be obtained.

Now, in this thirty-fourth year of its life, the new incumbent "set apart as its Pastor" found the little church with a somewhat more flourishing membership of sixty-two. The fact that in the fifteen years of his ministry "he received into fellowship one hundred and thirty-two members"[36] indicates that actually he was carrying on not so much a "settled" ministry as a successful missionary endeavor in a not too promising field. This must have been his true forte. We know that it was the strong pull of missionizing zeal which was to bring about his resignation and his removal to the comparative wilds of North America in 1835. Before another decade had elapsed the growing church, now part of a strong movement known as "the Congregational Union" of the northern English counties of Cumberland, Westmoreland and Northumberland, was to experience division in its own congregation and removal to more spacious new quarters in Lowther Street.

Old Carlisle

It is not surprising that Carlisle (Caer Luel in the old Brythonic tongue) should have been a small but important town in ancient times. It is at the confluence of two rivers, the Eden with the lesser Caldew, not far from where they flow into the inner reaches of the Solway Firth, that broad, deep estuary which penetrates the opposing coastal counties of southernmost Scotland and the northern English shire of Cumberland—almost directly across the Irish Sea from Belfast Lough, its smaller replica.

From near this strategic point, the Romans, during the first and second centuries of their occupation of Britain (which took place in the first and second centuries of the Christian era), began construction of their massive fortified wall which extended, punctuated by its *castella* and flanked by its military road, past the Pennine Chain of mountains and eastward across the narrowest northern neck of England to the mouth of the Tyne river on the North Sea. (In those early days, the territory later known as Northumbria, now the shire of Northumberland, lay within the wilds of Pictland, to the north of the Wall which took an almost direct west-east course.)

Ten centuries later, after the Norman conquest ended the long intervening rule of the Saxon kings of England, William II (the Red) built a Norman castle here at this important point for trade and defense. The massive twelfth century Keep still stands. Janet Woodrow, born in its shadow, told her son in reminiscences of her childhood, of how she and her younger brother James had played handball in their back garden, against the castle wall and next door to the Chapel in Annetwell Street. The dungeons, which held many a Scottish prisoner through the raiding years (including briefly the unhappy Mary Stuart, when she fled in ill-advised haste to a hoped-for sanctuary in England), may have been built after the twelfth century, for the castle withstood many assaults and batterings of siege and required various reconstructions. The latest such reconstruction, unfortunately for historic architectural remains, was effected with stones from the nearby Norman-style Cathedral which had been ruined partially during the Cromwellian Civil War.

In Henry VIII's time, the castle was manned regularly as a major stronghold against the Scots. Also dating from that era it has remained long in local memory as the scene of trials and executions of "the Commons" and certain gentry of the North whose "Pilgrimage of Grace" (an armed rising undertaken in protest against the despoiling of the abbeys and equally against Henry's assumption of Papal powers within his kingdom) was used by him as a dreadful object lesson in "treason." There too, and shortly thereafter, the Austin canons, whose priory had been founded four hundred years before, learned the full weight of Henry's spoliation program, and their priory church, enlarged through the years into a cathedral and a bishop's seat, was obliged to renounce the Roman affiliation and ritual in favor of the new English forms, which most of the clergy and people still looked upon as heresy.

Not until Elizabeth's time came the true "Establishment," and this only after her young half-brother Edward VI, in his short reign, had shown a disposition toward more extreme forms of Protestantism—even for a time favoring John Knox as his chaplain, and after her older half-sister and immediate predecessor, the Tudor "Bloody Mary," had (but only briefly) restored the Roman worship and beheaded many "heretics." Then the Anglican Church with its traditional rule by Bishops (the "Episcopacy") took root and flourished, carrying on its unremitting warfare, then and thereafter, against the non-conformist Covenanters and all other dissenting sects.

The Woodrow "Charge"

Yet even in so conservative an English center as Carlisle, a small scattering of Dissenters slowly grouped themselves, as we have seen, into a modest organization; and to this small but ardent congregation, surrounded and beset by severe "conformity," young Thomas Woodrow came to his first ministerial charge.

The early years were hard years as practical matters ran, but

195

infinitely rewarding as his preaching powers developed and evidenced themselves in a steady growth of converts. Although for him and the young wife, with their rapidly growing family, the chapel's resources offered only a meager living, still the early lean years were happy and challenging ones, and in the small home a quality of intensely living intimacy was generated which the young folk never forgot and which was to mark all their later relationships in a foreign land.

To moderate their financial stringency as the family grew, Thomas Woodrow opened an "academy" and taught the rudiments of secular knowledge as well as "the Faith" to young boys. In the latter half of his Annetwell Street incumbency, he was able to bring his family to the simple but solidly comfortable brick house at 83 Warwick Road—the house so noticeably similar to the solid and dignified Manse which the Scotch Presbyterians of Staunton, Virginia, were to build for their pastor some twenty years later, and where Thomas Woodrow's grandson was to be born.

There for fifteen years, the family knew the sorrows and joys of loss and birth—the death of an infant son (the youngest son, George) and the birth of the second and youngest daughter, Marion, six years younger than Janet. There was made the momentous decision to seek new missionary fields in the land where so many Scotch Presbyterians had gone before them, and from this home, the family embarked upon its hazardous voyage to America, with its disastrous concomitants noted elsewhere in these pages. There, three-quarters of a century later, Thomas Woodrow Wilson, President of the United States, was to make what he described as a "pilgrimage of the heart," and to be accorded signal honor in the church to which his grandfather had ministered so long ago. Outside the Lowther Street Congregational Church (successor to that on Annetwell Street) a tablet was placed to commemorate the historic event.

The Mother of
Thomas Woodrow Wilson
PRESIDENT OF THE UNITED STATES OF AMERICA
was born in Carlisle—Her
Father, The Revd Thomas Woodrow,
M.A. was Minister of this Church,
then worshipping in Annetwell
Street, from February 1820 to
June 1835.

Coming on this "pilgrimage" to his mother's birthplace in mid-season of the 1918 Peace Conference, the son—now revered by half the world as the "Covenanter" of the new ideal, the League of Nations—must have been deeply affected by the recollections of his mother's youth and his grandfather's ministry in that ancient little town, warmed and made vivid as they were by his mother's shared memories. The occasion would have been made for him the more poignant by her remembered stories of the dreadful voyage endured on their migration to the New World by this family—poor in worldly goods, not very strong in body, but great in valor and faith—true Covenanters from whom his own rock-firm faith and Covenanting spirit were derived.

"Mr. President," the Minister said on that Sunday morning in greeting him, "two-thirds of your name belongs to us." And in asking him to speak: "Mr. President, our prayers for you ascend. Our love for you is given, and our praise of you shall be sounded as long as we have breath. We all want to hear your voice ringing in these walls."[37]

To this unexpected summons, their guest, obviously touched (as his wife[38] records in her account of the occasion), opened his brief reply by saying: "It is with unaffected reluctance that I project myself into this solemn service. I remember my grandfather very well, and, remembering him as I do, I am confident that he would not approve of it. I remember how much he required. I remember the stern lessons of duty he spoke to me. I remember also painfully the things which he expected me to know which I did not know. I know there has come a change of times when a layman like myself is permitted to speak in a congregation. But I was reluctant because the feelings that have been excited in me are too intimate and too deep to permit of public expression. The memories that have come to me today of the mother who was born here are very affecting, and her quiet character, her sense of duty and dislike of ostentation, have come back to me with increasing force as those years of duty have accumulated."

After speaking briefly of the trials of war and problems of the peace, he closed by saying: "It is moral force that is irresistible. It is moral force as much as physical that has defeated the [late] effort to subdue the world. . . . It is from quiet places like this all over the world that the forces accumulate which presently will overbear any [future] attempt to accomplish evil on a large scale. Like the rivulets gathering into the river and the river into the seas, there come from communities like this streams that fertilize the consciences of men, and it is the conscience of the world that we are trying to place upon the throne which others would usurp."

Here were the authentic Covenanter spirit and phrase. Recognizing their true and valiant spirit, the Anglican Bishop of Carlisle,[39] present with other dignitaries of the town to do honor to the President, expressed the thanks of the community: "We thank you from our hearts for the simple stirring words you have just addressed to us which will ring throughout the world to purify and strengthen the consciences of men. We recognise in company with the whole God-fearing world the splendour of your ideals and the greatness of your achievements on behalf of humanity, the promotion of righteousness and freedom, of the blessing . . . of peace, and of the international brotherhood among men."

Heritage of Lowland Dissenters

That the Scotch and Scotch-Irish are more religious than their neighbors in England or Eire probably is not true, but it certainly is a fact that if they are actively Presbyterian they are intensely religious. The Wilson and the Woodrow heritages were not just Presbyterian—they were intensely Presbyterian. Development of this church has been wholly Scottish ethnically, for it grew out of the Keltic faith spread from the Scottish isle of Iona by St. Columba's disciples. Each stage in the history of this unique sect has been essentially Gaelic—the monastic era in Ireland following St. Patrick's mission to Tara in 433 A.D.: out of that, St. Columba's voyaging in 563 to the isle of Iona from Ulster (where he was born), his founding of the monastery there, his conversion of the Pictish King Brude in 565; and thereafter the spread of Keltic monasticism throughout what we now call Scotland.

This was a pristine form of Christianity which long antedated the coming of the Christian faith to Anglo-Saxon Britain; rooted in a pridefully cherished autonomy, and free of any ties with the Papal authority of Rome. Even after the mission of St. Augustine to convert the pagan King Ethelbert of Kent, in southeast England in 597, and 30 years later, that of Paulinus to the Anglian kingdom of Northumbria, Ionic Christianity still held sway in the Keltic North. Indeed, no Papal emissary came to Ireland until the Anglo-Norman occupation by "Strongbow" in 1170. And long before that happened, it was from Iona that a new apostolic mission came forth under the Gaelic monk Aidan in 635 to restore the Christian faith to Northern England after waves of pagan invaders from Southwest Britain and Scandinavia had ravaged the land, looted and burned the monasteries and slaughtered the Pauline monks. For seven years, Aidan journeyed and labored over the moors and dales of this rugged land on his mission of reconversion; established a monastery on the "Holy Isle of Lindisfarne," which became an English Iona; and by 664 the teaching had spread across all the pagan reaches of the Southwest, including Wales.

The Keltic Tradition

These Keltic missionaries worked by the light of their unaided consciences, rather than in accordance with the tenets of an institutionalized authority. They never lost this spirit. A thousand years later it asserted itself in the rallying of the Scottish Dissenters by John Knox and the subsequent crystallization of Presbyterianism by the Covenanters. The germ of this Protestant withdrawal from Rome lay in Keltic political and monastic history. The Scots were never brought to submission by the Roman Empire as had been all of southern Britain. On the side of monasticism, the issue was subtle but equally clear. St. Patrick's cult had been essentially Keltic. It was this that St. Columba and his monks and later disciples spread, first in Pictland and thence through the Lowlands of Scotland, and finally throughout the British North and West.

This history goes far toward explaining the vigor and astonishing progress of the Dissenters' doctrine in Scotland, under the inflamed and stubborn leadership of John Knox in the sixteenth century. It also explains why the Presbyterian Church which grew out of that doctrine cannot be regarded as an upstart or renegade sect. For Scottish Presbyterians, the break with Rome represents no break with original Christianity: they regard themselves as the inheritors of the Ionic mission and have never deleted the term "catholic" (i.e. universal) from the Creed to which they subscribe and which the congregation repeats at every service. But in their break with Papal authority, the Covenanters' teaching reemphasized the fierce adherence of the monks of St. Columba, St. Mungo and Aidan to liberty of conscience and the sacred right of privacy between the individual man and God. It is significant that the emergence of a comprehension of the rights of common folk was to follow gradually on the Covenanters' ceaseless proclaiming of the equality of every soul before God.

Directly from this heritage came those "powerful preachers," Thomas Woodrow and Joseph Wilson in America—and the Covenanter spirit of Woodrow Wilson. The personal and moral virtues that belong to the Presbyterian heritage are integrity and unflinching adherence to principle, staunchness in the faith, steadfast loyalty. Anyone who does not comprehend the strength of these principles, bred into him by generations of Covenanters, cannot assess the character of Woodrow Wilson rightly. He exemplified them personally and expected them in others. The seeming failure of his "mission" at the end of his active career was as much the result of the lack of these staunch principles in some of those adherents on whom he thought he could depend as it was on the rigidity within himself which such virtues tend to produce.

Qualities of the Heart

There is another quality—a quality of the heart and the spirit—that seems to distinguish the predominantly Keltic Scots and Irish (and Welsh) from other Britons with more of the Roman, Saxon and Norman in them. This manifests itself in more emotional spontaneity, greater depth and warmth of expressed feeling among kith and kin. To some extent this may be due to environmental factors such as isolation, which entails more intimate family and community identification, dependence and exclusiveness; and to historical causes related to environment, such as clannishness intensified by warring against the invaders (Roman, Saxon, Scandinavian, Anglo-Norman). But can environment and history completely explain the prominence of these qualities in all phases of culture and life? Love of locale and the halo of romantic lore surrounding places and antiquities (even stone relics of prehistoric exigence); the treasuring in ballads and laments of heroism and sufferings; the genealogies celebrated by the Welsh, and the place of family and clan tradition and allegiance in Ireland and Scotland—these characteristics are indelibly ingrained in Keltic folk. They glow in the lyrical and romantic poetic literature, from the legends of Tara to Thomas Moore and Yeats in Ireland, Scott and Burns in Scotland—literature which in both countries has a universal personal appeal. What other countries have powered a successful revolution with poetry and lyrical drama, or made the memorials to their national bards (as

200

Scott and Burns) their most revered shrines? The point need not be laboured—the Gaelic Scots and Irish are, and have been so long as tradition and history reveal them, romantic, tender—a *feeling* people.

The minister in the Manse at Staunton and his wife were like their forebears in these qualities of the heart. Joseph was the lively all-loving masculine Irish type toward his gentle, cultured young wife. Hers was the rather shy, deeply sensitive Scottish Lowland temperament, affectionate, dependent, possessive and exclusive. The child Tommy Wilson, in his years of infancy and childhood, was encompassed by these qualities of the heart—the exuberantly proud affection of his father, expressed in what to many more phlegmatic natures would seem extravagant phrases; the intense, possessive and exclusive devotion of his mother. Precisely those qualities that were and are characteristic of the Scotch and the Irish are those that were dominant in Woodrow Wilson himself, in his mature years. In the intimacy of his own home he was like his father, exuberantly affectionate, but with a touch of restraint that was like his mother's. They were not an outwardly demonstrative family. Feelings were too deeply rooted, too poignant, too private, to be fully expressed except in the most intimate moments of supreme emotion—or in letters when apart—those between father and son, mother and son, of Woodrow to his wife Ellen, and to his children in their later life, are rich with intense feeling. "That part is too sacred," Ellen would say, falling silent in reading aloud to her young daughters their father's letters—her cheeks suffused with delicate color and her eyes warmly misty, as the daughters well remembered.

These qualities of the heart—the word *sentiments* seems inadequate to express them—also were evident, sometimes in greater, sometimes in less degree, in the less immediate relationships with kin and with very congenial friends. Woodrow Wilson was a man whose lovingness was "without measure"—a favorite phrase of his. When he could give and receive such love he was *whole*. His spirit *required* such nourishment, for it had been so nourished throughout his life, until he came into the dark years of the World War. The exhaustion which then ensued was certainly as much a matter of spiritual depletion as of fatigue, mental and physical.

It is ironic that the few instances of broken friendship in his life should have been so magnified by some biographers as to give rise to the legend that Woodrow Wilson was a man incapable of deep, lasting and sustained attachment. Few men have been blessed with so many, so intimate, deep and lasting friendships. In his years at Princeton and elsewhere, as a student and teacher, he was, with truly congenial souls, extremely companionable and warm, forming attachments of lifelong duration. In the exuberance of the New Jersey campaign, exhilarated by his first plunge into active campaigning, he showed himself to be, with politicians, men of affairs and newspapermen, spontaneously friendly, almost always affable. He became popular not just for his ideas, or because he was a successful candidate, but as an engaging personality.

True to the Irish in him, the warm devotion of which he was capable could be turned, on provocation, into relentless antipathy. However, this occurred less on the level of personal feeling than as an aspect of his public life and principles. There were, so far as we know, few if any private personal detestations. His disappointment when, as he believed, Professor Hibben and later Colonel House failed him at critical moments and on crucial matters of principle, evoked not resentment or personal dislike, but rather deep discouragement and grief. But for "the little group of wilful men" in the Senate who played him false on the League of Nations issue; for Secretary Lansing when he realized that he was negotiating behind his back; for Poincaré whom he regarded as a fox, he developed an intense antipathy such as only a man of his forthright integrity and zeal inevitably feels towards individuals who, rightly or wrongly, he believes to have been false.

His ideal of loyalty, once given, was extremely exacting, and was richly rewarded by the many close attachments that never dimmed or waned—a host of early family friends; college-mates, notably Bridges, Talcott, Dabney, and of this same period, Stockton Axson his brother-in-law; certain professors and Princeton trustees from the teaching and administrative years; and new friends made at home and abroad in that period, such as Fred Yeats, the artist, in England. The long series of personal letters attest to the undiminished survival of these attachments. Then there were close friendships that never dimmed but that inevitably waned in their active phases because of the crowding and crushing circumstances of the War years.

A few friendships, through a complexity of causes, did dim or were tarnished, such as that with Jack Hibben, Mrs. Hulbert, Colonel House. Among the many devoted political adherents, most of whom gave him an unswerving devotion to the end, there were a very few, such as Tumulty, whose loyalties, through tragic misunderstandings growing

202

out of the aging man's illness and isolation, became for Wilson suspect, the relationship tragically eroded and skewed as the shrinkage of heart and will advanced with the progress of his invalidism. This process, in the few instances in which it occurred, was doubtless accelerated by the quality of "unforgivingness" which was a notable Woodrow characteristic—and Anglo-Norman Scotch. The Irish are hot, vengeful, vituperative when roused to anger (and *both* Joseph and James Wilson were like this); the Scots are apt to be cold, withdrawn, and dour toward what has injured or betrayed them, but no less ready to take action if need be. This was the *Woodrow* in Wilson. His very withdrawal, his coldness in the face of chicanery or presumption could wither an opponent more acutely than a hot blast of anger—and thereby beget legends of personal inaccessibility and steely self-righteousness.

This impression was augmented by a degree of reserve and a cherishing of personal privacy that too are characteristically Scotch, or Scotch-Irish as opposed to South Irish, and in strong contrast to the gregarious quality of the New World culture in which Woodrow Wilson grew up. Certainly these innate attitudes were the antithesis of the average politician's natural or cultivated heartiness, and likely to be little understood in political circles. Their presence in Wilson the administrator and statesman must have added measurably to his difficulties in pursuing the career he loved.

A Sense of Privacy

In Scotland and North Ireland, the long nights of the rigorously cold half of the year, for centuries upon centuries, have shut in the families of town and land alike into the snug privacy of home and workshop, the crofter's cottage and the walled domain of the larger land-holder. Throughout those centuries, internecine strife, piracy and Border raids intensified the need for security and privacy until those came to be a most prized possession. Reserved, distrustful of the too familiar approach, taciturn when intruded upon—these were attitudes bred inescapably by the nature of the life, until they became bone of the Scottish bone and strength of its sinew.

At the Manse in Staunton, as within a snug farmstead like that of Dergalt, or the solidly built town houses of Paisley and Glasgow, the exclusive privacy of family and person perpetuated the social and psychological pattern of millenia. In Jeanie and Joseph Wilson, these traits were inherent. In his home, even after he entered the official residence of the president at Princeton, and later the White House in Washington, Woodrow Wilson regarded his own and his family's private life as something that should be inviolate. The insistence of newsmen in making "news" out of his personal affairs and probing into the activities of his daughters; scandal-mongering as a partisan maneuver in the political campaigns; the readiness to exploit the story of his courtship of his second wife in 1915—all these experiences were so repugnant to him, angered him so much, that gradually he became uncompromisingly non-cooperative toward the Press.

In 1913, he was the first President to establish the White House Press Conferences. He liked and was stimulated by them, he depended on them as a link with "the people," in whom he had implicit confidence. In his governorship and first Presidential campaigns, his popularity with newsmen had been a big factor in his success; and throughout his second Administration he continued to give certain trusted news correspondents his complete confidence. But by 1919, when he personally took the issue of the League of Nations to the country, the enormous pressure of problems and events and his own consequent preoccupation with them had become such that many Capitol reporters sought their news through Congressional rather than White House channels. In consequence, the story of the tremendous response of the people on the Western Tour was poorly reported in both the national and the international press. As on some earlier occasions, the dourly stubborn taciturnity of his breed had asserted itself, to the detriment of his most cherished objective.

Here was made manifest the effect of an unresolved conflict in his nature which had been evident at the very beginning of his career in active politics—a personal dependence upon seclusion and privacy, and a great ambition for public service and esteem, with the inescapable publicity that has been made a *sine qua non* of the American Presidency.

Regnant Will

Toward the end of his public career, those qualities of unrelenting aversion and resentment became dominant factors in his nature and behavior, as resistance to his leadership grew and frustration cumulatively increased. They had not been *suppressed* in his more vigorous years: he had gallantly risen above them, as in the defeat of his larger plans for Princeton, and when the voting in the national election of

1916 seemed to have given the Presidency to Hughes. During the bitter, enfeebled years of invalidism, his aggravation even became quite personal, an inevitable situation when nervous exhaustion and age tend to neutralize a lifetime of self-discipline.

The story of the gradual ascendance of this type of behavior, under adverse conditions, probably is not unrelated to another strongly Scottish trait, that of intense self-respect which, when combined with a keen sensitivity to the attitudes of others, can cause equally strong reactions.

Amour propre is not peculiar to any breed, but there is a quality of self-esteem that is distinctively Irish and Scottish. It is not egotistical, does not express itself in personal vanity as it frequently does where associated with aristocratic status or wealth. It is rather a kind of self-respect that carries with it a high degree of sensitivity to others' opinions and qualities, and to moral issues. Robert Burns' awareness of his own gifts, and equally of his shortcomings and weaknesses, was a case in point. He is described by a literary contemporary as of

> . . . a sort of dignified plainness and simplicity . . . .His conversation expressed perfect self-confidence, without the slightest presumption . . . he expressed himself with perfect firmness, but without the least intrusive forwardness . . . .I never saw a man in company with his superiors more perfectly free from either the reality or the affectation of embarrassment.[40]

This quality is compounded of honor, deference, esteem due to others, and from others to oneself. It was present in Woodrow Wilson— one of the strong marks of distinction in one who made no aristocratic pretensions. It is essentially a social virtue. By contrast, vanity and arrogance are antisocial. Where respect was lacking in another, however, sensitivity induced response in kind. This was true, for instance, in Wilson's attitudes toward Theodore Roosevelt and Henry Cabot Lodge. It is difficult to know here in which direction the disrespect was first felt keenly; or whether personal antipathy preceded or grew out of political enmity.

Although Woodrow Wilson, and both sides of his family before him, had achieved an enviable status in the New World, their self-esteem and their sense of distinction were for them matters of individual worth rather than of place in society. Joseph Wilson, in the Presbyterian world of his time and hence in the Southern communities where he served as minister, preacher and teacher, was a man of superior status, but he thought of himself only in terms of intellectual distinction and achievement. The same was true of Jeanie, and for her scholarly father who, in terms of background, enjoyed in America the very real distinction for those days of being a graduate of the University of Glasgow. Their son and grandson always judged himself by the same set of values, and from the earliest years when his nature revealed itself, was engrossed in intellectual interests and in training himself in scholarship, in public speaking and writing. His eager desire to make his mark, to excel; his aspiration toward excellence—these undoubtedly were strengthened by the wish to make the best possible use of his talents for the good of his fellowmen, in the tradition of his preaching forebears. "Making a name for himself" was not a primary motivation for a child bred in the moral climate of "service." But if not so *animated*, he did undoubtedly *love* to shine! And when recognition came and shine he did, he was fully aware—always modestly, never pompously—of his own distinction.

There was an episode during his teaching at Princeton when he became self-conscious in his writing, trying to develop a "style." Hitherto, with significant exceptions, his writing had been largely the product of a hard-pressed professor needing to augment his income. But the absorption with "style" was brief and for him unrewarding. His composition (and speech) was truly distinguished when he was presenting or discussing with conviction and precision issues affecting political and civic or spiritual life. Such evidences may be found in his address at the sesquicentennial celebration of the founding of Princeton; in that at the finale of the Paris Peace Conference; in the last article he wrote—"The Road Away from Revolution"; and in this from his first inaugural:

> This is not a day of triumph, it is a day of dedication. Here muster, not the forces of party, but the forces of humanity. Men's hearts wait upon us; men's lives hang in the balance; men's hopes call upon us to say what we will do. Who shall live up to the great trust? I summon all honest men, all patriotic, all forward-looking men, to my side. God helping me, I will not fail them, if they will but counsel and sustain me.

His poignantly felt and expressed address to Congress asking for a declaration of war on Germany is a case in point. Indeed, there are countless passages in his public utterances that are as eloquent, as well wrought, as significant for the human race as were any expressed by Jefferson or Lincoln at their finest. They are fine because they are true reflections of the honor and sensitivity, the simplicity and distinction of his nature.

There is a basic characteristic as yet unmentioned here, and one from which stemmed other essential traits: Woodrow Wilson's temperament was wholly urban.

This strong strand in the warp of his heritage came directly from the Lowland Scottish Woodrows and Williamsons—from generations of Glasgow and Paisley town dwellers—artificers and burghers. This American offspring of theirs deeply enjoyed the beauties of lake and mountain landscape and the peace of the countryside—briefly, when hard pressed and in need of refreshment and rest—but he cared not at all for rural living. No bucolic pursuits appealed to him, not even the milder vestiges which survive in towns, such as gardening and the tending of pets. This cannot be said to be due merely to preoccupation with an intellectual career: many intellectuals combine with their scholarly or professional careers a strong taste for various other active pursuits or avocations. Woodrow Wilson, quite simply, was happier among urban surroundings and activities, and apparently felt no drawing toward any other. The land-loving traits of his Irish forbears, it would seem, were completely latent in his make-up.

This town-dwelling strain showed itself in the characteristic virtues of urbanity, civility, courtesy; but primarily, perhaps, in that strong sense of law and order which develops among burghers of upright breeding over the generations. Respect for the laws of the community by which neighbors live in peace, the habit of reducing relationships and rights and duties to a concise formula (or "constitution" or "covenant")—these were qualities inherent in the Roman background of the Anglo-Norman civic life of Lowland Scotland as distinct from the clan culture of the Highlands, and, equally as distinct from the country life and temperament of the Ulster Irish. In eighteenth century Glasgow, for example, the authenticity of this quality was lessened in no way by the coexistence of that fierce capacity for nonconformity in matters of faith, or the equal disregard of laws imposed *from without* and stubbornly resisted when believed to be unjust. The Covenanters, during their years of political ascendancy, were as zealous in enforcing the meticulous laws of their own theocracy as in resisting the encroachments of an alien authority and an intrusive faith.

Both of these seemingly contradictory traits Woodrow Wilson inherited in marked degree. He was an unwavering exponent of the reduction of all things to order in an explicitly delineated instrument—whether it be the rules for a debating society, the constitution of a college literary club, the parliamentary conduct of a faculty meeting, the setting up of a party "platform" of political commitments or a "Covenant" for the organization of a Society of Nations of the world. Along with this delight in order, and a respect for law that brooked no trifling with agreed rules, there went his incontinent contempt for unjustly imposed authority such, for example, as that imposed sectionally upon the South by the North in the American Civil War. With it went also a stubborn will to nonconformity wherever he detected authoritarian injustice, as in the case of the Presbytery's heresy trial of his scholarly uncle James Woodrow over the issue of evolution.

But in Woodrow Wilson even this tendency to nonconformity was moderated, in behavior, by an urbanity, a natural courtesy, which was certainly as much a product of the generations of Woodrow town culture as of his own childhood discipline—a native inclination, not learned. This trait—the opposite of the bluff outspeaking, the heartiness, real or assumed, characteristic of the political scene of his era—was marked throughout his career, in personal and public intercourse, and was violated only when a sense of outrage or frustration overpowered him. It was an *ingrained* gentility (in the literal sense of that word) which contrasted often with the equal "good breeding" of his father, who had a taste for overriding the opinions of others with the sometimes rough whip of his tongue and caustic wit. When the son arrived at positions of administrative leadership, he demonstrated an equally strong power of overriding opposition, and of flaying whatever he regarded as venal obstructionism. But, at least until his years of failing health, this was always expressed impersonally and courteously, if vigorously, and never indulged in for the purpose of wounding. For him, high office meant always obligation, not privilege—the duty of "righteously" administering the laws to which one subscribed and of safeguarding the civil authority of the community, be it "burgh," college, nation or the polity of humankind.

Political Motivations

As distinct from these traits which we have termed the civic-mindedness and conscientiousness of the town man, Woodrow Wilson's drive toward politics, which dominated him from earliest youth, came not from his Lowland Scot forbears, the Woodrows, but directly from his grandfather, the publicist James Wilson. It was accompanied in considerable measure by the partisan zeal, the "reforming" vigor of that pugnacious politician, who carried his passionate convictions into the legislature of the new mid-western state of Ohio, where he had settled, and where he was spoken of as one of the foremost public men of his time.

In the case of James Wilson's famous grandson, the propagation of his convictions did not take the form of ebullient and often vituperative attack. But never had a president of Princeton University so vigorously carried the written and spoken message of his reforming educational faith across the nation; and perhaps never before was a President of the United States so passionately concerned with swaying the electorate, not just to partisan support, but to a true understanding of his view of governmental principles. When it came to world leadership—that role so unexpectedly thrust upon him by the tragic events of 1914-1918—there was displayed not only this strong adherence to principle but a quality of self-dedication and crusading zeal, almost a will to martyrdom, which was his heritage equally from Lowland Scottish and Ulster Irish forbears. Both family lines, long before the two grandfathers emigrated to America, had been nurtured, throughout a century and a half of religious reform, struggle and persecution, upon zeal and steadfast faith, and had survived only through the stubborn will to fight.

To this stubborn will there was added, on the Irish side, an *exuberance* of fighting spirit, and of this quality, Woodrow Wilson also partook. For him it was the dynamic attraction of battle in which words and wits were the weapons—an enthusiasm as strong in its way as was his lifelong loathing for the senseless physical carnage of war. This dynamism, in large measure, was the source of his strength in action. It carried him triumphantly through all lesser conflicts, and up to the supreme contest in Paris when he found himself confronted by the devious maneuverings of Old World diplomacy in the battle of the Peace. Then, it would seem, enthusiasm died, and he had to rely solely, abroad and at home, upon the self-dedication and stubborn will which had always underlain it.

This stubborn will certainly took something of its quality of dominance from the paternal grandmother, that indomitable Scotch-Irish woman Ann Adams, who had aided her firebrand young husband so masterfully in the fulfillment of his pioneering dream. Her one-pointed, inflexible spirit surely found its echo in this son of her youngest son, the shy child whose gift for leadership was recognized so early and fostered carefully by his father throughout his youth. Onepointed in purpose and ideal, inflexible where principle was concerned, but with a difference—never wilful (a trait he detested), always ready to seek counsel from those near to him, to listen to and weigh advice, Woodrow Wilson, until the later unhappy years of his invalidism, was ever open to persuasion *unless* and *until* his conscience already had persuaded him. Then, like his Grandmother Wilson, he was adamant.

But his gift of leadership, his power to sway men, took equal strength from the other side of his heritage—from the "powerful preaching Woodrows." Although less aggressively expressed, the Woodrow strength of conviction also was ranged unalterably on the side of "the righteous." It expressed itself in a passion for freedom, religious and political, in the idealization of the land where they had found it, in an ardent patriotism and larger humanism. Surely the inheritor of this formidable array of qualities—from the intellectual appeal, the sense of the power and dignity of conviction so strong in the Lowland Scots, to the dynamism, the persuasive wit and charm of the Ulster Irish—came to his ultimate role well furnished. Yet the very multiplicity of these traits of leadership could be a weakness of a sort. For according to which set of qualities, through circumstance, was in the ascendant, he was judged—amenable or adamant, warmly human; or a cold "machine," practical or idealistic, even, to some, mercurial. He was right when he confessed to Joe Tumulty that "there are two natures combined in me," and that "when these two fellows get to quarrelling . . . it is hard to act as umpire between them."[41]

VII

THE COSMIC MILIEU

The Total Environment

We have described the environmental setting in which Woodrow Wilson was born and nurtured, and that of his forebears in Northern Ireland, Scotland and America. Now there remains to be considered the total environment of the biosphere of which he was physically a part, subject to the meteorological changes which produce the seasons and their weather cycles. The all-encompassing phases of the Earth's climate and weather we shall find to reflect the changes to which the sun is subject—its periods of turbulence when increased radiant energy is transmitted to Earth, affecting all forms of life; alternating with the periods of quiescence during which the sun emits far less energy and the earth and its atmosphere and biosphere, including mankind, enjoy episodes of relative calm and tranquility.

William F. Petersen, M.D., so far as we know, was the first scientist who devoted himself to studies of man in relationship to the meteorological phenomena of our planet and the influence of the waxing and waning of solar radiation affecting the earth. His earlier writings are found in a series of massive monographs describing the theoretical concepts which guided his studies, but mainly they present his clinical observations, as a pathologist, of patients in Chicago hospitals. In 1943 Dr. Petersen published a compact volume entitled *Lincoln-Douglas, the Weather as Destiny*.[1] This encompasses the whole range of his thought as applied to two political adversaries of contrasting physical type— Abraham Lincoln, tall and lean and weather-sensitive, and Stephen Douglas, short and stout, well "buffered" against the violent fluctuations of temperature, humidity and barometric pressure characteristic of the Middle West and Eastern Seaboard of the United States. The heredity and life history of the two men are described in some detail. The latter half of the book is taken up entirely with the story of Lincoln's life in Washington, first as a Congressman and later as President. Contemporary records of the time show that in Washington, while a Congressman, he was practically incapacitated during two successive cold waves in January, 1841.[2] Subsequent physical and psychological

211

crises in the lives of both Lincoln and his wife are shown to have occurred at times of sudden changes in temperature and barometric pressure.[3]

In this study of Lincoln, Petersen uses the cogent characterization of man as a "cosmic resonator."[4] The interrelation of the season of conception and birth of unusual offspring is, Petersen concluded, "probably due to the effects of the biochemical condition of the maternal organism (and her egg) when the organic pendulum is pushed to extremes."[5] It is not that the explosive emissions of energy in the sun's atmosphere have a direct effect upon humanity. Sunspots are evidence of turbulence and of increased outflow in radiation and energy from the sun. This induces increased turbulence in the Earth's atmosphere. To this, Man, as a "cosmic resonator," responds biologically, socially, politically, culturally. Mankind and civilization pass through cycles of stimulation and quiescence which coincide with the rise and fall of the sun's outpourings of radiant energy.

It would seem that a greater number of highly gifted persons are born when the sun is irradiating the earth with increased energy, than during periods of quiescence.[6] Referring to studies of the incidence of genius between 1750 and 1850, by Havelock Ellis, Catherine Cox and Lang-Eichbaum, Petersen writes:[7]

> Obviously we are dealing with a period when, with maximal social and political disturbance, we produced an unusual number of outstanding personalities; inventors, statesmen, scientists, philosophers, musicians and artists. All this unusual reproductive phase, this disturbance in the human mass, occurred at a time when the gaseous atmosphere of the sun was more disturbed and turbulent.

Certainly Woodrow Wilson was a gifted person, but he was not a genius. His every achievement required much expenditure of effort. When he was born, the gaseous atmosphere of the sun was quiescent—there were no eruptions of sunspots. It was just after the winter solstice, when the sun is farthest south of the equator, and days are very short; just after midnight, when the sun is on the other side of the earth; and at a time when the moon, which in its bright phase reflects some solar energy back to Earth, was dark, reflecting no sunlight. The life of the man born at this climax of quiescence on earth was one in which every episode of creativity was achieved only by means of great concentration of energy, at the cost of a maximum expenditure of effort. We shall show that his times of notable achievement coincided with the maximum outpourings of solar energy, and that periods of exhaustion induced by over-exertion came when the sun was quiescent. His was a life, then, which proved that a man who was not blessed by coming into the world at the most propitious time, by dedicated devotion to duty and with great effort, could overcome environmental handicaps and achieve greatness and full expression of unique gifts.

The Astrophysical Frame of Reference

For a man as weather-sensitive as Woodrow Wilson, the combined effects of barometric pressure, humidity and temperature which produce what we call weather, either stimulated or depressed his physique and nervous system. The story of this is plain throughout his life, as plain as it was in the life of Abraham Lincoln as described by Petersen. It therefore is both interesting and necessary to go in some detail into the consideration of the astrophysical influences which affected his behavior and his capabilities. Concerning the effect of barometric pressure Clarence A. Mills, in *Living with the Weather,*[8] has written:

> Few people realize the extent of pressure changes that take place every few days in central North America. If a building of ordinary construction were made air-tight and closed on one of our low pressure days, it would probably collapse [because of the weight of air inside] on the next high-pressure day. Or, if it were closed on a high-pressure day, it would explode outward as the outside pressure fell.

The human body, fortunately, is not hermetically sealed. It adjusts its internal pressure to that of the atmosphere by cellular expansion and contraction. The tissues take water, like a sponge, as pressure falls and humidity increases, and they squeeze it out as the barometer rises. It is obvious that the lowered nervous and mental efficiency that mark low-pressure days put an enormous burden on a man like Wilson, who had to face more critical situations in bad weather than in good. Because he was weather-sensitive, his personal occlusions coincided with those of weather and season.

It is not merely that the body is affected by or reacts to the weather. The same factors which produce the atmospheric changes that we call "weather" induce concurrent physiological and biochemical changes in living organisms, and the body adjusts itself to the weather.

213

When a low-pressure center prevails over an area, the air over the surface of the country is relatively warm and humid. The warmth opens the pores of the skin and the humidity keeps it moist, and as a result, the nervous system is not insulated. The electrical potential of the body is low like that of the air about it, which is very slightly ionized when the air is warm and humid. The cells of the body are relaxed, they expand, absorb moisture. The nerves are slack, the brain also. Breathing is reduced, and the blood carries less oxygen to the organs and tissues of the body. Literally, the body is heavy, a bit waterlogged, and feels sluggish. The air is moisture laden, and at the center of the low-pressure area it is motionless, so there is little evaporation.

Animals and human beings respond to a falling barometer (the condition that precedes a storm) with nervousness, irritability, restlessness. Waking at night, while the air is heavy and still, is a common experience. Dearth of oxygen makes it hard to breathe. The nerves and the mind seem stagnant, problems are worrisome. When a storm is brewing and the barometric pressure is low, livestock on a farm are uneasy, anxious—a condition that may result from millions of years of evolution, the need for taking refuge from coming storms; but their restlessness is due to a simple physiological factor: they are restless because, like a barometer, they are "depressed." In human organizations and operations, personnel problems, friction, gripes, coincide with low barometer. Comes the rising barometer, and the tensions and problems evaporate: a rising tide of energy, the clearing of heart and mind, keep pace with the barometer.

Weather changes affect man . . . . Violent and frequent storms bring to some regions major weather problems, with sudden atmospheric changes which wrack body and mind. In the earth's most active storm belts this turbulence becomes a very important factor of existence, adding spice to life but at the same time interfering with body functions and bringing on many serious ailments.[9]

When a low-pressure area is invaded by a high-pressure center, with crisp cooler or cold air (which is surcharged electrically by sunlight), the cool air thrusts in under the damp warm air mass lying lazily over the surface; turbulence results, clouds form and rain falls. The raindrops which have absorbed the positive electrical potential of the upper ionized air are dissipated as they strike the earth's surface and release their energy so that the air becomes ionized or charged with positive electricity. The turbulence also produces breezes or wind, the surface is cooled by the circulation of air, which increases evaporation. The moisture having been precipitated out of the air, the clouds clear, sun shines on wet surfaces, and the air is charged with ozone, which has a stimulating effect on all animate organisms.

What transpires in the body when this occurs is that the cooling causes the cells of the body to contract and the pores to close. The skin dries, insulating the body, which quite literally becomes a storage battery. The nervous system is gradually charged with positive electrical potential from the ionized air and ozone, and skin and lungs are stimulated and freshened by the cool breeze. The blood takes up more oxygen, which accelerates metabolism. All the organs and tissues are stimulated, and especially the nerves and the brain, which control animation; and the man feels the exhilaration of "good weather." The accelerated functioning of the internal organs induces increased combustion of food, with resulting increase of energy. Not only does the body feel "more lively," it actually has more life.

Change in distribution of the body's blood, coinciding with a syndrome of other changes, is the body's first response to change in temperature. In a lean type like Woodrow Wilson, in which the volume of blood is relatively less in proportion to the external area of the body and to the size of the organs, a greater adjustment is required than in a well-buffered, robust type with more proportionate blood volume, like Joseph Ruggles Wilson, his father. Petersen in his analysis of the effects of this syndrome of weather change says:

> With increasing environmental cold the body must diminish radiation of heat from the body surface. It does this by shutting down the blood flow in the peripheral tissues.[10]

Withdrawal of blood from the brain as part of the process of adjustment to cold weather involves a serious conflict in an intellectual of Wilson's type whose brain must function efficiently, regardless of weather. He was aware of the conflict, but never allowed his physical condition to affect his mental labors unless he was too ill to work at all.

Four main factors in the atmosphere produce the weather and physiological changes that affect the behavior, the tone and the quality of personality. These are barometric pressure, temperature, the amount of sunlight and the electricity in the air. These are not independent but are interrelated in their physiological effects. The mechanisms of adjustment, physical, chemical and so on, are very complex and have not been analyzed sufficiently as yet to permit of summary without over simplification and errors of unqualified statement. This is especially true with respect to the part played by a preponderance of positive ions (when pressure is high and it is clear, cool, dry), as contrasted with preponderance of negative ions (when pressure is low and humidity and temperature are high: i.e. bad weather brewing or breaking).

In certain respects, and although he was sound physically and nervously, Woodrow Wilson was abnormal in ways that made him extremely weather-sensitive. As a child, he was physically lazy, due no doubt to a certain lack of robustness in which he resembled his mother. Throughout his life, his energies were given to sedentary pursuits and the development of his intellectual capacities. This, in consequence, would mean that his circulation was relatively poor and he would be (and was) easily subject to chilling. Until Dr. Cary Grayson, as White House physician, built up his weight by means of diet and regular exercise (golf), and for the first time in his life relieved him of chronic dyspepsia, he was thin and undoubtedly in some fundamental ways undernourished, both conditions reducing his resistance to respiratory infection. He suffered much from deep colds from his youth onward; and the final collapse in the autumn of 1919 was in no small measure the consequence of having given himself no opportunity to recover from an attack of influenza in Paris the previous spring. His terminal illness in 1924 was due to chilling followed by bronchial pneumonia.

The weather, then, is an all-encompassing frame of reference in what we have termed the total environment of the person we are studying. But the weather, which results from turbulence in the atmosphere of our Earth, is generated by our sun.

In the discussion which follows, it will be seen that the changes in the sun which affect the earth, in part at least, are produced by the earth and other planets. It is a matter of interplay of cosmic forces in our solar system. That is why our total frame of reference, the whole background, for the life and times of Woodrow Wilson must include some understanding of the sun in its seasons, and of other astrophysical forces affecting the earth.

The Sun Has Its Seasons

Since all life on Earth is dependent directly upon solar energy, it is evident that the life of each organism on earth must be responsive to the ebb and flow of solar tides. The metaphysics of the seers of ancient India conceived of the energy of the universe as arising from the out-breathing and inbreathing of a Supreme Being whom they named, simply, Brahman, which means *breath*. Astrophysics in our time enables us to comprehend the fact that the primary energy which flows into the area of the cosmos of which we are a part, our Solar System, flows outward from the sun in the form of electrical energy, which is light and heat in rhythmic impulsions that might be likened to in-and-out-breathing.

Stupendous outpourings of incandescent gases on the surface of the sun, observable through a powerful telescope, are followed by equiva-lent episodes in reverse, when the incandescent gases breathed forth from the body of the sun swirl back into it in cyclones whose rotation is caused by the differential speed at which the glowing gaseous atmos-phere and incandescent surface of the sun moves as it rotates on its axis. At the time of its maximal outpourings, the corona of the sun is seen, on photographs taken through a telescope, to be very much wider and more brilliant than during quiescent episodes. These in-and-out-pourings of energy presumably are due in some degree to physical processes within the sun itself.

From Blumenstock's *The Ocean of Air*[11] we quote the following graphic description of the transfer of the sun's radiant energy to earth and its atmosphere:

> The warmth of the earth and its atmosphere is derived from the sun. Ninety-three billion miles away, within the sun, billions of hydrogen atoms are transformed into helium in a millionth of a second. In this reaction, which is like that of a hydrogen bomb, prodigious amounts of energy are released. From the surface regions of the sun, the energy rushes outward in the form of a pulsating wave of radiation that travels away from the sun at a speed of 186,000 miles per second. ... The earth's atmosphere intercepts the sun's radiation eight minutes and twenty seconds after it has left the sun ....
>
> Only partly diminished through running the gantlet of the high upper atmosphere and the ozone layers of the stratosphere, the pulsating wave of sun radiation sweeps on earthward. In less than one thousandth of a second it reaches the lowest atmos-phere ... On the average—about 50 per cent of the incoming solar radiation is absorbed by the earth's surface. About another 16 per cent is absorbed by the gases and clouds of the atmos-phere. The remainder is scattered back or reflected back into space. ...

During the eruption of solar flares and sunspots on the surface of the sun, the sun sends out its most powerful pulsations of energy. The nature of what are called "sunspots," as observed through a powerful telescope, is described as follows:[12]

At the lower atmospheric levels [of the surface of the sun], gases move upward and outward from a spot, while in the higher levels the movements are inward and downward, as if a spot were a sort of whirlpool into which the high-level gases are drawn. . . .

. . . Among the markings on the sun's surface, . . . flares [which are seen as outbursts of light visible above the normal surface] are the most significant from the standpoint of the direct effects of the sun on Earth. The outbreak of a flare, visible in hydrogen light, and accompanied exactly at the start of the visible disturbance by a sudden large increase in the solar radiation in the radio region of the spectrum often are followed by a magnetic storm on Earth. . . .

The effect of solar flares is described by Blumenstock as follows:[13]

Solar flares, which consist of the sudden energetic flaring up of small regions within the disc of the sun, produce an instantaneous burst of extremely intense ultraviolet light that excites the particles of the [Earth's] ionosphere.

Dr. R. Grant Athay has described the discovery and nature of solar flares:[14]

. . . Until fairly recently in the history of mankind the sun was thought of as constant and unchanging . . . [actually] manifestations of variability . . . are many and striking; and among the most important is the solar flare.

Quite by chance, in the year 1869, R.C. Carrington, an astronomer at the British Royal Observatory, while engaged in making routine sunspot observations, saw a small area of the sun brighten for a few minutes, then fade back to normal. . . .

The sunspot areas with which flares are associated, particularly those areas in which the spots are evolving rapidly, reveal several distinguishing features. . . . Flares are distinguished . . . by their extreme brightness and relatively short lifetime.

Apparently, brilliant flares eject streams of electrically charged particles from the sun, and these give rise to magnetic storms on the earth's surface. These storms intensify the Aurora Borealis or Northern Lights over the geomagnetic northern pole of the earth:[15]

The spectra of the auroras, when observed along the lines of force of the earth's magnetic field—which is the direction supposedly followed by the incoming particles—show features characteristic of hydrogen atoms hurtling toward us at speeds up to 2,000 miles per second. The sun is composed largely of hydrogen, and there can be little doubt but what it is the source ejecting electrons and protons from which these hydrogen atoms are formed.

Sometimes the intensification of the inflow of cosmic rays coincides with the flares. At these times there is "an intense outburst of noise at radio wave lengths." As solar radiation increases, the number of free electrons in the earth's atmosphere increases.

Elsewhere we read:[16]

> . . . Invisible particles and radiations stream to the earth, affecting the ionosphere and the earth's magnetic field and causing the brilliant northern and southern lights . . . The earth is thus an integral part of the universe whose forces, particles and radiations establish the conditions of human life and activity. . . .

The intensity of ultraviolet radiation in high levels of the earth's atmosphere waxes and wanes with the increase and decrease of sunspots.[17]

> . . . The Sun, our nearest star and the source of almost all the earth's energy emits a broad spectrum of radiations and particles that affect the earth and its atmosphere. Solar disturbances, particularly sunspots and flares, often result in magnetic storms, heightened auroral displays, ionospheric variations that frequently disrupt long-range radio communications and sometimes [cause] intensification of cosmic rays. . . . Weather and climate represent the end products of complicated interplay between the sun's energy and the lower atmosphere, the oceans, and snow and ice fields. . . .[18]

There are various theories about what causes turbulence on the sun's surface. These theories arise from and are dependent upon certain scientifically observed celestial phenomena. For instance, it is recognized that there are at least three ways in which the earth, and other planets of the sun, may affect the solar atmosphere:

(1) When Earth and Jupiter are in alignment, the increased gravitational pull may cause a tidal bulge on the molten surface of the sun, nearest to and facing the two planets. It is argued that upon reaching a certain degree of tension the surface bulge breaks, causing incandescent gases within the solar atmosphere to shoot upward, then, as they cool,

to spiral back into the surface of the sun—a process visible from our earth through powerful telescopes.

(2) A second hypothesis is based on the fact that throughout interplanetary space, great quantities of meteoric material exist. This material would be drawn toward the surface of the sun by the drag of gravity when the forces of Earth and Jupiter in alignment operate to stop these meteoric materials in their flight through space. Those nearest the sun would be drawn to its surface, would plunge into it and become volatilized, ejected, and when cooled would spiral back into the sun—the whole process causing the eruptive flares visible from Earth's astronomical observatories.

(3) A third theory is based upon the belief that the electrodynamic influences emanating from the planets when in conjunction (or opposition) in themselves may so modify the polarity of the sun's surface as to cause the eruptions and subsequently restore the sun's atmospheric balance.

Perhaps all three of the above processes may combine to cause the solar storms.

It is probable also that the sun is responsive to impulsions acting upon it from other parts of the universe as yet beyond our known observation. There are forces which we cannot measure, although we know they exist, because some, more penetrating than any rays from our sun, impinge upon our earth in the form of what we call "cosmic rays." These rays influence, intensify or obstruct the effectiveness of those energies which man has partly learned to harness and use in telephony, electric power, radio, radar and the electronic devices designed for safety and guidance in aerodynamics. They influence also the growth and effectiveness of that electrically charged and motivated being, Man himself.

Tides of Solar Energy

In its largest dimension, the ecological or environmental frame of reference in which the character and career of Woodrow Wilson has to be set is that of Earth in relation to the sun, its source of life-giving energy.

The graph on the figure referred to as the Life Line (fig. 5, page 227), which plots the increase and decrease in the frequency of sunspots, recorded originally at Geneva and now at other observatories, shows the rise and fall of the outpouring of light, heat and electrical energy of the sun, center of our solar system.

220

In the case of Woodrow Wilson, the existence of certain coincidences between crises throughout his life cycle and those astrophysical conditions affecting the atmosphere which are identified with sunspots, are worthy of attention as one of the potent environmental factors affecting his life and career. A few scientists in various fields are interested in discovering specifically what direct and indirect effects the sun, as cosmic "generator," has upon the human organism. To indicate the coincidences is quite simple; to evaluate them is very complex. Yet to disregard them—as do most biologists, social scientists and historians—is poor science.

We have described how the surface of the sun is constantly in a state of transition from a condition in which its outer atmosphere is relatively quiescent to episodes when violent eruptions of gases flame outward, creating incandescent cyclonic storms north and south of the sun's equator. Observation and study of the sun's gaseous surface have shown that when these flaming cyclonic storms occur, they follow the same pattern as do the vortices of our tropical windstorms. They revolve in opposite directions north and south of the equator of Earth and the sun respectively.

There are a number of ways in which there is a close correlation between solar disturbances and electrical phenomena on the earth. Our magnetic needle and compass records turbulence on the sun's surface. At maximum outpourings of solar energy, the Aurora Borealis appears in northern and southern skies. Radio reception is interfered with. The flow of magnetic earth currents waxes during the increase and wanes during the decrease of intensity of radiation (fig. 4). Weather cycles and phenomena are altered, storms are move violent, prevailing conditions of either drought or precipitation are intensified. And the degree of ionization of the air reflects the amount of the sun's outpourings. All of these variations profoundly affect the life and health of man and his behavior. Turbulence on the sun and in the atmosphere and on the surface of Earth are reflected in political and social upheavals, in phenomena of public health, in fact, in every aspect of the biosphere.

That President Wilson and his physician were unaware of astrophysical influences affecting his life was understandable, since not until after the President's death was the first research into these matters begun. While Wilson was in the White House, C.G. Abbott was at work at the Smithsonian Institution in Washington studying the relation of solar radiation to the weather.

Before 1924, medical men were little concerned with the relation of

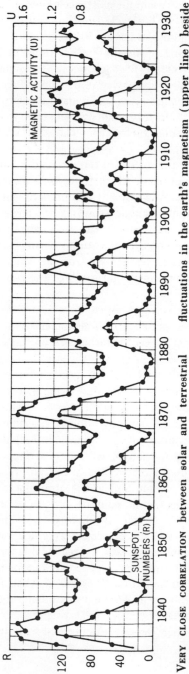

VERY CLOSE CORRELATION between solar and terrestrial phenomena is illustrated by the graph, *above*, which shows fluctuations in the earth's magnetism (upper line) beside sunspot activity (lower line), during the years 1835-1930.

Figure 4

From Athay, p. 481, see Bibliography.

meteorology to health or possible relationship of the behavior of man-kind to turbulence in the atmosphere of the sun. Both Woodrow Wilson and his physician, Dr. Cary Grayson, certainly would have dismissed with a shrug any suggestion that sunspots might have any direct rela-tionship to the life and career of the President. Woodrow Wilson's inclination to overexpend his nervous reserves might have been tempered could Dr. Grayson have included in the careful and rigorous routine he prescribed for the President certain ways of adjusting his episodes of intense effort to changes in temperature, air pressure and humidity which were extreme from 1917 to 1919, a period of major turbulence of the solar atmosphere. Had this been the,case, it may be that the President's campaign in America for the League of Nations might have been successful and he might have retained his health to complete his career. And that in turn might have meant that a League of Nations, reinforced by United States participation, could have tempered, even perhaps prevented, World War II and its continuing aftermath.

If, at this post-facto date, this seems but idle speculation, there may be some value in considering in the future the astrophysical factors that affect mankind, as components of environmental control. If we must regard our Presidents as expendable to the last degree we, in an era that prides itself on being scientific, at least ought to weigh the odds set up against them by atmospheric and astrophysical factors in times of unusual stress. Time is our master, but "the times" and seasons we should learn not wholly to disregard. The periodicity of life processes was pointed out by Aristotle, including the cycles of night and day, month and year, together with the fact that the waxing and waning of the moon is a "period" superimposed upon the diurnal and annual cycles of the sun in relation to Earth.[19]

In scheduling a President's time, as in all modern affairs, night and day are respected perforce in some degree, but seasons of the year are disregarded almost entirely and seasons of the sun not known at all to those responsible for the arrangements and health of the Chief Execu-tive or the affairs of the Nation, nor in the concepts of those who assess or criticize his decisions. Woodrow Wilson, after unabated over-exertion during the 1917-to-1919 outpouring of solar energy, repeated a pattern exhibited regularly from youth onwards in his career—that of a general breakdown in the 1920's when radiant energy flowing from the sun to earth was on the wane. Could he have been persuaded by a physician like Dr. Petersen that the ups and downs of his health were correlated with the waxing and waning of radiant energy received by Earth from the sun, the President might have been spared the fateful collapse suffered on his Western speaking tour in the autumn of 1919. But he refused to listen even to Dr. Grayson's blunt warning that the heavy travel schedule in the heat of August and early September, on top of his state of exhaustion on the return from Paris, might be fatal. He was convinced that the only hope for the entry of America into the League of Nations lay in rousing the people throughout the United States to an awareness of the fateful issues involved, and that he, its chief architect and champion, was the one to do it.

Dr. William F. Petersen coined the cogent phrase, "solar tides," to refer to the ebb and flow of electromagnetic energy from the sun into Earth's atmosphere and biosphere. The comparatively moderate effects of the diurnal and seasonal solar tides upon mankind, manifesting themselves in light and darkness, winter cold and summer heat, are obvious to all. But the longer solar tides, those of the maxima and minima of the sun's incandescence, also have their definite influence, mainly indirect, upon the organic world—and particularly, according to Dr. Petersen, upon "the more susceptible individuals."[20]

Woodrow Wilson throughout his life was peculiarly susceptible as a "weather-sensitive" organism. One of the most interesting aspects of these studies, for us, has been to discover whether the waxing and waning of the tides of solar energy did have definite effects on his career. There may be more than a figure of speech involved when it is said, as surely may be said of Wilson: "That man is a human dynamo." We, therefore, have studied most critically the relation of the solar tides to the inner and outer events of Wilson's life.

Sunspot Cycles and Earth's Weather

The larger solar cycle that affects Earth is the so-called "Sunspot Cycle." Light and heat, in the form of electrodynamic energy, enters and surcharges Earth's ionosphere or outermost layer of the atmosphere. Over the last 200 years, an average of 11.2 years has been recorded between successive sunspot maxima. However, this figure is variable—it may be as low as nine years, or as high as seventeen.[21]

C. G. Abbott,[22] studying periodicity in the solar tides, found that variations in temperature of Earth's surface are correlated with the solar tides, but not directly, as would be expected. Earth's surface and the air just above it become cooler as heat from the sun increases and warmer as the sun's radiation decreases. There is a correlation of rainfall with solar radiation—more rain when the air is warmer (less solar radiation), less when it is cooler (more solar radiation). This general rule, however, is reversed in some areas. In normally humid and warm regions where there is abundant vegetation, the evaporation is increased and there is more rain; where dryness normally prevails, drought and desert conditions are intensified.

Each major eruption on the sun causes in Earth's stratosphere a great increase in ultraviolet light, sufficient in fact to scorch the earth's surface were it not that the ionized particles drifting downwards into our atmosphere produce ozone, which in turn causes cloudiness and mist sufficient to shield the biosphere (the zone of plant and animal life). It is because of the heavier and more frequent overcast thus induced and the consequent increase in rain and snowfall, that the surface of Earth actually is cooler during the solar-flare episodes, when the stratosphere is hotter.

The main effect of all this upon life on Earth, including human life, is, as has been said, indirect—through increased rainfall and vegetable growth, *or* drought; storminess, heat and/or cold, etc. How much direct electromagnetic effect on living creatures is produced by the impact of increased solar radiation in our stratosphere has not been determined yet. But Petersen's research has convinced him that man responds organically to the surcharge and discharge of this cosmic energy in our atmosphere.

Of course, weather resulting from changes in the atmosphere is the chief channel through which solar radiation affects man, acting through barometric pressure, temperature, humidity, light, and electrical effects. The body and brain of a "human dynamo" like Wilson unquestionably is not only a receiving station but acts literally as a generator. In weather that is stimulating, the effects on human beings are cumulative because the direct physical influences are enhanced by psychological and social factors. The "stimulating atmosphere" produces more energy and élan, speeds up thought and action, and the social and psychological interplay of persons is accelerated. In "depressing weather," the negative effects are likewise cumulative.

An astrophysicist, Harlan True Stetson, through his study of the sun as the controlling factor affecting transmission of radio waves in the atmosphere, necessarily has concerned himself with the sun's effect on weather. Professional meteorologists have avoided involvement in this fascinating field of research. Theirs is the duty of *predicting* weather

225

THE LIFE LINE

Figure 5

A

YOUTH

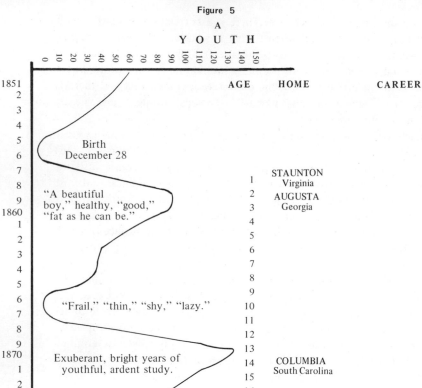

0 10 20 30 40 50 60 70 80 90 100 110 120 130 140 150

1851			AGE	HOME	CAREER
2					
3					
4					
5	Birth				
6	December 28				
7				STAUNTON	
8			1	Virginia	
9	"A beautiful		2	AUGUSTA	
1860	boy," healthy, "good,"		3	Georgia	
1	"fat as he can be."		4		
2			5		
3			6		
4			7		
5			8		
6			9		
7	"Frail," "thin," "shy," "lazy."		10		
8			11		
9			12		
1870	Exuberant, bright years of		13		
1	youthful, ardent study.		14	COLUMBIA	
2			15	South Carolina	
3			16		
4			17	WILMINGTON	DAVIDSON
5			18	North Carolina	College
6	Two "breakdowns":		19	PRINCETON	PRINCETON
7	gastro-intestinal and		20	New Jersey	student
8	nervous fatigue.		21	and	
9			22	WILMINGTON	
1880			23	North Carolina	UNIVERSITY of
1			24	CHARLOTTESVILLE	VIRGINIA
2	Masterful		25	Virginia	law student
3	student.		26	ATLANTA, Georgia	LAW OFFICE
4	Successful		27	BALTIMORE	JOHNS HOPKINS
5	authorship.		28	Maryland	student
6			29	PENNSYLVANIA	BRYN MAWR
7			30		Professor
8	Overwork		31		
9	poor health		32	MIDDLETOWN	WESLEYAN
	fatigue.		33	Connecticut	Professor

Smoothed Graph showing annual mean of WOLF "SUN SPOT" NUMBERS taken from *The Sun*, Gerald
Pieter Kuiper, Ed., Ch. 6, Solar Acitivty, by K.O. Kieppenhauer, pp. 331-2, Table 1; University of
Chicago Press, 1953

THE LIFE LINE

Figure 5

B
MATURITY

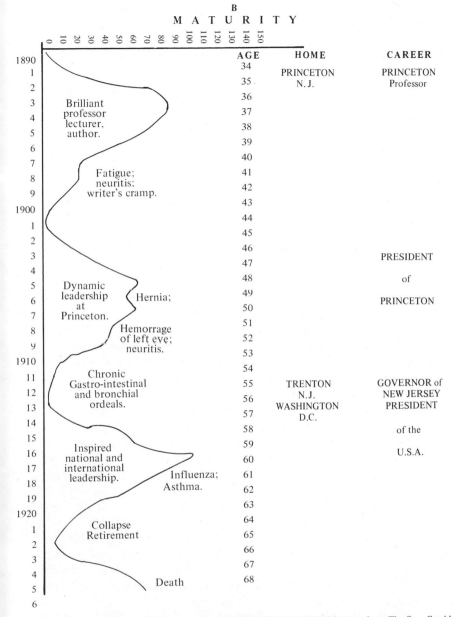

		AGE	HOME	CAREER
1890		34		
1		35	PRINCETON	PRINCETON
2		36	N. J.	Professor
3	Brilliant	37		
4	professor	38		
5	lecturer, author.	39		
6		40		
7		41		
8	Fatigue; neuritis;	42		
9	writer's cramp.	43		
1900		44		
1		45		
2		46		
3		47		PRESIDENT
4		48		of
5	Dynamic	49		
6	leadership at	50		PRINCETON
7	Princeton.	Hernia;	51	
8	Hemorrage	52		
9	of left eye; neuritis.	53		
1910		54		
11	Chronic	55	TRENTON	GOVERNOR of
12	Gastro-intestinal and bronchial	56	N.J.	NEW JERSEY
13	ordeals.	57	WASHINGTON D.C.	PRESIDENT
14		58		of the
15		59		
16	Inspired national and	60		U.S.A.
17	international	61		
18	leadership.	Influenza; Asthma.	62	
19		63		
1920		64		
1	Collapse	65		
2	Retirement	66		
3		67		
4		68		
5	Death			
6				

Smoothed Graph showing annual mean of WOLF "SUN SPOT" NUMBERS taken from *The Sun*, Gerald Pieter Kuiper, Ed., Ch. 6, Solar Activity, by K.O. Kieppenhauer, pp. 331-2, Table 1; University of Chicago Press, 1953 accurately, not estimating its effects, and that is a grave responsibility in itself. Although recognizing that the ultimate control of atmospheric changes on earth is solar radiation of light and heat, meteorologists base their predictions principally on the movements of air masses, without reference to the coincidental changes on the surface of the sun, as observable in "sunspots," until very recently a little-understood phase of astrophysics.

On the relation of sun to weather, Stetson[23] writes: "One certain thing is that all the weather on the earth is produced by the sun." In explanation, the following relationship has been shown between solar activity and Earth's atmospheric changes, beginning in the tropics:

As the sun over the tropics superheats these regions, the equatorial air rises and gives space to the inrush of polar air. These interchanging air masses are churned into swirling winds by the rotation of the earth, and from this the launching and patterning of storm tracks and of milder variable weather alike develop and are affected in turn by subsequent changes in the intensity of the sun's radiation. Radiation occurring during the enormous intensification of hydrogen eruption on the sun has been observed to affect not only our atmospheric temperature but Earth's barometric pressures as well, and these two factors are primary determinants of the nature and number of storm tracks in any given period of time and area of Earth's surface. If the degree of solar radiation were static and unvarying—in other words without this periodicity of fluctuating outbursts of energy—our own atmosphere would be relatively stable and predictable in its movements and the resultant weather changes more neatly patterned and less violent.[24]

The explanation here set forth represents a vast simplification of an extremely complex set of relationships, and all the details are by no means clear yet to man. Stetson believes its clarification may well be, for humankind, "one of the most important problems that science can solve."

Weather and Man

Out of his study of Stetson, Abbott and others, and from his own years of research on "Weather and the Patient," Petersen concludes that if man (and the organic world in general) reflects weather, and thereby reflects changing solar activity, then "the bridge from the sun to the weather and so to the human is a fairly direct one."[25]

In our own effort to understand Wilson, the particular human dynamo with whom we are concerned, and to take account of the multiple variables which molded or influenced his behavior, his health, in fact his entire character and career, we therefore must take into account the cycles of solar activity to which Earth was subjected during the sixty-eight years of his conscious life and activity on this planet, and examine whatever correlations exist. That is the purpose of Charts A. and B. of fig. 5, and of the explanatory sections entitled "Tides of Solar Energy" and "Sunspot Cycles and Earth's Weather."

Such astrophysical factors as do affect an individual are clearly components in a complex of physical and astrophysical controls extending even beyond the solar system. The effect of these, like other environmental factors, is always modified and sometimes largely governed by heredity, constitution, temperament, emotion, intellect. These in turn, in any person, are never independent of the other persons, times and conditions in his immediate milieu.

Two things are very clear in a whole view of Woodrow Wilson's life: One, that he was extremely weather-sensitive and his personal out-pourings of energy appear to have been correlated with the ups and downs of sunspot activity and the barometer and thermometer. But the second is equally, perhaps primarily important—that his somato-psychical behavior as an organism, and what he thought and did as a person throughout his life were basically the consequence of his being an American of recent Scotch and Scotch-Irish Presbyterian exigence, gifted with a keen mind that was well trained for the political leader-ship which he chose as a career in his youth—a choice entirely logical in view of his background and training and the times in which he lived. Along with the rest of humanity (if Petersen's theories are correct) and as a part of the biosphere responding to earth's atmosphere, Wilson's energies and activity seem to have been exhilarated during the sun's outpourings, and definitely were tempered by the reaction of his physique to genial and/or harsh weather. But always, irrespective of physical factors or conditions, he persisted in living intensely and being wholly himself. In a word, the mind and temperament of the man primarily determined his behavior. Physical environmental factors were variables significant as conditioners, but are not to be regarded as determinants.

The Life Span

Figure 6 shows that Woodrow Wilson's life spanned the interval in history between the years just preceding the American Civil War and those just following the First World War. He was acutely aware of the suffering that wars entail. His father was a chaplain in the Confederate Army, and his church in Augusta, Georgia, across the street from the Manse where the boy lived, served as a hospital. There the boy Tommy gazed with grief and pity upon soldiers young and old who had been wounded and maimed in battle. The abundance which the minister's family had known at Staunton, where he was born, was non-existent in the state which Sherman's army had scourged. Cowpea soup was often the best fare that Jeanie Wilson could offer her family.

A few years later, when the family had moved to Columbia, capital of South Carolina, Tommy Wilson knew at first hand what a half-ruined city with shattered and burnt buildings was like. As a small boy, he listened to the talk of the elders and was made aware of the political and social disruption of the community during the Reconstruction era. Probably these experiences were decisive in orienting the young mind and heart toward a life of public service in civics and politics rather than in the ministry.

Just as the birth of his physical life had started when astrophysical and environmental conditions were at their lowest, so his conditioning as a child occurred when the life of the communities in which he lived was at an all time low. Recollection of these times undoubtedly was a potent factor in his determination to keep America out of the First World War, in 1916 and 1917.

The growth and maturing of the mind and heart of Woodrow Wilson came during the years when the United States as a political entity matured as a nation. His nature and his character reflected the spiritual, social and cultural conditions in Georgia, South and North Carolina and Virginia during the Civil War and Reconstruction. In later years, he acquired a mature scholarly comprehension of the history of the United States before he was born. This came during the writing of his *History of the American People*, which covered the period beginning with the first settlement of Virginia and ending with the Civil War. In his studies and as an author, then, he spanned the times before his birth in 1856, while in his own life, he experienced at first hand what came after.

Ebb and Flow

During this period between the Civil War and the First World War, the United States endured the effects of six episodes of increased and diminished solar energy, and, as the chart which we call "The Life

230

Figure 6

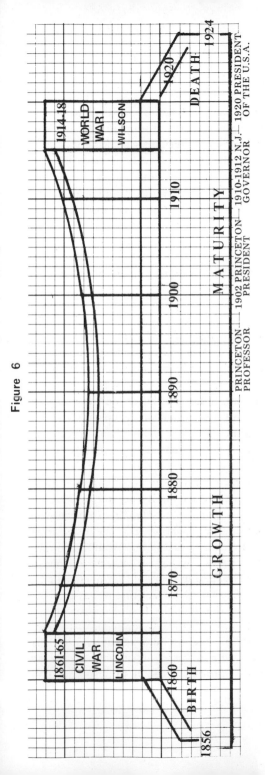

The life of Woodrow Wilson spanned the period of American history between and including the Civil War and World War I. His recollections of the war between the states and of the "Reconstruction" profoundly affected his philosophy and his policies during his Presidency — his determination to keep the United States out of the conflict, and his passion for a just peace and a League of Nations to prevent another and a worse war.

The figure also illustrates the fact that he did not reach full maturity until he was practically at the midpoint in his life span. The true beginning of his career as a public servant was his appointment at Princeton as Professor of Jurisprudence and Political Economy. The short episodes of teaching at Bryn Mawr and at Wesleyan, following his Ph.D. at Johns Hopkins, were in the nature of apprenticeship or internship. Nevertheless it must be remembered that his ability as a writer on government had made its mark while he was still an undergraduate at Princeton.

Line" (fig. 5) shows, the life of the child and man responded to the ebb and flow of these tides of solar radiation. The nature of the response is shown on the graph at the bottom of the chart.

The year of birth, 1856, was one of quiescence: the child came into the world during the calm that preceded the storm and turbulence of the Civil War. He was described in family letters as being very quiet in temperament and sound physically. The outbreak of the Civil War followed the maximum outpouring of energy from the sun in 1859. At this time, the child was in his fourth year, and his parents had moved farther south from Staunton in Virginia to Augusta in Georgia. The curve of the chart indicating the frequency of sunspots comes to its lowest point in 1867. At this time, the boy is described as frail, thin and shy.

From 1867 to 1871-2 the degree of sunspot intensity shows a rapid rise, and this was a period of exuberant growth of the mind of the child under his father's tutelage. After 1872 the graph showing the incidence of sunspots falls rapidly, until 1877-8, there is another period when Earth's biosphere was subject to a minimum of stimulation from the sun. During this time the youth experienced two periods of low vitality, one as a student enduring quite primitive living conditions at Davidson College in the mountains of North Carolina when he was in his upper teens, and the second while he was a law student in the University of Virginia. In both instances he returned home to recuperate, but his persistence in cultivating his mind continued, strengthened greatly in the first instance by four enriching years as an undergraduate at Princeton.

The next rise in the sunspot cycle reached its maximum in 1883-4. During these years, his superior intellectual ability became evident. He was an outstanding graduate student at Johns Hopkins University in Baltimore, when he wrote *Congressional Government* as the dissertation for his Ph.D. This work was received so favorably that from then on, he was a man who had made his mark as a writer on subjects relating to government and administration. His close scrutiny of the American plan of republican government did not make him feel that it was the best system, however. It was his conviction that the English parliamentary system was the best form of representative government. At Johns Hopkins, he revised the constitution of the Literary Society along the lines of the British Parliament, with a "government" that could be "supported" or "turned out" as it proved successful or unsuccessful in maintaining its position in the face of critical debate. The Literary Society, thus reconstituted, he named "The Hopkins House of Commons," and he assumed the role of prime minister, presiding over its meetings.

From the inspiring years as a graduate student at Johns Hopkins, he went on to teach at Bryn Mawr, the college for women recently established in Pennsylvania, and after that to Wesleyan College in Middletown, Connecticut. These first years of experience as a teacher coincided with the episode of minimum solar radiation in 1887-8. This perhaps explains in part the fact that at Bryn Mawr he felt a lack of inspiration in teaching young women and that his health was somewhat frail. It was a period of overstrain, exhaustion and some degree of frustration. Partly, this was a result of overwork due to the added burden of family responsibilities after marriage. At Wesleyan, he found the atmosphere more congenial and intellectually rewarding, but still it was necessary to supplement his income by writing.

During his years in Connecticut, the call came for him to join the faculty at Princeton, his beloved alma mater, and there, while the solar radiation again rose to a high level in 1895-6, he enjoyed a renewed surge of energy and enthusiasm for his work and a fresh outlet for his favorite mental pursuits. In his brilliant lectures on political science, he soon established himself as the most popular professor at Princeton. There remained, however, the financial necessities of a growing family and of aid to relatives near and dear. By continuing to carry a double load of work, he overexpended his reserves of energy and suffered a minor breakdown in health as the solar flares subsided. Thus the rise and fall of his creative endeavor continued to parallel the graph marking the rise and decline of solar radiation which results from increase and decrease in the recorded number of sunspots.

In 1896 and again in 1899, he made two trips to Europe for rest and refreshment, overfatigued by his excess of zeal for his work. The long sea voyages of those days were very restorative, and while abroad he restricted his travels to England and Scotland. In fact, the first trip was somewhat of a pilgrimage to places long revered for this association with men whose writings had inspired him—Wordsworth, Bagehot, Burke—the Lake Country, Edinburgh, Oxford and Cambridge. At this time his right arm and hand were so crippled from neuritis that he could not write, and had been compelled to learn to use his left hand for his letters home, letters which, when absent, were always a daily part of his life of sharing experience and thought. He returned to Princeton restored in body and spirit.

The second trip for rest and refreshment was made with his brother-in-law, Stockton Axson, also a professor at Princeton. Travelling by bicycle, they visited the former homes and haunts of Robert Burns in Scotland, and again Wordworth's Lake Country, which Wilson regarded as the most beautiful part of England. This time, in addition to enjoying the charm and dignity of Oxford and Cambridge, he already was contemplating the possibility of certain innovations at Princeton during his coming presidency, changes which would bring its plan of education more in line with the tutorial methods of the great English universities whose systems he greatly admired. Again he returned to America rejuvenated, and was able to say, as he worked on his inaugural address: ". . . As for my health, that is firm and excellent."

In 1902, when he became Princeton's new president, the curve of the graph showing sunspot frequency was rising rapidly again toward a new high which would continue longer than most, through 1905 and 1906. This period was one which taxed his intelligence, will and energy to the utmost, as he attempted to transform Princeton into a university that would be the equal of the other great "Ivy League" institutions, Harvard and Yale. It was a time of challenge, in which the conservatism of the old-guard trustees and alumni had to be overcome by his cease-less efforts, aided and abetted by the support of, for the most, an enthusiastic and loyal faculty. In the latter years of his Princeton administration there were some severe setbacks and disappointments; as, for example, when his hopes and plans for a graduate school closely affiliated with the college were defeated by the conservative and stubborn Dean West. As always, following periods of maximum out-pouring of his energies, he suffered the effects of overdrive and frustra-tion. Several times during this latter period, he had to retire for brief periods of rest in Bermuda.

After ten years of arduous accomplishment and fame as president of Princeton, he was persuaded to end his academic career and campaign for the governorship of New Jersey. The attention of political leaders had been attracted by speeches made before Princeton alumni gatherings across the country in the course of his urgent efforts for college reform. These forays turned out, quite unexpectedly, to be the beginning of his campaigns as a candidate for public office, though at the time he was unaware this was so. For years, however, he had longed to play a role of leadership in implementing some of the political ideas he had been preaching to his students, beginning with that ringing phrase from his inaugural address: "Princeton in the service of the Nation!"

The release from his academic career into the hurly-burly of the New Jersey political arena appears to have renewed his energies to such an extent that the momentum of his new career carried him through the next period of decreased solar stimulation without the usual recession. The campaign for election as governor of New Jersey and the period of his governorship came when the sunspot graph shows a minimal discharge of solar radiation.

Actually, the momentum generated during his presidency of Princeton carried him through the New Jersey campaign and the governorship, and through the hotly contested Democratic convention where he was nominated for the Presidency of the United States. His effectiveness as a campaigner in this climax of his career shows that whatever physical and nervous handicaps he had to contend with during his years as writer, teacher and academic leader were psychosomatic rather than indications of basic deficiencies, that when his career released his energies into channels of action, his stamina rallied to meet each crisis as it came.

Again observing the graph, which represents the incidence of sunspots, we see that he became President of the United States when sunspots were on the increase, and that the time when he, as President, became wartime commander-in-chief of the armed forces, coincided with the maximum discharge of solar energy. Through the vicissitudes of those years and the ceaseless pressure of events necessitating momentous decisions, his energy and dominant leadership never slackened until the ordeal was over. When the graph of the sunspot curve was descending rapidly, Woodrow Wilson, in a state of near exhaustion during the hot summer which followed the Paris Peace Conference, decided to take his campaign for support of the League of Nations Covenant to the people, and set out upon the grueling speaking tour of the Mid-west and far West. It was then that he suffered the cerebral incident that left him partly paralyzed. His determination to recover, for the sake of the League, and his refusal to admit that he was *hors de combat* coincided with the period of minimum solar discharge in 1922-3. And early in 1924 he died.

ENVOI

The Unique Individual

An appraisal of Woodrow Wilson's life reveals two qualities that typify men of unique gifts. Irrespective of factors of success and failure, it cannot be denied that he was original and creative in the sense that insight and vision beyond that of his contemporaries marked him as a unique person in relation to his times and to other leading men of the United States and the world during the years of his public service—at Princeton, in the governorship of New Jersey, in the Presidency of the United States and at the Peace Conference in Paris. This originality and creativeness were notably relevant to the dominant issues of his times, making him the exponent and champion of the more advanced humanitarian aspirations of the several areas of action in which his career was cast. This awareness of his times, which triggered his originality as a leader in his public life, appears to have been characteristic of his mind from a very early age.

The child born at the Manse in Staunton on December 28, 1856, had genius in the sense that he had talents peculiar to himself and a great capacity for concentration, but he was in no sense a prodigy. It was of the sort that is "ninety percent perspiration and ten percent inspiration," as Thomas A. Edison so aptly characterized what goes into the making of genius. The nature and source of the ten percent, whence it comes and how it functions, is one of the mysteries that psychologists can tell us little about as yet. Not a few men of unquestioned competence have described the operation of this faculty.[1] It functions differently with different individuals, and in different fields of endeavor. But in general, it may be said that it represents a level or faculty of the psyche that is relatively independent of the conscious reasoning intellect, although it depends upon the logical processes of the mind for the initiation of its activity and for implementation of its intuitions and insights. Call it what you will—there is no standard term—intuition, inspiration, the subliminal self—Woodrow Wilson had it, was aware of it, cultivated it, and was true to its dictates to as great a degree as his talents and opportunities and capacities permitted.

His talents, as we believe we have shown, were quite definitely of the order of those typical of his forebears, and they were shaped by his environment, channeled and matured by his times. That some exceptional qualities were notable from the time he was a small child is proven by the fact that his father very early recognized something in the boy deserving of especial fostering. Although the lad was superficially lazy and quite lacking in diligence in his studies, he responded fervently to his father's tutelage. His lack of interest in formal schooling well may have been due to the fact that it seemed rather dull in comparison with the stimulating comradeship of his father. (In later years, Woodrow Wilson always had a peculiar distaste for reiteration, and in early schooling, especially in those days, there was much of this, inevitably.) The languor in early youth, which was described as "laziness," undoubtedly was due, at least to a certain extent, to climate and a restricted diet, and to the fact that the boy preferred mental to physical exercise.

His father was responsible for bringing the boy's talents to early maturity, partly by setting up in him two conflicting motivations. Made acutely aware by the father of possessing unique potentialities, the son was (perhaps prematurely) spurred by the desire to excel; while the sobering yet stimulating effects of frustration, which is the lot of every child forced to outrun his own natural development, must frequently have affected him and brought with it both self-questioning and strengthened resolve. As a matter of fact, this unhappy psychological impasse is experienced at many stages of life by every individual who enjoys the blessings and sustains the burdens of genius in any degree or any field. The awareness of his powers or abilities gives a sureness of superior competence, but that very competence, which is beyond the average and ahead of the times, produces situations fraught with temporary frustration. Woodrow Wilson was to know this refinement of self-torture at moments throughout his life.

The masterful and companionable tutelage of Dr. Wilson, himself a gifted and very dynamic man and one accustomed as a minister to molding others to his ideal of behavior by censure and exhortation, was concentrated specially upon developing in the boy skill and accuracy in the use of the spoken and written word, an art in which Joseph Ruggles Wilson revelled and excelled. Our conception of this process of tutelage certainly is out of focus if we think of the father as an ideal and patient parent, lovingly and gently encouraging a gifted boy. Acerbity and rigor were peculiarly characteristic of the father in this enterprise. And in those days, in any situation, strictness and discipline were regarded as the only effective means to good training. Woodrow Wilson's daughter Margaret is reported to have said of her grandfather: "His idea was that if a lad was of fine-tempered steel, the more he was beaten the better."[2] The beatings in this instance were verbal, not physical, and they were of the order of systematic dialectic.

Not only did this tutelage produce an acuity in the choice of words, for which Woodrow Wilson was notable in his teaching and political careers, it also explains, perhaps, the extraordinary mental stamina during the severest ordeals of his life. However, it also may have been a factor in producing a certain rigidity which increasingly characterized his mind as he aged. The boy's mind and nervous system, like tempered steel, learned tautness as a means of sustaining his father's rigorous attack. That inflexibility, when he was pushed to the wall in crises of later life, may have lost him a number of engagements which might have been won by adroitness. Nevertheless, in assessing this possibility, it must be remembered that all his life long, and from the beginning, to be "uncompromising" was with him a matter of principle. For a Scottish Covenanter, the very word "compromise" smelled of Satan.

While Wilson's talents may be said to have been hereditary—and it is clear that his father's tutelage was the chief factor in sharpening them—neither his inheritance nor his education is sufficient to explain the definite channeling of his interests which led to the career he chose. Admiring his father and his grandfather as he did—both of them notable preachers—it would have been logical in view of his intensely religious nature and temperament for him to have chosen the ministry as a career. That he turned instead to politics was due, we believe, to the times and the region in which he was born and reared. When he was a boy in Georgia and the Carolinas, during and after the Civil War, political issues and social justice, war and its aftermath, economic and financial rehabilitation and orderly representative government were the topics and issues that filled the minds and dominated the conversation of his elders. As the boy's mind grew in the soil of his locale, he became aware that leadership would be needed and opportunity might be sought and found in these areas of activity. Once this was perceived—subconsciously at first, presumably—ambition grew apace. The boy's temperament being, as it was, histrionic, his mind projected the vision of a life of thought, action and service in the political arena. The vision naturally became egocentric, and remained so. This is not to say it was dominantly egotistical. That it was *not* basically so was always evidenced by an extraordinary humility and impersonality with respect to his major achievements.

The glowing embers of the boy's heart and mind were fanned by his father until maturity brought dedicated purposefulness. While Thomas was still a student, he wrote to his classmate and comrade, Charles Talcott, that he had become aware of "a sort of calm confidence in great things to be accomplished."

Gifted composers, musicians, artistic and scientific geniuses in such fields as mathematics, architecture and engineering are, unique in this, that from early life and throughout life they are one pointed. In the particular field in which they have genius, they manifest a serious pre-occupation and purpose and they sustain this interest, or rather their genius sustains it. As one reviews Wilson's life, this is seen to have been true of him. Even in childhood a predilection existed for the particular interests and activities to which his life became devoted in his mature years. In the years when he was still groping for the means to realize his ambition, he wrote to his fiancée, Ellen Axson, ". . . My heart's *first* primary ambition and purpose, which was to take an active, if possible a leading, part in public life, and strike out for myself, if I had the ability, a *statesman's* career. . . . I have a strong instinct for leadership, an unmistakably oratorical temperament and the keenest delight in affairs . . . ."[3] We base our summary of Wilson's talent for leadership and his perfecting of the art of speech as his primary tool, on Ray Stannard Baker's *Life and Letters (of Woodrow Wilson)*, and Eleanor Wilson MacAdoo's *The Priceless Gift*.

At Staunton, the child christened Thomas Woodrow had impressed his grandfather, whose name he bore, as being "dignified enough to be Moderator of the General Assembly." The minister did not know how prophetic his words were. The man this child was to become would preside over the greatest conclaves known to man in his times. In so functioning, that man was ever to be notable for a peculiar dignity, arising out of a keen sense—a sort of inspired awareness—of the significance of the occasion, and of his part in it.

The boy Tommy, before he was an adolescent, was fonder of his own imaginative life of the mind than of physical play. Not much of an athlete, he chose a role among his playmates that revealed his latent proclivities. He organized his little gang into the "Lightfoot Club," which held its meetings in the hayloft of his father's stable, opposite the big church in Augusta, Georgia. He presided over debates conducted strictly in accordance with rules laid down in a "Constitution" which he had written. All this took place under the eye of His Satanic Majesty, torn from an advertisement of devilled ham. (Thereby the Club certainly established a healthy juvenile counterpoise, in its relationship to the church across the street and to the father of its president.)

Some years later, from Columbia, South Carolina (where his family had moved in 1870, and where his mind and spirit had been stirred by great words and thoughts in the sermons and lectures of his father and other notable preachers and teachers at the theological seminary where his father taught), young Tommy went to Davidson College in North Carolina, in his seventeenth year. Davidson was a Presbyterian school in the mountains, where life was physically rugged and discipline severe. A fellow student later described him at this time as "witty, genial, superior, but languid."[4] At Davidson, the debating club, known as the Ecumenean Society, interested him more than either his studies or sport. Meeting in a room furnished in a style of "sedate magnificence appropriate to the seriousness with which the youths of those days burned offerings on the altar of oratory,"[5] the debating society elected him president, and he proceeded to rewrite its constitution—all this in his first term at the school!

One of the first books that Tommy had read to himself in his father's library in Augusta was Weems' *Life of Washington*. He had devoured the speeches of Gladstone before he was in his teens. That great orator's portrait hung over the desk where he studied. Once he told his cousin Marion Woodrow, who was eyeing the portrait of Gladstone with curiosity, that he too intended to become a great statesman. Between his terms at Davidson and before he went to Princeton, he was fond of discussing with his chum John Bellamy at Wilmington, North Carolina, where his father was then minister of the Presbyterian Church, the careers of famous men he admired—Cromwell and Gladstone, Stonewall Jackson and Robert E. Lee—eagerly speculating about the qualities that made them great.

Entering Princeton as an undergraduate in 1875, he interested himself in the Whig Society, that debating club organized by James Madison nearly a century before. In October of that year, he made his first speech: his subject, "Rome Was Not Built in a Day!" A fellow member of the club reported to Ray Stannard Baker many years later that "he steadily grew in the estimation of his fellow members until he was recognized as the best debater in the Society—always with a full and ready knowledge of the question and with unequalled facility in clear expression. He was especially effective in extemporaneous debate."

Not content with the Whig Society's possibilities as a forum for his talents, he promoted the founding of a new organization, the Liberal Debating Club. For this, he wrote a constitution reflecting his growing interest in the British parliamentary system, which, in the course of his reading, he had learned to admire. His chief colleague in this enterprise was his classmate, Charles Talcott. Charlie was elected president, and T. W. Wilson secretary of state, with functions approximating quite closely those of the prime minister in the English Parliament. With Talcott, he entered into a "solemn covenant" which pledged that they should "school all our powers and passions for the work of establishing the principles that we hold in common," that they would "acquire knowledge that we might have power and . . . drill ourselves in all the arts of persuasion, but especially in oratory . . . that we might have facility in leading others into our ways of thinking and enlisting them in our purposes. . . . " During this period, he privately wrote out a number of cards in his carefully practiced, graceful script:

Thomas Woodrow Wilson
Senator from Virginia

The occasions of formal debate or informal discussion were only a part of his training and practice in the art of oratory. He used to walk in Potter's Wood near the college, repeating aloud one of Burke's orations. In his sophomore year, he published an article on oratory in which he asked "What is the object of oratory?" and answered, "Its object is persuasion and conviction—the control of other minds by a strange personal influence and power." Then he proceeded to define "the chief and best means of training," saying "the greatest and truest model for all orators is Demosthenes. . . . Only as the constant companions of Demosthenes, Cicero, Burke, Fox, Canning and Webster, can we hope to become orators." At home in Wilmington during vacations, he would go every weekday into his father's church and deliver from the pulpit to the empty pews the speeches of Gladstone, Bright, Patrick Henry, Daniel Webster—and Demosthenes!

241

Entering the University of Virginia in 1879 to study law (a logical decision for a young man who hoped one day to be a Senator from Virginia), he joined the Jefferson Society, one of the University's two debating clubs. Four days after joining, he was elected its secretary. In less than four months, when he was scheduled to deliver an address on John Bright, he had become so notable as a speaker that the wives of faculty members petitioned to attend. He spoke to an enthusiastic overflow audience of his fellow students, faculty and their wives. The address, which showed a great deal of accurate and intimate acquaintance with current English politics, was published in the university magazine. Mr. Baker[6] describes the article as "judged by any standard, a remarkable production." "It exhibits," he writes, "an unusual grasp of English politics and English leadership, and sets forth with a maturity that is magisterial, and with a finished and somewhat flowery grace of expression, the essentials of good oratory, true liberalism, and great statesmanship."

The most notable feature of this oratorical triumph, in its time and setting, lay in a carefully reasoned persuasive appeal to Southerners to regard the defeat of the Confederacy and the preservation of the Union as a fortunate event. To say this forthrightly to an audience of Virginians, but a decade and a half after war's end, showed not only courage but maturity and integrity of a high order, even though he prefaced his point by saying: "I yield to no one precedence in love for the South."

In October of 1880, he was elected president of the Jefferson Society. At his instigation, the meetings for many weeks were devoted to discussing a revision of the constitution, as proposed by him. While that was going on, two meetings were devoted to the consideration of topics that were of special interest to the new president—the tariff, and the feasibility of adapting the British scheme of ministerial responsibility to the political system of the United States. The revised constitution for the debating club was adopted—although the national Constitution remained unchanged!

In the year after his withdrawal from the University of Virginia (because of poor health due mainly to inadequate diet), he completed his study of the law at home in Wilmington, passed the bar examination in Georgia and hung out his shingle in Atlanta. There, it became plain to him that routine practice would be intolerable and certainly not the road to the career he desired. In 1883, therefore, he entered Johns

Hopkins University at Baltimore as a graduate student in political science and government. Organized only seven years before, and with a faculty of superior ability, Johns Hopkins seemed the "best place in America to study," as he wrote his Virginia chum, Heath Dabney.

This opinion was well founded. The head of the department in which he enrolled was Dr. Herbert B. Adams, America's leading scholar and teacher in the field in which Wilson desired to make a career. The young man by this time had decided that the academic path was best suited to his tastes and ambitions. With Professor Adams' approval, he set about the writing of *Congressional Government*, his first book. It was published and received by reviewers with acclaim even before it was accepted as a dissertation for the degree of doctor in philosophy.

At Johns Hopkins, his zest for debate and his gift as an organizer and leader again manifested themselves. The equivalent of a debating club there was the Johns Hopkins Literary Society. With this group, he affiliated himself, and soon wrote a new constitution for the Literary Society, converting it into the "Hopkins House of Commons." Over this, he presided as "prime minister." All the evidence points to the fact that in this new venture his fellow students shared his enthusiasm. During this period, he wrote exuberantly to his fiancée, his beloved Ellen with whom he shared all his ambitions, exaltations and depressions of spirit: "I have a sense of power in dealing with men collectively . . . absolute joy in facing and conquering a hostile audience . . . or thawing out a cold one."[7] In his subsequent career as a leader in academic and political affairs, he was to experience many occasions on which these abilities would be demonstrated in notable fashion.

At Wesleyan University in Connecticut, where he taught political science from 1888 to 1890, he again organized an enthusiastic band of students into a "House of Commons." The meeting always drew a full turnout, issues were hotly debated, "governments" were formed, defeated and turned out. The debates of the Wesleyan House of Commons in those days are said almost to have rivaled football games in popularity with the student body.

After teaching but two years in the congenial atmosphere of Wesleyan, he was invited to come to Princeton as full professor to fill the newly established chair of jurisprudence and political economy (a chair which in fact had been tailored to fit his special abilities). Then, he felt that gates truly were opening to opportunity of rich promise.

243

Actually his rise from graduate student at Johns Hopkins to full professor at Princeton was so swift—a mere five years, three at Bryn Mawr and two at Wesleyan—that the invitation to join the Princeton faculty in itself was a remarkable recognition of ability.

Raymond B. Fosdick, a student under Wilson at Princeton who later served in his Administration at Washington during the First World War, regards Woodrow Wilson as the greatest orator of his time. Fosdick was in a position to judge, for he knew personally or had listened to the other notable reformers, politicians and statesmen of his era. He writes:[8] "I would be inclined to say that he was the greatest orator I have ever heard. . . . His power lay in the precision of his mind, in the matchless lucidity of his argument, and in his passionate sincerity. His influence on his listeners was almost hypnotic, and he could fairly bring them to their feet with a stirring phrase."

This precision of Wilson's mental processes and the lucidity of his argument had been in course of development ever since his father dedicated himself to cutting and polishing the "gem-like mind" (as he described it) of his small son in Georgia so long before. The passionate sincerity was inherent, but certainly his Presbyterian heritage and up-bringing were very much to be thanked, insofar as extrinsic factors are concerned. Fosdick's characterization continues: "In sheer ability and power it seems to me that Wilson towered above them all. He was a scholar in action, a prophet touched by fire, with unmatched strength to move and persuade his listeners." Here one is reminded of the "solemn covenant" with Charlie Talcott in student days: ". . . that we would drill ourselves in all the arts of persuasion, but especially in oratory . . . that we might have facility in leading others into our ways of thinking and enlisting them in our purpose."[9] It need not be said, however, that in later years he did not always succeed in leading others into his way of thinking; that sometimes his carefully chosen words, as weapons, were in the final critical test twisted and turned against him by adroit personal and political enemies at the climax of his career.

Fosdick's assertion that his "influence on his listeners was almost hypnotic" is of peculiar interest. There was in Wilson, in youth, a quality which he termed (as we have quoted above from a letter to Ellen from Johns Hopkins) "a sense of power in dealing with men collectively." This quality he had earlier described, in the Princeton article previously mentioned, as "the control of other minds by a strange influence and power," and had named it as a *sine qua non* of the true orator. While he was a law student at the University of Virginia, an incident occurred which illustrates the fact that he himself really possessed this power.

A circus had come to town, and a few students had got into a row with some of the roustabouts. The entire student body had come together to decide what to do for the University's honor. Hotheads were all for marching in a body to the circus grounds to beat up the roustabouts. "Just as the excitement reached its height," records Baker,[10] "the slender figure of young Wilson arose, standing upon a chair, with hand uplifted until there was silence. 'I have listened,' he said, 'with much attention to the plan you have outlined to whip the circus. I want to make a remark on how *not* to do it.' He made a powerful but quiet speech that [as an onlooker reports] 'had the effect of sending the students all quietly home to bed.' "

In writing of this persuasive power, Walworth says: ". . . His most intimate and incisive weapon was The Word." During the Paris Peace Conference there were many occasions on which he used this weapon effectively. Those on which it was most notable appear to have been times when he spoke spontaneously, without preparation. A good instance of this was during an evening meeting with the commission charged with drafting the Constitution of the League of Nations. The problem was to persuade the other members of the commission to include a clause protecting the American Monroe Doctrine. The discussion seemed to reach a complete impasse. At eleven o'clock, the members were ready to quit in despair. But Wilson and Colonel House insisted that the discussion must continue. Walworth[11] describes the finale:

> It was near midnight when there was a pause and the President rose and gave the occasion its setting in the spiritual history of the race. A Century before, he said, when the world was in the grip of tyranny, England had suggested to the United States that they take a step to keep this evil from the American continent. And so principles had been laid down that from that day to this had proved an effective barrier against absolutism. The Monroe Doctrine was the forerunner of the League of Nations. Absolutism had been ended by a world war that the United States had entered in accordance with the principles that she always had honored. Now a document was being written that extended the Monroe Doctrine logically to the whole world. Was the United States to be refused recognition of her leadership in this glorious cause? Was there to be denied her, Wilson asked, the small gift of

245

a few words which, after all, only state the undoubted fact that her policy for the past hundred years had been devoted to principles of liberty and independence? Indeed, were they not assembled at Paris to consecrate and extend the horizon of this Document as a perpetual charter for all the world?

Americans who heard it thought this the most moving speech of the Peace Conference. It left the secretaries breathless, gasping with surprise and admiration, their pencils quiet in their hands and hardly a word set down. . . .

Thus the long night meeting ended on a note of understanding which later led to a satisfactory formula for the moot point.

As a final illustration, let us quote from descriptions of his "valedictory," another extempore speech said to have been of remarkable power. It would seem that this last speech of his Western tour on behalf of the League of Nations, in September of 1919, indicated that "the strange influence and power" with which he was endowed lay as much in his projection of intense feeling as in his words: that the chief secret of his power was the histrionic gift of valid articulate emotion.

At Pueblo, Colorado, on September 25 of that year, when he had returned from the long ordeal of the Paris Peace Conference to meet the concerted and aggressive enmity of political opposition to the League Covenant, he made what was to be his last public address as President before a vast assemblage, not many hours before the collapse which would incapacitate him physically for the remainder of his term. Both his faithful secretary Joseph Tumulty and Mrs. Wilson were very near him on the platform. Mrs. Wilson watched her husband anxiously, aware of his extreme fatigue and of the severe headache which had caused him to confess to her that he would be unequal to more than a few words on this occasion of the city's roaring Victory celebration. In her *Memoir*[12] she describes the occasion, and writes:

> Strangely, the speech . . . was one of the longest, one of the most vigorous and touching he had made on the tour, and again I do not venture this opinion without consulting the impression of more detached hearers. As he warmed to his subject, the President's weariness seemed to leave him. New and undiscovered reservoirs of strength seemed to reinforce his efforts. Tears were on my cheeks, and not mine alone.

Tumulty agrees with Mrs. Wilson, but he prefaces his description by saying that the "fine newspaper men" who accompanied the Presidential tour stated in their dispatches that evidence of an imminent breakdown was to them "plainly visible" in the course of this address. Tumulty writes:[13]

> ... This last speech ... was ... one of the best and most passionate appeals he made for the League of Nations. ... In the peroration of the speech he drew a picture of his visit on Decoration Day, 1919, to ... a beautiful hillside near Paris, where was located the cemetery of Suresnes, a cemetery given over to the burial of the American dead. As he spoke of the purposes for which those departed American soldiers had given their lives a great wave of emotion, such as I have never witnessed at a public meeting, swept through the whole amphitheatre. As he continued ... I looked at Mrs. Wilson and saw tears in her eyes. I then turned to see the effect upon some of the "hard-boiled" newspaper men, to whom great speeches were ordinary things, and they were alike deeply moved. Down in the amphitheatre I saw men sneak their handkerchiefs out of their pockets and wipe the tears from their eyes. The President was like a great organist playing upon the heart emotions of the thousands of people who were held spell-bound by what he said.

On reading these and other impressions, and the recorded speech as it has been preserved, it would seem that the President's hearers were affected mainly by the emotional intensity and fervor of this, Woodrow Wilson's swan song—by feelings evoked rather than by words alone. The speech was spontaneous, unprepared. The concluding sentences summoned the audience to contemplate for themselves the vision that had driven him to this, his act of supreme ordeal, as it had sustained him throughout the war years of self-expenditure:

> Now that the mists of this great question have cleared away, I believe that men will see the truth, eye to eye and face to face. There is one thing that the American people always rise to and extend their hand to, and that is the truth of justice and of liberty and of peace. We have accepted that truth and we are going to be led by it; and it is going to lead us—and through us the world—out into pastures of quietness and peace such as the world never dreamed of before.[14]

247

NOTES AND REFERENCES

Chapter I

1. Baker and Dodd, 1925, vol. II, p. 178.
2. Op. cit., pp. 178-181.
3. Op. cit., pp. 178-181.
4. Galton, 1914.
5. Baker, 1927, vol. I, p. 118.
6. McAdoo, 1962, p. 55.
7. Galton, pp. 360, 1.
8. Wilson, 1901.
9. Smuts, 1936, Foreword.
10. Taine, 1871.
11. Galton, p. 360.
12. Taine, pp. 2, 3.
13. Handy, 1952.

Chapter II

1. Baker, 1927, vol. I, p. 54.
2. Loc. cit., vol. I, p. 82.
3. McAdoo, 1962, p. 56.
4. Waddell, 1902, pp. 530-33.
5. Ibid.
6. "The attack on uncle James Woodrow which I predicted has begun, and very much in the way—though not from the quarter—I expected . . . It *must* be reckoned wicked to bring upon God's church, such reproach of spite and bigotry . . . If Uncle J. is to be read out of the Seminary, Dr. McCosh ought to be driven out of the church, and all private members like myself ought to withdraw without waiting for the expulsion which should follow belief in evolution. If the brethren of the Mississippi Valley have so precarious a hold upon their faith in God that they are afraid to have their sons hear aught of modern scientific belief, by all means let them drive Dr. Woodrow to the wall."

A little later he wrote:

"You will be disgusted and bitterly disappointed to learn that *Dr. Mack* has been elected to fill Uncle James's place! I hope that the Seminary *will* die, and die soon, if such pestiferous fellows as he are to be put into its hitherto honoured chairs. *He* in the chair of Science and Religion! He knows about as much of the facts of the one as about the true spirit of the other! What is to become of our dear church! She has indeed fallen upon evil times of ignorance and folly!—But enough of that—my thoughts are too harsh for the pages of this letter." (See Baker, 1927, vol. I pp. 208-210).

7. Jefferson, 1825, p. 28.

8. Hotchkiss, in Waddell, 1885, p. 31.

9. Thomas Jefferson had written (1825, pp. 26-7):

"It is worthy of notice that our mountains . . . are disposed in ridges, one behind another, running nearly parallel with the sea-coast, though rather approaching it as they advance north-eastwardly. . . .

"In the same direction generally are the veins of limestone, coal, and other minerals hitherto discovered; and so range the falls of our great rivers. But the courses of the great rivers are at right angles with these. James and Potowmac penetrate through all the ridges of mountains eastward of the Alleghaney . . . The passage of the Potowmac through the Blue Ridge is perhaps one of the most stupendous scenes in nature."

10. It is certain that the minister had read *Uncle Tom's Cabin*, which first appeared in 1852. In 1855 the bloody battle for abolitionism in Kansas had begun, incited by John Brown and his sons, who had settled near Ossawatomie in that state. This dedicated but impractical zealot, having brought about a state of anarchy in Kansas (of which the Federal Government washed its hands), then planned the seizure of the U. S. Army arsenal at Harper's Ferry, situated at the juncture of the Shenandoah and Potomac rivers, a few miles north of Washington. He began to drill fellow zealots for this dramatic "incident" designed to precipitate a government crisis. In 1859 he actually did seize the arsenal, was caught by a local posse, jailed, tried and hung. A U. S. Army engineer named Robert E. Lee was sent from Washington with a company of Marines to reoccupy the arsenal and restore order.

11. Waddell, 1902, p. 441.

12. Wernli, p. 21.

Chapter III

1. Handy, 1927, p. 14.

2. Petersen, 1936, pp. i, xxxi, 521.

3. Wyld.

4. Huntington, 1938, p. 330.

5. Ibid., pp. 304, 306.

6. Petersen, 1947, p. 434.

7. When the male and female nuclei unite, the 46 chromosomes line up in an orderly fashion, so that each, containing corresponding genes, is aligned with its opposite partner. But they cannot unite as they are. If they did, they would double the number of genes. So each chromosome is halved, and half joins opposite half, and there are 23 distinct pairs which unite to form a new 46. The unused halves disintegrate. The die is cast. Thenceforth, they remain the same for the new individual, will control his characteristics, will compose the formula for his or her germ-plasm to be passed on as nucleus of sperm or ovum in the breeding of the next generation.

8. Identical twins are formed by the fusion of a single pair of nuclei. Physically such twins are the same in sex, in features such as nose, ears, eyes, teeth, in form of skull, hair, skin, hands and feet, palm and fingerprints, and blood type. If they are separated, their behavior is less identical than if the two are raised in an identical environment. Yet they remain unique and similar in nonphysical characteristics which are essentially personal in the sense that they determine personal and cultural behavior—gait, gestures, timbre of voice, and mannerisms.

9. Sherrington, p. 294.

10. Op. cit., p. 277.

11. Muller, p. 48.

12. The sensory parts of the eyes appear first as a pair of bulblike protrusions from the sides of the forebrain, the optic vesicles. Each grows outward until it is marked off from the brain by a definite stalk. This continues to lengthen until the bulb comes into contact with the external ectoderm (or surface layer which will become skin) of the embryo. Where it presses against the surface from underneath, the ectoderm thickens and forms a crystalline lens. (Guyer, pp. 67, 68.) By the fifth week, the lens cups are formed, by the sixth they are detached, and pigment is present in the retina, and in the seventh week nerve fibres are invading the optic stalk. (Arey, pp. 397 ff., figs. 350, 351, 353, and pp. 453-464.)

13. Old, p. 1.

14. Arey, Fig. 112.

15. Shree and Yeats, pp. 17, 70.

16. Cannon, See Bibliography.

17. A brief description of the developmental history of the digestive system of any human being might be that it consists of a complex of organs derived from a primitive tube which at the head end is termed the fore-gut and at the tail end the hind-gut. The exposed ends are lined with cells derived from the ectoderm, but the gut itself is derived entirely from the endoderm, the inner or infolded layer, as are the organs of digestion: the liver (which is budding by the 4th week), esophagus, stomach, intestines (5th week). (See Arey, pp. 168-209).

18. Day, p. 29.

19. The hypophysis or pituitary gland is an extension hanging on a tiny stalk, or pedicle, from the base of the brain, and socketed, for safety, in a little cup of bone set in the floor of the braincase. From the front part of the master gland (the part which develops from the pharynx) hormones will be secreted which regulate body growth and size. The middle portion of the gland secretes hormones that affect the bladder. From the posterior section, a direct extension of the base of the brain substance, come hormones which will exercise an enormously important control. These hormones, through their regulation of the contraction of the smooth muscles, directly control the functioning of the autonomic nervous system which in turn regulates the breathing and digestive functions of the organism.

20. Crile, pp. 17, 18.

21. Mottram, p. 68.

22. The hormones of the gonads derived from the sex glands, acting in concert with those of the pituitary, control and animate the organism in every phase of its life as a male or female, be it manifested in affection or passion, intellectual stimulation and companionship, uxoriousness, flirtatiousness or fondness for children. A man with subnormal sex glands is dull, unresponsive. An excess means all the unpleasant behavior identified with being oversexed.

23. Recent research has cast new light upon this matter of the production of hormones. It is now indicated that the endocrine glands may be *reservoirs* and *distributors* of particular hormones, rather than production centers. By means of modern electronic microscopy, the existence and role of certain specialized nerve tissue, known as neurosecretory cells, has been discovered, their role being the production of hormones of particular types. This is a function hitherto unsuspected in connection with the known main functions of the tissues and ganglia of the nervous system as pathways and centers of communication connecting the endocrine glands with other parts of the organism. (Scharrer, pp. 1396-1398).

24. The adrenal glands, "resting atop each kidney like a cap," consists of a medulla (marroe) or enclosed layer of tissue derived from the celiac (solar) plexus of the nervous system, the center of the innervation for the stomach, intestines, liver and kidneys: and a cortex or outer layer, which is a growth out of the same tissue from which all six endocrine glands of the body are formed. The medulla maintains the balance of sodium chloride (salt) and potassium in the body fluids. This balance must remain the same as that in sea water. Upon the normal secretion of adrenalin from the medulla depends the circulation of the blood (pressure and rate of heartbeat) and peristalsis or intestinal movement on which digestion depends. Too much adrenalin causes blood pressure to rise, the heartbeat to quicken, and stops peristalsis; when there is too little, these symptoms are reversed. (Tokay, p. 168).

25. The thyroid gland, at the base of the throat, is both a dependent and collaborator of the master gland, the small tripartite tripotent pituitary. The thyroid is a gross organ compared with the pituitary. It is a large purplish mass having two lobes which contain a veritable network of fine blood vessels. It absorbs from the blood and stores up in its tissues the iodine which is essential in the formation of the thyroid hormones. These particular hormones maintain energy and tone throughout the whole nervous system. Through them the thyroid gland controls the conversion of nutrients into energy in every cell. An excess of hormones (hyperthyroidism) makes man overactive, overexuberant, too energetic and aggressive. If the gland is sluggish in its production of hormones—hypothyroidism results; the man is lacking in nervous energy and stamina, lazy or apt to "go off the deep end" nervously.

251

26. Elliott, p. 237.
27. Sugrue and Starling, p. 87.
28. McAdoo, 1937, pp. 122, 3.
29. Wilson, E. B., 1938, pp. 77, 8.
30. Handy, 1927, p. 14.
31. Ibid.
32. Baker, 1927, vol. I, p. 231.
33. Elliott, p. 237.
34. Alderman, pp. 2, 4.
35. Tumulty, p. 20.
36. White, p. 351.
37. Wilson, E. B., 1938, p. 145.
38. Sugrue and Starling, pp. 51, 56.
39. Wilson, E. B., 1938, p. 260.
40. Op. cit., p. 268.

Chapter IV

1. Waddell, 1902, pp. 448-9.
2. Murrill, p. 19.
3. Huntington, 1938, p. 304.
4. Shree and Yates, p. 17.
5. Baker, 1927, vol. I, p. 35.
6. Gesell and Ilg, pp. 28 ff.
7. Allport, p. 115.
8. Op. cit., p. 101.
9. Op. cit., p. 107.
10. *New York Times*, October 17, 1931.
11. Baker, 1927, vol. I, pp. 318, 9.
12. "Although many of its determinants are congenital, personality as such is not inherited. Only when the original stream of activity meets the environment, acting upon it and being acted upon by it, do the first habits, conscious desires, and incipient traits emerge." (Allport, p. 122.) Results of one set of tests indicate that not until the second month does the baby react positively to the human voice: that is, hear in the sense of identifying the sound with the person, and with some inner sensation, pleasurable or the opposite. (See Greene, Table 26.) Not until the third month is he capable of focusing upon the adult's face, catching his glance and responding with a smile or cooing sound; not until the fifth month does this random response become sustained to the point where baby's gaze follows the movements of a person about the room; and another month probably will elapse before the infant's own facial expressions will begin to reflect the expressions of friendliness or anger on the faces around him.
13. "(1) Personality, defined as the distinctive mode of adjustment adopted by each individual in his efforts to live, is not formed at birth, but may be said to begin at birth. (2) The earliest distinctive adjust-

ments in respect to which infants can be said to differ are in the intensity and frequency of their spontaneous activity (motility) and in their emotional expression (temperament). Both these factors are primarily products of inheritance. (3) Probably not before the fourth month is there sufficient learning and maturation to form distinctive *habits* of adjustment or rudimentary traits; but by the second half of the first year adaptive responses to the physical environment and to people show marked distinctiveness. (4) Distinctive qualities noticed early in life tend to persist; the child seems predisposed to learn certain modes of adjustment and to reject others. Even before these adaptive modes are clearly defined an observer can often by the method of 'prophecy' predict later traits." (Allport, pp. 129-130).

Chapter V

1. Ewen, Black, Woulfe.

2. See for example "Ulster and the City of Belfast," p. 146, in the series *This is Ireland* by Richard Hayward; *Ulster Sails West*, p. 46, by W. F. Marshall; *Strabane Official Guide*, pp. 6-10; and *Ulster Links with the White House*, p. 79, *Belfast Evening Telegraph; Strabane Festival, 1952*, historical sketch of the town by James Bradley, pp. 9-13, and of the Presbyterian Church by Edward McIntyre, p. 41; "Landmarks of Strabane," a lecture by Mr. John Lowrey in 1921; the Strabane Urban Council Minute Book recording the congratulatory cable sent to Woodrow Wilson upon his Inauguration and, under date of April, 1913, the receipt of an acknowledgment.

Mr. Kelley wrote voluminous notes summarizing the results of his inquiries, study of documentary records, interviews with informed persons, including much genealogical and historical data. From these, together with our own notes, we have pieced together our account of the forebears of Woodrow Wilson's grandfather James Wilson and of his grandmother Ann Adams.

3. In the Records Office at Belfast is an abstract of a Will which may have bearing on the coming of the Wilsons to County Tyrone. This is the will of Archibald Wilson, to which there has been attached an unsigned memorandum as follows:

"Archibald Wilson, *the ancestor of President Woodrow Wilson* . . . was born in Island Magee, County Antrim [just north of the Belfast Lough] but moved to Tyrone County to follow his trade of linen weaving."

His will, signed and witnessed March 2, 1745, and probated in Londonderry April 5, 1746, desires that he be buried at Donaghmore, County Tyrone, which is six or eight miles west of Dungannon. There are specific bequests to three brothers, Daniel, John and Thomas, and to others whose relationship is not specified. Were it not for the memorandum (of which no one now knows the origin) stating that this Archibald Wilson was the ancestor of the President, and that he moved to Tyrone County before James Wilson was born, there would be little reason for giving more credence to this document as possible evidence than to many another such which fails of direct genealogical connection. The possibility of its having bearing is strengthened, however, by the fact that a brother in the present elder generation of Dergalt Wilsons is named Archibald.

4. For the present generation of Wilsons who occupied the old home at Dergalt the Government of Northern Ireland has built a new and comfortable modern home nearby. This must seem quite luxurious compared with the old farmhouse, for it has four bedrooms, two reception rooms, bath and toilet, a kitchen and pantry. Miss Susan Wilson is housekeeper in the new home, and caretaker of the old house; and in addition, has 2,000 hens in battery cages—a busy life indeed! Her brother William still farms the land. A letter from Mrs. Robert Wilson in Strabane tells us that there have been many visitors since the dedication of the old home where Woodrow Wilson's grandfather James was born and grew up.

A leaflet commemorating the dedication was published at Gray's Printing Shop in Strabane, where James Wilson learned to set type before emigrating to America. This leaflet presumably was printed on the old manually operated press that is said to have been there when James Wilson learned his trade. Gray's Printing Shop also was taken over as an historical site by the National Trust. Doubtless this leaflet will be the last item printed there. The leaflet reads as follows:

"THE GOVERNMENT OF NORTHERN IRELAND
THE NATIONAL TRUST AND
THE ULSTER-SCOT HISTORICAL SOCIETY

"At a Ceremony on 17th June, 1966, the Very Rev. Francis B. Sayre, D.D., Dean of Washington Cathedral and grandson of President Woodrow Wilson, opened to the public Gray's Printing Shop, Strabane, Co. Tyrone, where John Dunlap, Printer of the Declaration of Independence, and James Wilson, grandfather of President Wilson, are said to have learned their trades.

"Dean Sayre also declared open the farmhouse at Dergault, Strabane, associated with the ancestors of President Wilson.

"The Ceremony was presided over by the Prime Minister of Northern Ireland, Captain The Rt. Hon. Terence O'Neill, D.L., M.P., and amongst those present were members of the Scotch-Irish Society of the United States of America."

5. McIntyre, p. 41.
6. Marshall, p. 9.
7. Op. cit., pp. 10-11.
8. Hayward, pp. 29-30.
9. Marshall, p. 11.

10. Hayward, p. 30.
11. Camblin, p. 1.
12. Baker, 1927, vol. II, p. 5.
13. White, pp. 3 ff.
14. Hooton, vol. 1, p. 212.
15. Camblin, p. 21.
16. Ewen, p. 264.
17. Black.
18. Baker, 1927, vol. I. p. 8; and White, p. 5. James Wilson and Ann Adams were married on November 1, 1808, in Philadelphia by the Rev. George C. Polk, Minister of the Fourth Presbyterian Church.
19. Kelley Research Notes, 1956, Belfast and Glasgow.
20. Ibid.
21. Hayward, p. 80.
22. Coon, pp. 186-189.
23. Hooton, vol. 1, p. 203.
24. Dalton, vol. 1, p. 22.
25. Joyce, vol. 1, pp. 81-2.
26. Callary, p. 31.
27. Guyer, p. 1, paraphrased from a verse by Barker.
28. Hayward, p. 34.
29. Sugrue and Starling, p. 37.

Chapter VI

1 Coon, p. 375.
2. Op, cit., pp. 370-72.
3. Kelley MS notes, under "Patrick Wodrow Line"; and to:
"The *Fasti Ecclesiae Scotianae* for the three synods of Glasgow and Ayr records that 'Patrick Wodriuf had orders in the Roman Church and was vicar of Eaglesham. He conformed [i.e. to the reformed Church of England] and was reader at Eaglesham from 1574.' (David H. Kelley Notes, 1956.)"
4. Baker, 1927, vol. I, Chapter 1.
5. Black, p. 613.
6. *Glasgow Herald*, 8 Feb., 1924, p. 8.
7. Black, p. 822.
8. Ewen, p. 264.
9. Black, p. 824.
10. Woodrow Genealogical Sources: David H. Kelley, 1956 *Notes on Research*. National Registry Office, Edinburgh: vital statistics, shire maps and records, antiquities. *Fasti Ecclesiae Scotianae* (for the three synods of Glasgow and Ayr). *Matriculation Albums of the University of Glasgow*, transcribed and annotated by W. Innes Addison, Glasgow, 1913. The Rev. H. B. M. Reid, *Divinity Professors in the University of Glasgow, 1640-1903*, Glasgow, 1923. *Senex Glasgow Past and Present*, 1884. *Glasgow Parish Records, 1719-1737. Govan Parish Records,*

Gorbals Parish Records (relevant dates), being parishes adjacent to Glasgow. Paisley "Low Church" *Register* (for Sclaters, Mortons, Widrows, Wodrows, Woodrows). *The Burgesses of Glasgow*, official lists (for relevant dates). *The Paisley Corporation of Merchants, Founded 1725*, official records. *Glasgow Journal*, and *Glasgow Herald*, files for relevant dates. *Edinburgh Evening Courant*, files for relevant dates. MSS and news clippings, Paisley Library. *Poll Tax Records*, Glasgow and Paisley. *Paisley Directory*, present day (listing many Mortons, Sclaters, Wodrows and Woodrows). Private family records of Mr. John Woodrow, director (1956) of the Coats Observatory, Paisley; and of Miss Peggy Kirkwood of Paisley, who had a Woodrow grandfather. Robert Brown, *The History of the Paisley Grammar School, 1576—*, Paisley, 1875. W. M. Metcalfe, *A History of Paisley*, 1909. *Crawford's Renfrewshire*, ed. by Robertson. James E. Shaw, *Ayrshire, 1745-1950*, Edinburgh, 1953. *Dictionary of National Biography* (Scottish). Robert Wodrow, *The Life of James Wodrow* (written before 1725); and *Analecta* (printed for the Maitland Club, 1842). L. W. Sharp, editor, *Early Letters of Robert Wodrow, 1698-1709*, Edinburgh University Press, 1937. The Rev. Robert Burns, *A Biography of Robert Wodrow (the younger) of Eastwood*.

11. Marwick, p. 15.

12. Op. cit., p. 36.

13. Lockhart, 1819, vol. 3, p. 286.

14. Marwick, Glasgow Charters, p. 1.

15. Lockhart, 1819, vol. 3, pp. 66, 77, 264-5, 270-73.

16. Addison, p. 286.

17. Mackie, pp. 246-57.

18. *Reformation*: (in Scotland), 1560, Catholicism abolished by the Scottish Parliament under the influence of John Knox and his converts; *"Solemn League and Covenant:"* 1648, between the Scottish Parliament and English Commons to oppose authoritarian policy of Charles I in religious matters (based on the Scottish National Covenant of 1638); *Restoration*: of Charles II after the Cromwellian interregnum, 1660; *Re-establishment*: of the Episcopal Church and rule of the Bishops, by Charles II in England and Scotland, 1661; *Revolution* and the *"Kirk Triumphant."* Presbyterian faith again the State Church of Scotland at overthrow of James VII (Scotland) and II (England), and accession of William and Mary to throne of England and Scotland, 1689; *Disruption*: between the "Auld Kirk" of Scotland and the new "Free Kirk," 1843; *Re-union*: of "Auld Kirk" and "Free Kirk," 1929.

19. Renwick and Lindsey, p. 216.

20. Innes, vol. 1, Doc. 2.

21. This etching is reproduced from Renwick's *Glasgow Memorials*.

22. Innes, Doc. 4, and Mackie, p. 45.

23. MS in the Archives of the University of Glasgow entitled *Liber Decani Facultatis Artium*, pp. 102-3.

24. Mackie, p. 45.

25. Op. cit., pp. 92-106.

26. Op. cit., p. 128.
27. Op. cit., p. 103.
28. Wodrow, 1828, pp. 6-10.
29. *Glasgow Herald*, 17 December, 1918.
30. Mackie, pp. 215-36.
31. Pryde.
32. Brown, pp. 497-8.
33. Ibid.
34. Baker, 1927, vol. I, pp. 82-3.
35. Op. cit., vol. II, p. 35.
36. Thomas and Porteus, pp. 22-9.
37. Op. cit., p. 28.
38. Wilson, E. B., 1938, pp. 205-6.
39. Thomas and Porteus, p. 29.
40. Lockhart, 1956, pp. 209-10.
41. Tumulty, p. 457. These remarks to Mr. Tumulty are very revealing, and may be here quoted in full. "You know, Tumulty," he said, "there are two natures combined in me that every day fight for supremacy and control. On the one side, there is the Irish in me, quick, generous, impulsive, anxious always to help and sympathize with those in distress." As he continued his description of himself, his voice took on an Irish brogue, "And like the Irishman at the Donnybrook Fair, always willin' to raise me shillalah and hit any head which stands forninst me. Then, on the other side," he said, "there is the Scotch—canny, tenacious, cold, and perhaps a little exclusive. I tell you, my dear friend, that when these two fellows get to quarreling among themselves, it is hard to act as umpire between them."

Chapter VII

1. Petersen, 1943.
2. Op. cit., pp. 74-6.
3. Op. cit., p. 116.
4. Op. cit., Chap. XI.
5. Op. cit., pp. 134, 139.
6. Op. cit., pp. 136 ff.
7. Op. cit., p. 138
8. Mills, 1934, p. 35.
9. Mills, 1942, p. 7.
10. Petersen, 1943, p. 173.
11. Blumenstock, pp. 19-21.
12. Dingle and Mohler, pp. 562-3.
13. Blumenstock, p. 174.
14. Athay, pp. 475-6.
15. Op. cit., pp. 478-9.
16. Oldishaw, p. 514 B.
17. Appleton, p. iv.
18. Oldishaw, pp. 516-7.

19. Petersen, 1947, pp. 239-40.
20. Op. cit., p. 242.
21. Op. cit., p. 316.
22. Abbott, Smithsonian Misc. Coll., vol. 95, No. 12.
23. Stetson, 1937, p. 102.
24. Abbott, Smithsonian Misc. Coll., vol. 84, No. 14.
25. Petersen, 1947, p. 244.

Envoi

1. Ghiselin, see Bibliography.
2. Baker, Papers, Series B.
3. McAdoo, 1962, p. 118.
4. Baker, 1927, vol. I, p. 74.
5. Op. cit., vol. I. p. 75.
6. Op. cit., vol. I. pp. 119-20.
7. McAdoo, 1962, p. 55, 103.
8. Fosdick, pp. 44-5.
9. Baker, 1927, vol. I, p. 184.
10. Op. cit., vol. I, pp. 127-8.
11. Walworth, vol. II, pp. 302-3.
12. Wilson, E. B., p. 283.
13. Tumulty, pp. 449-50.
14. Op. cit., p. 451.

BIBLIOGRAPHY

Abbott, C. G., *Sunspots and Weather*. Smithsonian Miscellaneous Collections, vol. 87, No. 18.
The Dependence of Terrestrial Temperatures on the Variations of the Sun's Radiation. Smithsonian Miscellaneous Collections, vol. 95, No. 12.

Addison, W. Innes, editor, *The Matriculation Albums of the University of Glasgow, from 1728 to 1858*. James Maclehose & Sons, Glasgow, 1913.

Alderman, Edwin Anderson, *Memorial Address* (before a joint session of Congress, December 15, 1924), in honor of Woodrow Wilson. Doubleday, Page & Company, Garden City, N.Y., 1925.

Allport, Gordon W., *Personality: A Psychological Interpretation*. Henry Holt & Company, New York, 1939,

Anonymous, Woodrow Wilson at his Grandfather's Church at Carlysle. Overbrook Press, Stamford, Conn., 1956.

Appleton, E. V., Foreword to Harlan True Stetson's *Sunspots in Action*.

Archives of the University of Glasgow, Manuscript entitled *Liber Decani Facultatis Artium*, in the University Library.

Arey, L. B., *Developmental Anatomy*. W. B. Saunders, London and Philadelphia, 1934.

Athay, R. Grant, "The Sun's Flares and Earth," *Natural History*, LXVII, No. 9, November, 1958.

Baker, Ray Stannard, Papers, Series 1B, in the Manuscript Division of the Library of Congress, Washington, D.C. *Memorandum of a Conversation with Margaret Wilson*.
Woodrow Wilson, Life and Letters. Doubleday, Page & Co., Garden City, N.Y., 1927, vols. 1 and 2.

Baker, Ray Stannard, and William E. Dodd, editors, *The Public Papers of Woodrow Wilson, College and State, 1875-1913*. Harper Brothers, New York, 1925.

Black, George Frazer, *The Surnames of Scotland: their Origins, Meaning and History*. The New York Public Library, New York, 1946.

Blumenstock, David L., *The Ocean of Air*. Rutgers University Press, 1959.

Bradley, James, "Chronological Outline of Strabane," in *Strabane Festival*, 1952, pp. 9-11. Published by the Roman Catholic Diocese of Derry, Northern Ireland.

Brown, J. Douglas, "Princeton University," Encyclopaedia Britannica, 1963 Edition, vol. 18, pp. 497, 8.

259

Bühler and Hetger, in Greene, Edward B., 1941.

Callary, Robert R., *The Hill of Tara*. Meath Archaeological and Historical Society, Dublin, 1955.

Camblin, Gilbert, *The Town in Ulster*. William Mullin and Son, Ltd., Belfast, 1951.

Cannon, Walter B., *Bodily Changes in Pain, Hunger, Fear and Rage*. D. Appleton & Co., New York, 1915.

Coon, Carleton S., *The Races of Europe*. The Macmillan Company, New York, 1939.

Crile, G. W., *Intelligence, Power and Personality*. McGraw-Hill Book Company Inc., New York, 1941.

D'Alton, Edward A., *A History of Ireland*. Sealy, Bryers and Walker, Dublin, 1903-6.

Day, Donald, *Woodrow Wilson's Own Story*. Little, Brown & Co., Boston, 1952.

Dingle, Herbert, and Orren C. Mohler, "Sun," Encyclopaedia Britannica, 1963 Edition, vol. 21, pp. 562, 3.

Elliott, Margaret Axson, *My Aunt Louisa and Woodrow Wilson*. University of North Carolina Press, Chapel Hill, N.C., 1944.

Ewen, C. L'Estrange, *A History of Surnames in the British Isles*. London, 1931.

Fosdick, Raymond B., *Chronicle of a Generation, an Autobiography*. Harper and Brothers, New York, 1958.

Galton, Francis, *Hereditary Genius*. Macmillan & Co., London, 1914.

Gesell, Arnold, and Frances L. Ilg, *Infant and Child in the Culture of Today*. Harper and Brothers, New York and London, 1943.

Ghiselin, Brewster, *The Creative Process, a Symposium*. University of California Press, Berkeley, California, 1955.

Glasgow Herald, 8 February, 1924; 10 April, 1917; 17 December, 1918.

Greene, Edward B., *Measurements of Human Behavior*. The Odyssey Press, New York, 1941.

Guyer, Michael F., *Being Well-Born*. Bobbs-Merrill Company, New York, 1927.

Handy, E. S. Craighill, *Polynesian Religion*. Bernice P. Bishop Museum, Honolulu, Hawaii, 1927. Quoting John White's *The Ancient History of the Maori*, Wellington, N. Z., 1887-1890, vol. I.

Handy, E. S. Craighill and Elizabeth Green, *Genethnics Manual No. 1, The Genethnics Screen*, Richmond, Virginia, 1951.

Hayward, Richard, *Ulster*, in "This is Ireland" series, Arthur Baker Ltd., London, 1950.

Henry, Robert Williamson, Letter in the Glasgow *Herald*, issue of December 17, 1918.

Hickey, Elizabeth, *The Legend of Tara*. Dunalgan Press, Dundalk, Ireland, 1955.

Hooton, Earnest A., and C. Wesley Dupertius, *The Physical Anthropology of Ireland*, Harvard University Press, Cambridge, Mass., 1955.

260

Hotchkiss, J. E. D., "The Physiography of Augusta County," in *An Illustrated Historical Atlas of Augusta County, Virginia*, by Joseph A. Waddell, Staunton, Va., 1885.

Huntington, Ellsworth, *Earth and Sun*, Yale University Press, New Haven, Conn., 1923. Chapter IX is by H. H. Clayton.

Seasons of Birth, John Wiley and Sons, New York, 1938.

Innes, G., editor, *Munimenta Alme Universitatis Glasguensis*, Records of the University of Glasgow from its foundation till 1727, vol. 1, Docs. 1, 2 and 4.

Jefferson, Thomas, *Notes on the State of Virginia*, H. C. Carey and I. Lea, Philadelphia, 1825.

Joyce, Patrick W., *A Social History of Ireland*. Dublin, 1913.

Kelley, David H., Research Notes in manuscripts and letters, sent from Belfast and Glasgow in 1956.

Liber Decani Facultatis Artium, vol. I. Manuscript in the Library of Glasgow University.

Lockhart, J. G., *Peter's Letters to his Kinfolk*. Edinburg, 1819.

"Life of Burns," in G. F. Maine's *A Book of Scotland*, Collins Clear Type Press, London and Glasgow, 1956.

Macalister, R. A. S., *Ancient Ireland*. Methuen & Co., London, 1935.

Mackie, J. D., *The University of Glasgow, 1451-1951*. Jackson & Son, Glasgow, 1954.

Marshall, W. F., *Ulster Sails West*. The Belfast News-Letter, Belfast, N. Ireland, 1950.

Marwick, James. D., *The River Clyde and the Clyde Burgs*. J. Maclehose and Sons, Glasgow, 1909.

Glasgow Charters. Glasgow, 1909.

McAdoo, Eleanor Randolph Wilson, in collaboration with Margaret Y. Gaffey, *The Woodrow Wilsons*. The Macmillan Co., New York, 1937.

McAdoo, Eleanor Wilson, *The Priceless Gift*. McGraw-Hill Book Company, Inc., New York, 1962.

McIntyre, Edward, "The Presbyterian Church," in the pamphlet entitled *Strabane Festival*, published by the Roman Catholic Diocese of Derry, Northern Ireland in 1952.

Mills, Clarence A., *Living with the Weather*. Caxton Press, Cincinnati, Ohio, 1934.

Climate Makes the Man. Harper and Brothers, New York and London, 1942.

Mottram, V. H., *The Physical Basis of Personality*. Penguin Books, Hammondsworth, Middlesex, England, 1952.

Muller, F. Max, *The Sacred Books of the East*, vol. 1, *The Upanishads*, Part I, *The Khandogya Upanishad*. Oxford University Press, London, 1926.

Murrill, William A., *The Natural History of Staunton, Virginia*. New York, 1919.

Oldishaw, Hugh, "The International Geophysical Year," Encyclopaedia

Britannica, 1963 Edition, vol. 12, pp. 514B-518.

Old, W. G., *The Simple Way, Laotze*. David McKay, Philadelphia, 1939.

O'Riordan, Sean P., *Tara, the Monuments on the Hill*. Dunalgan Press, Dundalk, Ireland, 1954.

Petersen, William F., *Weather and the Patient*, vol. 1, Part 1. Edwards Brothers, Inc., Ann Arbor, Michigan, 1936.

Lincoln-Douglas, the Weather as Destiny. Charles C. Thomas Co., Springfield, Illinois, 1943.

Man, Weather, Sun. Charles C. Thomas, Springfield, Illinois, 1947.

Pryde, George S., *The Scottish Universities and the Colleges of Colonial America*. Glasgow University Publications, New Series No. 1, Jackson Sons & Co., Glasgow, 1957.

Renwick, Robert, *Glasgow Memorials*. Glasgow, 1908.

Renwick, Robert, and John Lindsey, *History of Glasgow*. Maclehose, Jackson & Co., Glasgow, 1921.

Scharren, Ernst and Berta, "Neurosecretion," in *Science*, vol. 127, No. 334, pp. 1396-98, Washington, D. C., 13 June, 1958.

Sherrington, C. S., *Man and his Nature*. Doubleday and Co., Garden City, N. Y., 1923.

Shree Prohit Swami and W. B. Yeats, translators, *The Ten Principle Upanishads*. The Macmillan Co., New York, 1937.

Smuts, Jan Christian, *Holism and Evolution*. The Macmillan Co., New York, 1936.

Spenser, Edmund, *A View of the State of Ireland*. London, 1633.

Starling, see Sugrue and Starling.

Stetson, Harlan True, *Sunspots and their Effects*. McGraw-Hill Book Company, Inc., New York, 1937.

Sugrue, Thomas, and Edmund W. Starling, *Starling in the White House*. Simon and Shuster, New York, 1916.

Taine, H. A., *A History of English Literature*, translated by H. Van Laun. Holt and Williams, New York, 1871.

Thomas, John, and Charles A. Porteus, *Memorial of Lowther Street Congregational Church (formerly Annetwell Street Chapel), Carlisle, 1786-1936*. Charles Thurman and Sons, Carlisle, England, 1936.

Tokay, Elbert, *The Human Body and How it Works*. Doubleday & Co., 1957.

Tumulty, Joseph A., *Woodrow Wilson as I Know Him*. Doubleday, Page and Co., Garden City, N. Y., 1921.

Waddell, Joseph A., *An Illustrated Historical Atlas of Augusta County, Virginia*. Staunton, Virginia, 1885.

Annals of Augusta County, Virginia, 1726-1871. C. R. Caldwell, Staunton, Virginia, 1902.

Walworth, Arthur, *Woodrow Wilson, World Prophet* (vol. 2 of the biography entitled *Woodrow Wilson*). Longmans, Green & Co., New York, 1958.

Wernli, Hans J., *Biorythm*, translated by Rosemary Colmers. Crown Publishers, New York, 1961.

White, William Allen, *Woodrow Wilson*. Houghton Mifflin & Co., Boston and New York, 1924.

Wilson, Edith Bolling, *My Memoir*. Bobbs-Merrill Co., Indianapolis, Indiana, 1938.

Wilson, Woodrow, *Address at his Grandfather's Church in Carlisle, England*. The Overbrook Press, Stamford, Connecticut, 1956.

Congressional Government, a Study in American Politics. Houghton, Mifflin & Co., Boston, 1885.

History of the American People, volumes 1 to 5. Harper and Brothers, New York and London, 1908.

Letter to his father, quoted in an article in the *New York Times* of October 17, 1931.

When a Man Comes to Himself. Harper and Brothers, New York, 1901.

Wodrow, Robert, *Life of James Wodrow*. Edinburgh, 1828.

A History of the Sufferings of the Church. Blackie, Glasgow, 1830-35.

Woulfe, Patrick, *Irish Names and Surnames*. Dublin, 1923.

Wyld, H. C., editor, *The Universal Dictionary of the English Language*. G. Routledge & Sons, London, 1932.

Yeats, W. B., see Shree Prohit Swami.

ABOUT THE AUTHORS

Elizabeth Green Handy, who was educated at Rice University and the University of Chicago, is a former editor of *Pacific Affairs*. From 1924 to 1926 she was a Lecturer on Western Literature at the Chinese Government College of Foreign Studies in Peking. Her interest in Chinese social and political life began during this time, and she has written and published many articles on this subject.

Since 1934, she has been engaged in Hawaiian ethnological research—both field work and writing—in collaboration with her husband, the co-author of this book, under the auspices of the Bishop Museum of Honolulu and the Polynesian Society of New Zealand.

Dr. E. S. Craighill Handy, a graduate of Harvard, received his Ph. D. in anthropology in 1920 from that institution. He led two anthropological expeditions in the Polynesian islands for the Bishop Museum. His books, *Polynesian Religion* and *The Native Culture in the Marguesas*, as well as numerous monographs on the culture of the Polynesian islands and of Hawaii have been published by the Bishop Museum Press.

Dr. and Mrs. Handy now live on a farm in northern Virginia. They continue with their joint ethnological research and writing and make periodic trips to Hawaii.